Courtney C. Brown
In Memory

October 15, 1904 – April 28, 1990

Courtney C. Brown
In Memory

Edited by James W. Kuhn
and Chauncey G. Olinger, Jr.

Columbia Business School
New York, New York

Selections from Putting the Corporate Board to Work by Courtney C. Brown have been reprinted with the permission of the Free Press, an imprint of Simon & Schuster. Copyright ©1976 by The Trustees of Columbia University in the City of New York.

Selections from Beyond the Bottom Line by Courtney C. Brown have been reprinted with the permission of the Free Press, an imprint of Simon & Schuster. Copyright © 1979 by The Trustees of Columbia University in the City of New York.

Selections from The Dean Meant Business by Courtney C. Brown have been reprinted with the permission of Columbia University in the City of New York. Copyright ©1983 by The Trustees of Columbia University in the City of New York.

Selections from various reports of the Dean of the Graduate School of Business of Columbia University have been reprinted with the permission of Columbia University in the City of New York. Copyrights ©1958,1959,1960,1961,1962,1963, 1964,1965,1968,1969.

"A Corporate Dilemma: Materialism vs. Humanism," The Future of Business: Global Issues in the 80s and 90s, Max Ways, ed. (New York: Pergamon Press, 1978), reprinted with the permission of Mrs. Constance Ways.

Library of Congress Card Catalog Number: 94-69937

ISBN 0-9644274-0-0

Designed and produced by Stevan A. Baron

Printed in the United States of America by Quinn Woodbine, Woodbine, New Jersey

FIRST EDITION

Contents

Foreword

WHEN COURTNEY BROWN LEFT STANDARD OIL OF NEW JERSEY to assume the deanship of Columbia's Business School, the university could hardly have imagined the kind of man it was getting. Although he had earned his doctorate in economics at Columbia, he came to the deanship not after an academic career but with a decade and a half of a successful and varied managerial career behind him.

By nature a strong personality with a willingness to lead, Courtney Brown was bound to interact strongly with Columbia's community of scholars and administrators. But, if he was frustrated with the managerially inefficient ways of a university, he was also deeply dedicated to its goals of teaching and research.

It was my happy experience to meet Dean Brown in 1964 while I was still a graduate student in philosophy. As president of the university student council I had proposed that the university print a statement on its examination booklets encouraging academic honesty. Of all the administrators in the university, Courtney Brown stood out most strongly in his belief that students should be urged to do their own work.

Our official relationship grew into a deep friendship. I edited three of his books (*Putting the Corporate Board to Work*, *Beyond the Bottom Line*, and his autobiography, *The Dean Meant Business*) and did a long oral history interview of him for Columbia's Oral History program. Then active in alumni affairs, I was successful in having him elected a Trustee of Columbia. My wife Carla and I spent a number of wonderful weeks with the Brown's at Treasure Cay.

When, in the months following his death in April of 1990, Marjorie Brown began to raise the possibility of a published memorial to Courtney, I was delighted to help. We decided right away that we wanted to include the remarks from the memorial service for him, to have a personal memoir by his old friend and colleague Clarence C. Walton, and to publish a collection of Courtney's writings on the major themes of his thought.

To guide us in the selection of passages that reflected his strongest interests, we turned to his old friend, and now Courtney C. Brown

Professor at Columbia, James W. Kuhn for advice and counsel. The book that follows is a result of our discussions to identify the major themes in Courtney's writing and Jim's thorough review of the whole corpus of Courtney's written legacy to select those passages that best illustrated the major directions in his thinking. (Titles enclosed in brackets have been provided by the editors.)

On behalf of Marjorie Brown and of so many of Courtney's friends who will be glad to have this final summing up of his thought, I express our very deep appreciation to Jim Kuhn for his fine work on behalf of Courtney's memory.

January 16, 1995   Chauncey G. Olinger, Jr.

Preface

WHEN MARJORIE BROWN ASKED ME to select the best and most enduring portions of Courtney Brown's writings to include in a memorial volume, I was honored. As one of the first young professors hired by Courtney and thus greatly influenced by him over the following years of his deanship, I was well acquainted with his ideas and scholarly activities.

As I reread his various books, articles, and reports in preparation for selecting articles for this volume I was surprised how familiar they were—many of the ideas he proposed, notions explored, and analyses presented had become a part of my own thinking. I had not previously realized the degree to which I had borrowed, adapted, and incorporated his thinking into my own approach to, and philosophy of, business.

Long before most business managers or business scholars perceived a need for a re-examination of corporate governance, Courtney argued that passive directors and boards subservient to operating officials would not well serve American business. He was an early advocate of an independent, activist board of directors, offering detailed recommendations for achieving the autonomy he believed was required for healthy, efficient, and effective corporate organizations.

Courtney, also, had always recognized the business need for values beyond those of the bottom line. Using the language of his time, he referred to them under the rubric of corporate social responsibility—an informed, sensitive concern for the rights of the many community constituents, upon whose sufferance business depends.

That responsibility could best be defined by seeking guidance from what he called "the liberating arts"; economics, accounting, finance, and marketing had to be informed, he asserted, by broader, more humane values than those of their own narrow assumptions. The academy's responsibility was not merely to prepare its graduates with technical skills, but also to help them understand both the constraints imposed by, and the opportunities offered through, the larger social setting within which they would work.

In making the initial selections of his writings I left out dated illustrations and contemporary references whose meanings would now be obscure. I selected those ideas and analyses that are relevant to today's and the likely future's issues, leaving out his personal reminiscences and details of his administrative accomplishments; those can be found in his autobiography, *The Dean Meant Business*. This memorial volume presents his ideas: reflections on and recommendations for a "business society." To Courtney, the word *society* was quite as important as the word *business*. The enduring contribution of his writings arises from that linkage, ever present and obvious in the ideas about which he wrote and that are contained in this volume.

January 4,1995   James W. Kuhn
                                         Courtney C. Brown Professor of
                                         Management and Organization

Courtney C. Brown

In Memory

The Story
of Courtney Brown's Life

COURTNEY BROWN WAS THE SON OF A ST. LOUIS STOCKBROKER and a Texas-born music teacher. Raised by his paternal grandmother after his mother died when he was four, he attended Staunton Military Academy and then Dartmouth, where he was a gentlemanly student who reveled in the joys of the Roaring Twenties. Following graduation in 1926, he began a stint on Wall Street in the same firm that his father worked for, and in 1930 he married Marjorie Warren Lawbaugh of Meriden, Connecticut, and began the family that was to include daughters Joanne Lyman Brown, Roxanne Griswold Brown, and son Courtney Warren Brown. The next several years he devoted to Banker's Trust before becoming a very serious student in Columbia's graduate economics department where he earned a doctorate in 1940. He spent the war years in Washington, guiding the government's purchase of strategic materials.

Back in New York City after the war, he became the chief petroleum economist for Standard Oil of New Jersey and personal assistant to chairman Frank Abrams, with whom he worked on the landmark A. P. Smith Manufacturing Company case that brought judicial recognition of corporate philanthropy and on the founding of the Council for Financial Aid to Education. His association with Abrams brought Courtney in touch with many of the leading figures in American business life and prepared him for his major life's work, his deanship of Columbia's Graduate School of Business.

In a flurry of activity beginning in 1954, he persuaded the school's faculty to completely overhaul the curriculum to meet the current and emerging challenges to corporate managers, launched a vigorous and successful program of fund-raising, and built the school's new home, Uris Hall, on Columbia's Morningside campus. With his extensive business background, Courtney did not view academic administration as an unending effort to balance and placate highly articulate—and often managerially inexperienced—faculty members. While he appreciated the merits of intellectual

3

discussion—he had taught in Columbia College's Contemporary Civilization program—he became well known on the Columbia campus for his willingness to take definitive action.

In addition to his deaning, teaching, and writing, he served on the boards of five major corporations (American Electric Power, Associated Dry Goods, the Borden Company, CBS, and Union Pacific) and of many not-for-profit organizations, including Columbia's Board of Trustees, becoming a respected commentator on the corporate board of directors. Travel and golf with Marjorie and friends were his major escapes from a very heavy schedule.

Courtney Brown: A Winter's Man

Clarence C. Walton

WHO IS COURTNEY BROWN? Before the answer, an observation: the present tense is used for a person four years in the grave. Why, then, distort fact? Part of the reason for thinking Courtney Brown lives is religiously rooted: Courtney enjoying eternal life with his Creator. However, for those who do not accept the theological premise, using the present tense is justified because, in strictly temporal terms, Courtney Brown's thoughts and works are still with us, affecting the lives of Columbia scholars and Columbia students, the behavior of corporate executives, and the policies of professional associations in graduate business education.

Were one to ask what quality most characterized him, the answer would be simple: commitment to *excellence*, no triviality in a world where excellence has been too often supplanted by trendiness, and where commitment has been subordinated to convenience. In describing Courtney's life, emphasis will be on the personal over the professional, a separation, however, virtually impossible to maintain consistently because it was through our professional relationship that I came to know his personal traits.

Judging another person's character is not simply risky, it is downright presumptuous. The effort may be pardoned, however, when the judge has a long and close association with the judged, and when the appraisals, on the basis of those experiences, are most positive. In trying to delineate the character of this extraordinary individual, the old Greek quadrangle offers criteria on which reasonable assessments can be made. The qualities especially important to the Athenians were four: justice, prudence (born with temperance), fortitude (as revealed in steadfastness), and courage. While providing convenient starting points, these qualities do not, of course, exhaust the catalog, since the Greeks paid minimal attention to three virtues dear to nineteenth- and twentieth-century Americans: hard work, conscientiousness, and thrift—all abundantly clear in Courtney's comportment. Nevertheless, a good understanding of the man is gotten simply by applying the ancients' quadrangle to his life.

5

The Just Man

Perceptions of Courtney's sense of justice began even before we ever met. An anecdote is apposite. In 1953 I had become dean of the School of Business at Duquesne University in Pittsburgh. Part of my own preparation, for what turned out to be challenging and rewarding years, was to assimilate as rapidly as possible the thoughts of others in the field.

One of the first things that struck me at the Pittsburgh institution was the number of professors who were moonlighting—and moonlighting for longer periods than they were spending in the classrooms or in their offices. The first reaction was annoyance, indeed, anger, at such unprofessional behavior. But probing into the problem elicited unpleasant information: the professors' salaries were so low that moonlighting was necessary for them if financial sunlight was to become possible in their lives.

Seeking guidance on how to handle this manifest injustice, I turned to the report of the Arden House conference (Arden House is Columbia's Catskill mountain center for executive education and for similar purposes) sponsored by the American Association of Collegiate Schools of Business. One of the essays was authored by Courtney and a young assistant professor of statistics, Oscar Serbein. A sense of outrage at the dismal salary scales of business professors was clear in their very first paragraph.

> The economic position of teachers of business in colleges and universities, measured in terms of the purchasing power of the dollar, has declined considerably since 1941. Not only have teachers been unable to maintain pre-war living standards, but they have also failed to maintain their position in relation to other professionally trained groups. The steady worsening of the financial plight of the business teacher has been a source of continuing alarm to deans of business schools as well as to the teachers themselves.[1]

Painful facts were exposed. The typical salary of a full professor for which a doctorate was usually required was in the range of $7,100 to $7,500 a year. What was ironic about the depressed salary levels of 1954 was that there was even then clear evidence of a teacher shortage—only some 5,000 teachers were in the ranks. If the law of supply and demand was not working, something beyond market factors was at work. Part of that "something" was that business schools were not attracting the best students because their curricula were not attuned to the needs of business.

While the overall report was quite statistically detailed (comparisons, for example, between salaries of professors at research-oriented schools of business versus salaries in what were considered primarily teaching institutions), behind the cold statistics was evident revulsion at the injustices that were being imposed on business professors. That Courtney Brown removed those injustices at the Columbia University Graduate School of Business—and removed them quickly—is powerful evidence of unwavering dedication to fairness.

It is also worth noting that, even when some long-tenured professors began to rebel against their new brisk, sometimes brusque, dean, the vocabulary of their negative descriptions had included adjectives like "imperious," "impatient," and "idiosyncratic," but never "indifferent" or "unfair." The omissions told the tale.

Another testimony to Courtney's sense of justice was his refusal to play the competitive bidding game which allowed the academic market to determine a professor's salary. If another university made an offer for a Columbia teacher, who then used it as leverage for a salary increment, Courtney would simply shrug his shoulders and tell the individual that if he or she wished to leave Columbia and its potential in favor of a few extra dollars elsewhere, please do so. Few left.

Faculty heard the message: income would be directly related to output. Skeptical of the then-prevailing publish-or-perish criterion as the only norm for measurement, Courtney developed his own guidelines: meaningful research resulting in *significant* publications; work with the students inside and outside the classroom; and involvement with colleagues on important school and campus projects. And when fund raising became better organized under Harris Wofford's leadership, Courtney persuaded the administration to allow him to use 20 percent of the annual contribution for salary increments instead of the customary 5 percent.

Fuller knowledge of Courtney came when, in 1958, he invited me to become the associate dean, succeeding the kindly Roger Murray who wished to return to teaching. Why that invitation came about was, for a time, somewhat of a mystery because, when pressed to explain his decision, a cryptic response was given: "I liked what you said in Philadelphia." Precisely what I had said remained unclear to me. Whatever it was, its full effect on Dean Brown became known only when his memoirs appeared in 1983. In a most generous entry, which now reported seems to be an act of egregious self-indulgence, Courtney wrote:

> It occurred to me to invite Clarence C. Walton, the dean of the
> business school at Duquesne University, to take over Murray's position.
> I had met Walton at a conference that Tom Carroll, a vice president of
> the Ford Foundation, had arranged in Philadelphia for a group of twen-

ty business deans to discuss two books on changes in business education: one book sponsored by the Carnegie Corporation, the other by
the Ford Foundation. . . .

    The most impressive discussant at the table seemed to me to be
the dean from Duquesne. Needless to say, I recorded his name for
future reference. It was one of the most important entries I ever made,
and I was delighted when he accepted the offer to become our associate dean.[2]

If Courtney was delighted, I was thrilled. And the thrill never left—
despite the initial uncertainties about living in frantic and frenetic New
York. On that score it need only be recorded that Betty and I arrived in the
city on a sultry Labor Day afternoon in 1958 with two preschool children
who had the run of the garden in our Pittsburgh suburban home, regular
visits by grandparents, and where my wife was beginning to establish a
modest reputation as an artist. The decision to come to New York had not
been easy for her.

    We were prepared for a shock, and we were not disappointed. Soft-
ening the rigors of adjustment was Marjorie Brown. She had made great
efforts to find a Columbia apartment in an area where walking to work was
easy for me and where shopping (Betty did not drive) was easy for her. It
was the first of so many generous acts by Marjorie on our behalf that enu-
merating all of them is impossible.

    But Marjorie's help (finding the right furniture, choosing the right gro-
cery store, providing tips on places to visit and things to do) was invaluable.
Courtney was at her side when advice and help were rendered, and we soon
learned that to speak to one was to speak to the other, to work with one
was to work with the other. The Browns were not simply husband and
wife, father and mother to three gifted children, they were a team (emotional, spiritual, intellectual, and social) in every sense of the word. Unlike
similar couples whose intrusions into the office routine often annoyed or
frustrated other administrators, this team kept a respectful distance. Their
family policy (no assistance proffered unless wanted and no help denied
unless needed) enriched all.

The Steadfast Man

    Our warm reception by the Browns was complemented by a warm
reception from the business school faculty. But I soon learned that some of
the most distinguished senior professors were beginning to question the
wisdom of drastic curricular reform. In the struggle of minds and wills that
ensued, I learned of Courtney's second great virtue: fortitude. At the previ-

ously cited 1954 Arden House conference for the deans of the nation's best-known institutions, a recommendation was made to the effect that "schools of business must provide curricula to equip young men and women for the world of their future—as well as the world of today. This task will require a complete reexamination of the present educational programs."[3] One cannot say who was the primary source for this recommendation. One can say with certainty that Courtney Brown, if not its author, was one of its major supporters. It was this philosophy that prompted him to embark on a project that always raises faculty concern—curricular revision.

In this venture—one might appropriately call it an adventure—Courtney Brown was, in important respects, ahead of the times. This is not to suggest that Courtney alone was the academic pioneer. A previous Columbia business dean, Robert Calkins (who left to become president of the Brookings Institution in Washington), spoke of educating students in "economics as well as business administration."[4] Courtney and the Columbia faculty had already produced a blueprint that anticipated the proposals found in both the Carnegie Corporation and Ford Foundation reports.[5] But a considerable distance existed between blueprint and building, and some of the professional architects were voicing doubts about the new house of intellect. Given these circumstances, the temptation to "wait it out," even quit, might have been strong.

If ever tempted, Courtney showed no sign of it. He had initiated a project he thought was necessary; he was convinced that the project was doable; he had mustered financial resources from external sources to relieve undue pressures on faculty who were giving time from the classroom for the work. To the criticism, Courtney's unvoiced retort was the same: damn the torpedoes.

One major obstacle to curriculum changes was the faculty's traditional view of education. Composed overwhelmingly of specialists, the faculty tended to believe that having first-rate professors teaching first-rate courses in areas of concentration made for an excellent educational program. Although in 1954–55 the largest enrollments were in general administration and accounting, there were "majors" in advertising management, finance, investment management, foreign trade, labor relations, production management, and general marketing.

Courtney recognized the strength of faculty objections to his ideas for professional education because their adoption meant substantial reductions in the number of courses offered in the areas of specialization. In the view of some teachers, reductions meant retooling or resigning. Knowing this, the dean made every effort to reassure the faculty that this would not occur. Here, fortitude was now wed to justice.

Very diplomatically, Courtney told the Committee on Instruction, the power on curriculum in the business school, that he would like to share some suggestions "that might be helpful to the committee in developing its own ideas regarding such corrective actions as may seem desirable."[6] The camel's nose was in the curricular tent. Once in, he pressed forward with his own agenda. Signs of progress had come on March 16, 1956, when the Committee on Instruction announced its willingness to consider a core of courses that, cutting across departments, would cover materials clearly needed by managers: (1) world resources, (2) economic theory and business history, (3) management, and (4) the social and political institutions through which business was conducted. The dean was enthusiastic, the faculty still circumspect. Whenever Courtney sensed strong faculty resistance, he compromised on a single goal rather than sacrifice his overall goal.

When tensions between curricular reformers and those supporting specialized studies heightened, the dean used a series of Arden House conferences in 1957-58 to bring the two sides toward consensus. But the battle was far from over. Some senior faculty increased their criticisms of Brown for his alleged "high-handedness" and even went so far as to make representations to President Grayson Kirk to the effect that Brown was destroying faculty morale. Lesser men might have crumbled. Courtney never whimpered. And when a few professors used a technicality in the university by-laws to deny the dean a vote on curriculum matters, the dean took the issue to the trustees—and won. The university by-laws were changed to make clear the fact that, while only teaching faculty had voted in the past, officers of the administration would also vote in the future. Since the chief officer of administration was the dean, Courtney's fortitude paid off handsomely, including dividends to other members of administrations in the schools and to other deans. The academic "battle of the bulge" was won. It was no small victory.

The Temperate Man?

So far as temperance is involved, Courtney had shortcomings. He was intemperate in his public criticism of the Columbia University president, intemperate in his denunciations of a few powerful trustees, and intemperate in his decision to force the resignation of a tenured professor who had denounced him. Dislikes colored his objectivity. Intemperance and impulsiveness go hand in hand. Courtney was impulsive, although not in the sense of jumping into serious affairs without much thought. This he never did. But he was impulsive in being an individual so freighted with imaginative ideas that anyone who got in the way of their implementation was at risk. He acted frequently like a man who sought to do yesterday what he had just thought of today—not a sound formula for consistently prudent behavior.

The Brave Man

As is the case with most character flaws, the imprudent aspect of Courtney's character was essentially an expression of another quality he possessed in the extreme—courage, the final virtue in the Athenian quadrangle. When Courtney felt called upon to act, he acted fearlessly. When called upon to speak, he spoke fearlessly. Associates of the dean came to know that Courtney and courage were synonymous. Anecdotes illustrate this point.

On two particular occasions I saw him face down hostile audiences. One occurred at Mackinac Island where he told a group (led by an Oxford graduate) that their religious profession was based not on a love of God but on a hate of the Soviet Union. The thunderous silence following his remarks eloquently testified how the message hit home. That it was heard but not believed was due to no lack of clarity in the dean's remarks.

Another example came during the student uprising in 1968. Instead of taking shelter in his office where he could have done so comfortably because the business students were minimally concerned with the protest, the dean walked to the front of Low Library where a crowd of angry students had gathered at the sundial. Mounting one of the steps, Courtney told the students what they very much needed to hear: he would listen. But he quickly followed the opening statement by telling them what some of their SDS leaders did not want them to hear: behave civilly—or else!

The most dramatic reflection of Courtney's courage came in a somewhat unusual, but deeply personal, way. After a few years in the dean's office, Courtney told me on several occasions that, when he retired, he wanted me as his successor. On the basis of such reassurance, I had discouraged offers from other institutions. When I became dean of the School of General Studies, Courtney felt that the move was a good one because it would enlarge my contacts with members of senior administration, encourage activities with other outside communities, and permit regular interchanges with faculty from departments in the School of the Arts and Sciences. Meanwhile, by continuing to teach the doctoral colloquium, a required course for those preparing for their comprehensive examinations, I would maintain my contacts with the business school.

My days at General Studies were fruitful. My friendship with Courtney was constant. My reputation with the university's central administration was enhanced. Then the unexpected happened. One day Courtney invited me to his office for, as he expressed it, a "very serious discussion." Courtney opened the conversation by saying something like this: "I am planning to retire and I remember the conversations we have had about succession. A dean's job here has two requirements: scholarship and fund-raising capability. You rate an A on the first and a C on the second. I shall not recommend you for the school's deanship."

Stunned into speechlessness, I could only look at my "betrayer." I said nothing and left. Around noon, Courtney appeared unexpectedly in my office to ask whether I would join him for lunch at the Faculty Club. He then came to my desk and, putting his arms on my shoulders, said in a low voice: "this was the hardest decision of my life at Columbia." Tears welled in his eyes.

When Courtney left, I spent a few minutes in thought and the realization dawned that I was indeed not a good outside man. I played no golf, belonged to no downtown clubs, and was a very private person. In short, I did not move in the same business-social circles as Courtney. But, to my surprise, the short reflection brought comfort. I had gotten to admire the GS faculty and students, leaving them for another deanship would have been unlikely because it would have been heartbreaking. As was so often the case, Courtney led me to look more carefully at myself. What he said was true. So I raced and caught up with him just as he was reaching the club. He extended his arms in greeting and said gently, "You are a second son to me." At that moment the realization dawned—Courtney had exhibited, possibly more fully than ever, his commitment and courage: commitment to what he perceived to be the business school's welfare and courage to deny the position to a surrogate son.

The story, of course, did not end there. When the new occupant of the dean's office ran into trouble with the faculty, and it was evident that the incumbent's days were numbered, Courtney called me for another "serious discussion." In the presence of Associate Dean Chester Owens, Courtney said that he had made a serious mistake the first time, and that he hoped I would consider "coming home." Career development precluded accepting the invitation, but the incident revealed another aspect of Courtney's character, namely, a courage to admit mistakes and a courage to correct them.

The foregoing account provides a modest glimpse into the behavior of a remarkable man. The emphasis has been on how Courtney reacted, not what he achieved. The consequence is that the character sketch tells only part of the story of his accomplishments. He had, for example, remarkable talent in an ability to sell. He was an entrepreneur by instinct. Once the new curriculum was in place, what he wished to sell most was the idea of a new building to house the business faculty and students. To this end, he persuaded Percy and Harold Uris to donate approximately one third of the estimated $9 million cost for the project; another third came from private foundations, and the final third from business organizations, alumni, and friends. In this accomplishment Courtney used no professional consultants and no professional staffs. He "sold" the program and monitored the construction. The amount spent on fund-raising was approximately $25,000, an astoundingly low expenditure compared to the six, nearly seven, figures expended on similar ventures.

While he was working downtown on a four-day-a-week schedule (the fifth was spent on campus), I was in charge of the home front. He always kept in touch. Each day the phone would ring and the inquiry was always the same: "Anything new or worrisome?" Fortunately, my answers were consistently "No."

Courtney, of course, had his disappointments. He was almost certain of getting over $2 million from the widow of Samuel J. Woods whose fortune had come from the creation of a chain of proprietary schools to teach typing, filing, and shorthand. Mrs. Woods came to the campus, was wined and dined, seemed impressed, but then changed her mind and gave the money to build a new wing for a New York hospital. There were other disappointments. His close associates at Jersey Standard, Frank Abrams and Gerry Stanford, had seemingly cleared the way for a $2.5 million grant from the Alfred Sloan Foundation. But at the last minute Sloan disapproved of the Columbia grant, sending the money instead to his alma mater, M.I.T.

Never, however, did disappointment impair the dean's determination to make things better. One innovation was the development of a three-semester program to provide flexibility for students to study and for professors to teach. In his very practical way, he also knew that a three-semester schedule meant more efficient use for Uris Hall. Without the trimester a beautiful new facility would stand idle for four months. His criteria for admission to the MBA program did not follow the stereotypical entrance-by-test-score only. Not only was the academic record of the applicant considered, but maturity, extracurricular activities, and other signs of leadership, plus evidences of sound moral character, were also reviewed. Courtney made real the old-fashioned ideal of liberal learning—education for the whole person.

Other matters revealed his wisdom. Long before affirmative action became mandatory, he pushed forward so that when he retired, women constituted about a third of the faculty and an even higher percentage of the student population. He and Marjorie used their Scarsdale home for student parties, making lonely foreign students especially welcome. Through the Distinguished Speaker programs that Courtney instituted, some of the best business minds in the metropolitan area came to campus to share their experiences with students; a "dean's hour" was used regularly to involve students, faculty, and administrators in informal, but frank, discussions about the school's strengths and weaknesses.

Summing Up

Measuring the immeasurable is futile. Dean Brown was not the perfect man. When affairs did not go his way, he could pout; and when a subordinate posted a poor performance, he could shout. Perhaps such peccadilloes kept him from becoming a modern Thomas More—a man of all seasons. Metaphorically speaking, spring, summer, and fall were not his best times. In such benign seasons, people can easily care for themselves.

But when winter winds of disappointment or defeat howled against others, and when the ice of despair thickened over other lives, Courtney responded. Like Jesuit scholar Martin Oxford, Courtney was a fire at Columbia—a fire around which the students who were his "children" played, the young danced, and the old sought warmth while remembering their dreams.

The fire still burns.

Notes

1. The American Association of Collegiate Schools of Business, *Faculty Requirements and Standards in Collegiate Schools of Business* (St. Louis, Missouri: 1954), p.184.

2. Courtney C. Brown, *The Dean Meant Business* (New York: Columbia University, Graduate School of Business, 1983), p.181.

3. AACSB, *Faculty Requirements*, p. 4.

4. Robert D. Calkins, "A Proposed Program for Future Development," (New York: Columbia University, School of Business, 1954), mimeographed. See also Robert J. Senkier, *Revising the Business Curriculum: The Columbia Experience* (New York: Columbia University, Graduate School of Business, 1954).

5. Robert A. Gordon and James E. Howell, *Higher Education for Business* (New York: Columbia University Press, 1949); and Frank C. Pierson, *et al.*, *The Education of American Businessmen* (New York: McGraw Hill, 1959).

6. Senkier, p.19.

Recollections
from
the Service
in Celebration of the Life
of

Courtney C. Brown
Dean Emeritus
Graduate School of Business
Columbia University

Monday, the first of October
Nineteen hundred and ninety
at four thirty o'clock
St. Paul's Chapel
Columbia University in the City of New York

Recollections

Meyer Feldberg
Dean, Columbia Business School

GOOD AFTERNOON LADIES AND GENTLEMEN, welcome to Columbia University and to St. Paul's Chapel. We are here this afternoon in celebration of the life of Courtney Conrades Brown, Dean Emeritus of the Columbia Graduate School of Business, who passed away on April 28, 1990. We will hear this afternoon from friends of Courtney Brown, as well as from students that he taught and influenced over the years.

Peter McE. Buchanan
Vice President for University Development and Alumni Relations
Columbia University

COURTNEY BROWN: THE SPARKLING BLUE EYES, the ceaseless energy; a stubborn, tenacious, effervescent, restless spirit: they were Courtney Brown. Colleagues at Columbia, and I am sure friends of Courtney's everywhere, remember those qualities of twenty, thirty, forty years ago, as vividly today as if Courtney were here with us; and I am sure he is. At the height of his powers, he was everywhere, and on top of everything.

How else could it have been for a man who, among other duties and responsibilities, served his country as a War Food Administrator in Washington in World War II; was chief petroleum economist for Standard Oil; worked for the company while earning a Columbia Ph.D. in economics at the age of 36; served simultaneously as Columbia's Vice President for Business and Dean of the Business School; led the struggle to legitimize and legalize corporate giving to the nonprofit community; was a cofounder of the Council for Financial Aid to Education; pioneered today's corporate matching gift program for employees; developed an innovative business curriculum that the 1958 Ford Foundation and Carnegie Corporation studies of business education affirmed; served on the boards of the Interracial

17

Council for Business Opportunities, the Advisory Board of the Salvation Army, CBS, the Union Pacific Corporation; and who was a Governor of the New York Stock Exchange and chaired the American Assembly.

Courtney built a subway night-school into a thriving full-time graduate business school. He found the money for a new home for it and recruited, among a group of remarkable administrators, a quite unremarkable Columbia MBA, who in 1969 after meeting with Courtney, was persuaded that a career in education was better than one in business.

When I first met Courtney, his Associate Dean was Clarence Walton, later to become Dean of General Studies at Columbia and President of Catholic University. Chester Owens, who is here with us today, was his able and devoted replacement. His Associate Dean of Placement was J. Fredric Way, [who was] I remember, recruited by Harvard incessantly in the 1970s but to no avail. Bill Heffernan, whose life was synonymous with the school he served so well before his untimely death, was another staff member as was Karin Paulson Brocksbank, one of Columbia's finest admissions officers and fund-raisers. Last but not least is Hoke Simpson who we now acknowledge as the dean of continuing business education in the country.

The early death of Walter Smith made me part of that team, Courtney's senior group of administrators: special people, bound uniquely to the school by his magnetism and by a faculty who elected its senior administrators to membership in its body. I always thought that Courtney gave me that gift. For one very brief shining period in time, I was a bona fide member of this University's faculty.

Courtney was a whirling dervish, in and out of corporate boardrooms raising money, raising hell with us when things did not suit him, giving the faculty fits with a spate of new ideas, never at rest, except of course, with Marjorie. How proud Courtney was of Marjorie and of their children. I think the only time I ever saw him sit still was when Marjorie was there.

He was a man who took chances and risked to do better, never worrying about the down-side. He didn't have a down-side unless it was a poor round of golf, and even that didn't happen often. The legendary fund-raiser, whose deeds others will chronicle, even turned generous donor when I became his aggressive solicitor. As openly angry as he was with me when I left the Business School to work for the President of the University, he always welcomed me personally as a father would a son in the same business, comrades in arms doing their damndest, no matter how imperfect, for what they believed in and for Columbia.

Even in the midst of awful illness, those clear blue eyes never lost the inner brightness that drove his mind and energized his spirit. Though he could not speak at the end when I saw him last, I affirmed, and he knew, that my life in education was his doing.

Kathleen Harriman Mortimer

COURTNEY BROWN WAS A FRIEND, ADVISOR, AND SUPPORTER of both Averell and Roland Harriman. Their interest was three-pronged—the Union Pacific Railroad; the American Assembly; and its home, Arden House. As the representative of all the Harrimans, I wish to honor Courtney today and acknowledge our deep debt to him.

Courtney, with all his sophistication in hard-nosed business affairs and ivory-towered academia, understood Arden House and its potential, and with his incredible energy and focus, set out to make it the finest conference center. The tone of elegance combined with informality prevailed.

Not a man for the sidelines, Courtney took on the Woodbury tax assessors. He never missed a session with them and bulldozed an agreement no one believed could be fashioned. It still stands today.

Courtney foresaw the need for an auditorium and got it built. With Marjorie, who could make even the coldest marble hall cozy, Arden House became a haven where thoughtful men and women gathered to focus attention on some pressing problems.

Tradition did not deter him when he deemed action in order. In the early days of the executive summer session at Arden, the final exam became the bugaboo of a growing number of young multinational participants. Extreme panic found outlet in physical symptoms similar to heart attacks. Courtney's solution: Don't hire a shrink, do away with the exam. That warmed the cockles of my Bennington heart.

As chairman of the American Assembly, he was a dynamo of energy and determination. To Courtney, everything was possible. Once, as we were leaving a meeting together, Courtney spotted the name of a foundation high on the elevator wall. "Look!" he exclaimed and pressed its floor button. "Kathy, want to come?" To watch a master fund-raiser work his magic—this time uninvited, unannounced—was a chance in a lifetime. Of course I accepted. We got off at the designated floor, and he talked his way into the foundation executive's office without a wait. Courtney's pitch was smooth and devastatingly effective. Twenty minutes later we emerged with a commitment from a completely overwhelmed enthusiast.

To me, Courtney was a dear, dear man. I wonder how many of you came in contact with his puckish humor. Some eighteen years ago, he felt that a staid, entrenched board he was serving on should join the vanguard and have women represented. He wished to propose my name. When I protested my total ignorance of the workings of a multifaceted corporation, his face screwed up into a marvellous giggle. "It would do them some good," was his rejoinder.

Arden House stands as a testament of Averell's and Roland's dreams and intents. Thank you, Courtney; thank you Marjorie. We are grateful.

Jacques Barzun
University Professor Emeritus
Columbia University

In response to the invitation to speak today, Dr. Barzun wrote:

To MY IMMENSE REGRET several physical disabilities have combined to preclude my appearance to speak about Courtney Brown. Since I have always had great affection and admiration for Courtney, I am prompted to write a few words about him, which you might want to read to the gathering [at the memorial service].

From the day when Courtney appeared in Hamilton Hall as a young instructor in economics—which was the day I first met him—to the end of his splendid career, I felt that here was a man of uncommon mould. My early admiration for his mental powers and wise temper were soon coupled with affectionate friendship. It was clear that Columbia had made a recruit who would serve with distinction to himself and benefit to the institution. The years proved the truth of this judgment, which was not hard to make.

I recall that at the dinner celebrating the opening of the new Business School building that Courtney had planned and made possible, I said that perhaps any dean could raise funds and carry out such a purpose, but only Courtney Brown could have got rid of University Hall, the old, ugly, never-completed structure shaped like a ferryboat with two smokestacks, that generations had tried to hide or demolish.

And now, in its central campus position, was the new Business School, bright and efficient both within and without, the crowning achievement of a true builder in higher education.

A university is always in need of such men as Courtney Brown: they are not to be had on demand; one can only hope for them.

James W. Kuhn
Courtney C. Brown Professor of Management and Organization
Columbia Business School

To THOSE OF US WHOSE CHILDHOOD WAS BRACKETED by the Great Depression, Franklin Roosevelt was the President against whom all other Presidents before and after are measured. Roosevelt's natural home seemed to us to be the White House and he the only person who really measured up to the office. For those of us who joined the faculty of the Graduate School of Business in the 1950s, whose professional careers spanned the expansion years of business education and the rise of the MBA to a kind of secular glory, Courtney became the dean against whom all other deans, before and after, are measured. His natural place seemed to be in the Dean's Office, that room, though occupied by a succession of other deans, really is in some fundamental way, to me anyway, *his* office.

Courtney loomed, and still looms, large in my teaching experience at Columbia. The school's curriculum, its buildings, its administrative structure, and the overall purposes of the school and the faculty's motivating ethos still reflect the inspiration and vision that Courtney provided. He strangely believed that we were, first of all, to serve our students by teaching ably and well. Only after we fulfilled our teaching responsibilities were we researchers of excellence. He expressed and practiced a concern for the school's junior faculty, protecting them against exploitation and assisting them in establishing their professional careers and their reputations through research.

In my days as a junior faculty member, seldom a week went by that he did not see me and ask about how my BOOK was coming along. In those days, books rather than articles were the high road to tenure and professional recognition. No matter what I answered and however many times I assured him I was pursuing the book diligently, he would chucklingly exclaim, "Well, Jim, remember a book, is a book, is a book."

For Courtney, providing a business education was a high calling. We were no mere technicians, filling students' heads full of rules and theorems, however useful they might be. Along with the conventionally practiced knowledge of the business world, he insisted that we infuse our approach, our lessons, and our teaching with what he aptly called "the liberating arts." Managing requires an act of imagination, a projection of meaning and vision for the organization; if it is to be truly practical in human and a humane society, it is necessarily also an artistic and moral endeavor.

On the plinth of Uris Hall before the addition, he had inscribed a quotation from Alfred Whitehead's speech at the inauguration of the Harvard Business School in 1929: "A great society is one in which its business [managers]. . . think greatly of their functions." I believe that both Whitehead and Courtney understood those functions about which the managers could—and should—think greatly were service and serving. They were not profit and the bottom line, as important and necessary as they are. But management and managers should rightly consider as their great function the services they render in providing efficiently and effectively food, clothing, shelter, transportation, health, and all the other multitudinous goods and services of an industrial world.

The greatness of managers and thus of society lies not in the rate of return, or high position, large salaries or public prominence, but in their efforts in a poor world to improve life and living for all. I am grateful to Courtney for helping me realize this vision of what we in the school and our students and our graduates are all about.

Donald G. Morrison
Professor of Marketing, UCLA
Former Armand G. Erpf Professor of Business, Columbia Business School

AS YOU HAVE HEARD, COURTNEY BROWN WAS MANY THINGS to many people. I'd like to focus on "Courtney the Golfer" and "Courtney the Stroke Patient." In these recollections you will detect a common theme—Courtney never gave up; Courtney always kept his sense of humor; and if he loved you, he showed it.

Courtney was an excellent golfer. He carried a six handicap, he made it to the finals of the Club Championship at the Scarsdale Golf Club, he was a Senior Champion, and he was an absolute wizard around the green. However, as his age and physical ailments took their toll, Courtney could only hit the ball about 100 yards. But he was still tough. One of the last rounds I played with him, we had a friendly nine-hole wager. I had to give Courtney some strokes, of course, but after the first eight holes we were all even. We were playing for a dollar, and Courtney really wanted to win. Well, he got up and hit his usual tee shot, bisecting the fairway. As the ball was in the air, he turned to me and said, "No hook, no slice, no distance." I hit a pretty good tee shot. We got up to Courtney's ball, and his second shot was just a carbon copy of the first one. But he was still short of my drive. As we got to his ball, he mumbles about being old and not having any distance and he hits his third shot, same thing. But now he's still about thirty or forty yards from the green. I hit my second shot on the green, about twenty-five feet from the hole, and I'm feeling pretty good. Then Courtney gets up and hits this patented little punch-shot: he punches the ball up on the green about six feet from the hole. Remember I have to give him a stroke on this hole. Well, the inevitable happened. I took three putts for my five. Courtney made his putt for a five. He won the hole, he won the match. And as we were walking off the green, with his bright twinkling blue eyes, he looks at me and throws his arm around my shoulder and says, "Well, Don, looks like the tortoise just caught the hare. Where's my dollar?"

I knew Courtney pretty well, but when I really got to know and appreciate him and Marjorie and their relationship was after his stroke. When he returned to New York, he was in White Plains Hospital, which is only about a mile from my house, so I made it a habit to drop by on the way home from school. Some people would say, "Gee, Don, doesn't that depress you seeing Courtney like that?" And I would always answer, "No." Courtney was always delighted to see me; he kept trying to learn new words. He would push himself to regain the use of his right side and up close I could see firsthand the love and affection between Courtney and Marjorie. No, those visits were not depressing; they were a real inspiration to me.

Courtney moved from White Plains to the Burke Rehabilitation Center, which was still near my house. I saw him frequently, but eventually he had to go to a nursing home. Well, Marjorie hunted all around, and although it was not anywhere near the nearest, she settled on Sleepy Hollow, which is a very cheery place with an upbeat staff who grew to love Courtney. During my visits, I'd usually have lunch with him, then take a stroll around. On one particularly beautiful day we came back to his room, and Marjorie was waiting there for us. All of a sudden, Courtney got very agitated. I said, "Courtney, do you want to go back outside?" And Marjorie said, "Do you want to watch football on TV with Don?" "No." We tried a few other things, and finally Marjorie said, "The wine!" His eyes lit up. I went and got a bottle of wine from the closet. There were two little glasses, Marjorie declined to have a drink. I filled up the glasses. It took a real effort, but he said, "Cheers!" We clinked the glasses. There he was, a gracious host to the end.

My last visit was about a year ago. I was in New York for a conference. I drove up to Connecticut to see Barbara and George Thompson, and then the three of us drove to Sleepy Hollow. We had a great visit, reminiscing about the old times. George, of course, had been on the faculty for over forty years; Barbara used to be Courtney's secretary at the school. Eventually it was time to leave. Courtney knew it would be a long time until he saw me again, and perhaps he knew it might be our last visit. When we were about to go, he grabbed my hand and just held it. He held it for about a minute, and then he leaned over and kissed the back of my hand. I loved the old guy, and in the only way he had left, he showed his love for me.

Boris Yavitz
Paul Garrett Professor of Public Policy and Business Responsibility
Former Dean, Columbia Business School

WELL, YOU HAVE NOW SEEN Courtney Brown through five different pairs of eyes, five different witnesses, five different perspectives. They offer a remarkable diversity, but all of those views, I think, serve to sketch out and give good form to a portrait of a truly remarkable man. Let me add a sixth dimension to the five you've heard. I'd like to outline, at least in a few strokes, a sketch of Courtney Brown as a major contributor to the art and science of Deaning: the mystical craft of being a Dean. I was one of many who benefitted directly from this dimension of Courtney's wisdom. I had served on this faculty for a decade or so while Courtney was our Dean. I watched him in action, and then had the benefit of his advice and council when it came to be my turn to serve as the school's dean.

I learned much from him—more than I could possibly cover in this brief tribute—and much, much more than I'd care to reveal even if I had the time. Let me, however, cite three lessons which are both insightful and amusing.

Lesson #1. How to gain a realistic perspective of a dean's perceived status in the pecking order of academe. Courtney told me that several times. He had just made the transition from big-time executive of Standard Oil, New Jersey, to become dean of the school. On his first day on the job, he went into his new office, looked around the new empire, and he noticed in the middle of his desk was a strange, large buzzer. He kept looking for how to activate it, but couldn't figure it out. So he went out and saw his secretary, whom I did not know personally, but they told me she was a severe lady who had trained several deans before Courtney. He said, "How do you make this buzzer work?" And she said, "Oh, that's simple. The button for it is in the front room on my desk. And when I need you, I buzz it." True story. Now if you knew Courtney, you can guess that the position of the buzzer and the button was soon reversed. But, the lesson for any new dean, I think, is unmistakable. I think you will remember that pride goeth before a fall, or to put it another way, don't succumb to any delusions of adequacy.

Lesson #2. All faculty are created equal. Or at least all publicly visible trappings should so imply. It takes a sharp architectural eye, but if you have it, you will notice that Uris Hall is one of the few buildings in New York City which has no corner offices. All faculty offices on all floors from the third floor up are identical in size; same number and shape of windows, same furnishings. And Courtney was quite explicit in specifying this layout. As he said to me, "Can you imagine how long it would take otherwise to assign faculty offices when we move to the new building? And how would you select the four professors to receive the four corner offices on each floor and even more pointedly how do you tell the other 21 why they didn't get that office?" I thought that was a great lesson in both democracy and equal treatment. I should add a P.S. that there is indeed one corner office in Uris Hall, and that's the Dean's office. But, there is only one Dean competing for it at a time, and more importantly, as several speakers have noted,

Courtney paid his rent and his dues in full. He practically raised the money and financed that building himself.

Lesson #3. There is no limit to the personal sacrifice a Dean is prepared to undertake for the sake of his faculty. The move to Uris Hall consumed just about every penny in our piggybank, and little was left for the small amenities of life once we moved in. We had a nice new faculty lounge, we had pleasant furnishings in it, but we didn't even have the money to serve afternoon tea and cookies for the faculty. Courtney saw his opportunity and seized it. You heard about Courtney's excellent golf game, and he practiced it well. He was playing one summer day with Percy Uris, for whom the Hall is named. Percy mentioned to him when they got into the clubhouse that Courtney should really lose some weight for his health's sake. Courtney immediately pounced on that and said, "OK, I will lose ten pounds in two weeks, but I have to have a bet with you that if I make it, you will provide tea and cookies for the faculty for one full year." Percy Uris agreed, and the deed was done. Courtney worked hard at dieting, but he was still a couple of pounds off the target when the day of reckoning came. Percy Uris wanted to weigh Courtney at that point, and Courtney said, "No, you weighed me last time after we had our game, you will weigh me again at the conclusion of this round." Percy agreed. Courtney went out, and on a hot, blistering, humid summer day, played eighteen holes in his wooly underwear with a wind-breaker that wouldn't let the air penetrate through. By the time they got back to the clubhouse and Courtney stepped on the scale, he had indeed made it. He met the weight hurdle, and the faculty lived high and mighty on tea and cookies for the next year.

In many other ways, for the fifteen years that Courtney served as our Dean, he gave us a pound of flesh and more, much more. He was glad to do it for the faculty he so carefully built up. I might add here that Courtney did not only add to the knowledge of the art of Deaning, he also added to the list of its distinguished practitioners. It's interesting that Peter Buchanan mentioned several of the names of a strong cadre of administrators that Courtney built for the school. Let me repeat a couple of those names as I think they are worth mentioning: Chester Owens is here, Bill Heffernan, Karin Paulson, Fred Way, John Barch, Hoke Simpson, and many others. He also built a number of strong outside deans and presidents. Let me just name Bob Senkier, Sam Richmond, and Clarence Walton who was also mentioned.

From my own perspective as a former dean, Courtney personified a managerial philosophy that can be summarized in just a few words: Listen to as many points of view as you can muster, but then be clear about what you want to do and push hard for it whenever an opportunity arises. Work hard, never give up, but above all never lose your sense of humor or that special Courtney Brown twinkle in your eye.

Themes
from
the Writings
of
Courtney C. Brown

I
The Changing World of Business

The Merits of Moderate Growth*

THE TIMES ARE OUT OF JOINT. Political structures, laboriously designed by mankind over millennia to preserve individual expression in open societies, confront countervailing pressure groups and authoritarian governments. Enormous military outlays continue to grow when national arsenals are already able to obliterate whole peoples, even life itself. International discussion of arms control or reduction is superficial at best. Inflation, stimulated by efforts to reach maximum economic strength, has become permanent, varying only by alternating periods of moderation and acceleration. Long forgotten are the virtues of stabilization or of a sustained move of prices downward to match improved productivity and lower unit costs of production.

The evidence of social and political turbulence is present or barely below the societal surface throughout the globe. But the cause of this turbulence is by no means clear. I want to propose here that part of the difficulty comes from an excessive enthusiasm for growth in all its forms—beliefs so long and so firmly held that they now qualify as traditional attitudes. This essay is a plea for the moderation of several types of growth that otherwise can be pernicious.

The Concept of Growth

Growth had little or no role in Medieval thought. The idea of growth did not begin to awaken the European mind until the arrival of the Age of Reason and the Enlightenment. For several hundred years, it has been the prime mover of material well-being. Affluence, it was realized, increased mobility and enlarged the range of alternative opportunities. Its identification with the achievement of human happiness focused intellectual interest and inquiry on the means of achieving and maintaining growth.

But the concept that rapid growth in general brings social progress and individual happiness is now being challenged and qualified. Technical progress, it is said, has replaced the mutually satisfying relations between people that were typical of an earlier day with a rootlessness and a sense of

31

insecurity. Collective affluence does not necessarily mean individual happiness. There is no convincing reason to believe mankind is any happier than he was a thousand years ago. Bewildering as it seems, many in the less-developed world still seem to prefer a stable, tradition-directed though impoverished life to one of mobility and uncertain change.

In the developed world, exponential growth now creates serious problems for the natural as well as the social environment. It is becoming a question of whether some kinds of growth may not have become, on balance, debilitating to well-being. But growth per se cannot fail to be an ameliorating influence. Before growth, life was a "zero-sum game." One individual, one group, one nation got ahead at the cost of another. Unfortunately, much of this attitude still governs popular thought, particularly in matters of national political relations. The amount of land is finite and the territorial imperative continues to be one of the strongest influences in foreign policy. Not so in economics, which is based on growth. A suitable transaction is capable of providing an incremental benefit to both parties. If no decrement of equal magnitude for third parties is involved, growth has occurred. But the public is now beginning to notice the decrement that it suffers in many economic transactions.

There are types of growth in which the benefits are unquestionably overwhelming. All forms of the arts and culture have unlimited potentials for the improvement of well-being. Knowledge, including technology, is like an expanding balloon—what is known being the inside of the balloon and the unknown the outside. We shall never know as much as we do not know. Perhaps it is just as well, for some of the recently gained knowledge in the fields of nuclear power and biochemistry have vast potentials, both for good and evil. Some feel that advancing technology simply results in modern man's grasping for more material goods. Others hold that technology has now reached a stage where it can create a new and happier life—if only man were fit for such a world. The choice is yet to be made.

Three Forms of Growth

Three forms of accelerating growth that have negative implications illustrate the penalties of excess. Unfortunately, each has secured a very firm place in the traditional or conventional wisdom. Much contemporary public policy is based on them. Officeholders are elected by endorsing them. Unless modified they can be subtly pernicious. Without restraint, they become tyrannical traditions. They are:

(1) The growth of self-seeking organizations with sufficient influence to significantly bias political and economic behavior has resulted in an

interwoven network of countervailing private powers. Appeals of special interests and single-issue politics result in trade-offs that impose a kind of social and economic arteriosclerosis on societies. Part of the flexibility and adaptability of society is lost.

(2) The competitive growth of the power of nations is comparable to the growth of the countervailing power of organizations within nations, except that it is at a higher level and occurs for the most part within the context of what we have come to call a zero-sum game. One nation's gain is construed as another's loss—in land, in resources, or in trade. Rarely is aggression acknowledged. The competitive growth of the military is alleged to serve several purposes: to redress past grievances, or to defend against feared aggression for land, trade, or hegemony. Under the guise of self-defense, the growth of military power has now exceeded all possibility of sustained conflict by the major nations; total destruction is more likely. An alternative use of resources for beneficent purposes is frustrated by this military excess.

(3) The attempt of the more-developed nations to achieve and sustain maximum economic growth is a result of the desire for more material wealth, for full employment, and of the self-seeking of nations and of organizations within nations. The competitive effort to enlarge the cornucopia of wealth has been extraordinarily successful in the twentieth century, but not without the cost of sustained inflation. Resulting distortions in the distribution of gross production among claimant groups have intensified countervailing claims, usually ameliorated by more growth and inflation. Excessive growth among the populations of the lesser-developed parts of the world has impaired individual well-being despite the stimulation of inflation.

In years gone by, all three of these forms of growth have made major contributions to human development. Many feel that they will continue to do so. To challenge growth and the attitudes toward its encouragement in any form hackles the plumage of many. For the lesser-developed world, most forms of growth, excepting population growth, are probably right. Elsewhere, circumstances have changed. Organizations have become so ubiquitous that a need is felt to protect the individual against them, to curb organizational power. Increments to material abundance are now not so much the end sought as is the level of employment. Assuring full satisfaction of consumers' wants and needs is often secondary. Military production makes a large contribution to employment, but the potential for total destruction cancels the possibility of its being beneficial. Yet there are those who would test the limits of growth in all three of these forms. While a case can be made that the quantitative growth of organizations, of the military, and of total production should slow down, innovation working toward the improvement of the quality of life certainly should not and, indeed, must not stop.

It is now public policy to approve, indeed encourage, groups to organize and seek for themselves larger shares of the national product, i.e., a larger share of the public pie. To increase the size of the pie, maximum economic growth is an accepted public objective, even though accompanied by the inevitability of undesirable pollution, depletion, and inflation. Many believe that the resulting inflation can be controlled. A "little bit" of inflation is even felt to be desirable. But the belief that maximum growth and full employment can be reconciled with price stability has proved to be an illusion. The form of growth that has proved to be the most pernicious of all—military might—is made acceptable as national defense. But defense to one nation looks like offense to the neighbor.

Acceded to without serious question, these notions of the continued desirability of vigorous growth of private, self-seeking organizations, of military strength, and the total economy combine to make a major contribution to the instability of our times. Interactive, each reinforces the others. The ratchet effect of group struggle for larger shares has made aggregate growth more imperative. Contention and societal conflict have been ameliorated but not eliminated. Inflation when controlled has stimulated total growth, but in much of the world it is now out of control. In earlier times, military aggression resulted in territorial aggrandizement or extended hegemony and was a stimulant to total growth. Unfortunately, and without full realization, these several notions that have for centuries underpinned much of the economic and social progress of the Western world, in their present excesses, have now become disordering. That they are no longer constructive when carried to the current extent, but have become subtly debilitating, is a root cause of the confusion of public policy that continues to be based on them. The elaboration of each will help clarify some of the contradictions of our times.

The Growth of Private Organizations

The right of assembly and association is one of the most cherished in civilized society; it is a keystone of democracy. It is embedded in the constitutions of the United States and of other nations. No tradition has older roots. Its appearance in the medieval guilds is the progenitor of many of its present forms. Yet it is a right that can become injurious when unrestrained. It has become just that in some instances in contemporary society.

Organized groups can serve the interests of society at large, or they may use their power in the narrow interests only of their members. It is not easy to find a dividing line between an association's self-serving and public-serving activities. Most activities of organizations blend as a mixture—sometimes more of one than of the other. But it may be observed that less attention to respective beneficiaries is given by the typical legislator that provides the sanction than to the political rewards of the sponsorship. Politicians cannot be relied upon to impose appropriate restraint.

Associations tend to concentrate on promoting the immediate and parochial interests of their members. Usually that is the reason for their being. The dominating purpose is the pursuit of self-interest through the power of group action, which is usually more effective than individual effort. The public interest is usually secondary.

Self-interest, however, is not always, or necessarily, at the expense of the public. Trade associations may exercise close control of the qualifications of new members, but they achieve an orderliness and standard that otherwise would be lacking. A business corporation, a major type of voluntary association, usually does—but not always—serve a public purpose in its pursuit of self-interest. Professional associations of doctors, lawyers, and academics develop procedures and practices of a restrictive nature that contribute to higher standards of performance. Labor unions serve their members and the public by limiting hazards and grievances in the workplace. Their members achieve a sense of belonging and participation in decisions related to their jobs.

Greater orderliness may result in a society dominated by associations, but the cost is a stiffness in the economy and a pollution in the body politic. A society with extensive countervailing pressure groups seeking self-interests will lose some of its dynamism and become defensively static. Individualism becomes more difficult to assert. Meritocracy is discouraged, timely decisions are harder to make, and there is an increase in bureaucracy and intervention in open markets. Protecting the individual against the activities of organizations may become an increasing concern in years to come.

Single-issue politics emerges to satisfy the wants and needs of special groups. Their efforts usually lead to higher social and financial costs imposed on those who are not members. The current malaise of England and Western Europe has been attributed to powerful groups demanding more and more: more pay, more fringe benefits, more job security; or more market protection, more barriers to professional entry, and more state-provided support of various aspects of daily living. Groups have become accustomed to getting more each year. The end result takes the form of a nation living beyond its means.

The deeply embedded tradition of associating and organizing in democracies has been more stressed than the proper limits to the purposes served. Unfortunately, the longer a society has freedom of organization, the more self-serving groups seem to accumulate. Thus, for example, Professor Marcus Olson has observed, ". . . with age British society has acquired so many organizations and collusions that it suffers from an institutional sclerosis."

The professions of medicine, law, and academe, together with organized labor, provide the most conspicuous instances of collusive strength. Public concern about incompetent practitioners provides doctors, lawyers, and academics an ideal cover for their associations' policies that otherwise would be described as monopolistic. Labor unions, deliberately given many monopolistic powers in the early decades of this century, have enforced work rules that resist change, compel work to be done more than once, and, in the United States, have given steel, railroads, and automobiles wage rates that are noncompetitive with other parts of the world.

But the professions and organized labor do not by any means occupy these roles of cupidity alone. The capitols of many nations swarm with lobbyists that represent the self-interests of enormous numbers of associations. Countervailing groups are the characteristic pattern of life. Intertwined action and reaction among them results in a ratchet-lifting of the costs to provide the goods and services that are produced and offered for sale.

The resulting sustained movement of costs and prices upward must necessarily be accompanied by expansive monetary and fiscal policies—policies that are usually misconstrued as the primary cause of inflation, rather than the manifestations of inflation already built into the economy. Creditors, pensioners, the handicapped, and the other unorganized find themselves disadvantaged. To an undesirable degree, free markets have been replaced in the distribution of the social product by the not too subtle cupidity of a maze of collusive associations and their lobbyists, or by political agencies responding to their pressures.

Among the self-seeking organizations is the corporation—most would point to it as the dominant self-seeking institution. Fortunately, its self-seeking has provided the competitive drive for an enormous increment in the material well-being of a large part of the world. Where the corporation has no role, or a minor role, deprivation is the normal pattern of life. That is true in both capitalistic and socialistic societies. In its basic essentials, the corporation is nothing more than a means of marshalling deferred consumption and organizing it to produce additional goods and services. To some extent, its self-seeking has taken the form of exacting quasi-monopoly compensation for its activities. But, for several centuries, it has gotten its chief reward from converting raw materials and technology into desired goods and services at lower costs with ever greater efficiency. Society at large has been the ultimate beneficiary.

In the more developed and more economically mature parts of the world, the corporation must now face the need to serve the interests of more than just its legal owners. Its own success compels it. But decrements to the well-being of those not immediately involved in its activities appear with increasing frequency—what economists call externalities. The corporation's dramatic success in expanding material wealth is of such a magnitude that it has been placed in a position of not yet fully realized public trust. Its self-seeking must now necessarily include those associated as employees, consumers, suppliers, the community at large, as well as the stockholders and management. That will require a major readjustment in the corporation's internal power structure, including a more independent board of directors with diversified backgrounds.

Even though less tractability through working through groups seems to be a dominant direction of societal change, there are offsetting influences. Flexibility in the economy has been preserved by the rapid advance of technology. Associations may resist but ultimately they are compelled to adapt. Business corporations, heretofore concerned almost exclusively with the self-serving bottom line for stockholders, are extending their horizons to include the welfare of both blue- and white-collar employees and the community at large. Governments do not always succumb to special interest groups and frequently deal rationally with broad public concerns. In depression phases of the business cycle, associations, including labor unions, moderate their insistent demands for more and more. Increased awareness of exploding medical costs has led to efforts for their control through the collaboration of employers, unions, health administrators, and government officials.

But the tradition of free assembly and association with only limited restraint is strong in democracies. It will continue to be asserted in its many forms as a seldomly inhibited right as long as society at large is unaware of its negative aspects.

No clear-cut remedy is available, but awareness is the first step toward amelioration. Perhaps before the charters of all significant organizations are issued or renewed, they should be carefully analyzed to determine the balance of self-interest versus societal-interest implied for their members. Most can be expected to have powerful incentives to seek larger shares of the national product even though it may be at the expense of the public well-being. That does not mean that such charters should be denied. In most cases, it might be well for the balance between self-interest and soci-etal-interest to fall within certain limits. How the right of assembly, an almost sacred tradition, might be modified and restrained is a matter of high legislative and judicial importance.

The Growth of Military Power

Conflict is inherent in nature. The process of minimizing conflict and the consequences of conflict is, in a sense, the essence of civility or civiliza-tion. The development of law underpins the process, but at best, law among nations, unlike domestic law, is very ambiguous. Law among nations is based on the notion of the sanctity of sovereignty, but that notion is rapidly becoming a fluid concept. In the modern world, governments that are perceived to violate human rights, itself an imprecise concept, are said to forfeit the moral protection of sovereignty. Other nations feel uninhibit-ed to take an overt or covert part in foreign civil wars. The Brezhnev Doctrine held that the Soviet sphere only expands, never retreats. The Reagan Doctrine proclaims that support for foreign (domestic) rebels is in fact self-defense and sanctioned by the law among nations.

A less dangerous confrontation of countervailing power among nations is found in international trade. As transportation has become more rapid and more available, as instantaneous communication has become more widespread, trading across national borders has become more competitive. Restraints—and encouragements—of numerous kinds are now imposed on the flow of goods by all nations to gain advantages, but the ultimate win-ners are those whose populations are dedicated to work and have the best skills. World trade is a vast competitive race for advantage over other nations, a race fortunately better protected by international commercial law than by ambiguous political law. But conflict rather than civility among nations has been, and is, a way of life. In matters of foreign policy, whether commercial or political, there are no friends—only interests.

When contesting nations rather than private organizations are the countervailing power groups, the dangers to civilized survival become an issue. Not relying on ambiguous international law for resolution, nations resort to their traditional source of strength: military might. But the dimin-ished ability of military power to contribute to security or well-being, and the questionable benefits of political domination of other nations, are truly seminal events that have emerged in the twentieth century. This insight is new and as yet is little noticed—certainly not appreciated.

For as long as recorded history, men have joined in tribes, principalities, and more recently in nations to win political control or hegemony over their neighbors; or, alternatively, to prevent others from doing so. The prize was once land, gold, or other treasure. More recently, it has been access to resources that could be exploited, raw materials to be converted or to populations that could be worked or taxed. But political control of other people was a game of the nineteenth century or before, and its time has now passed. In terms of costs and benefits, even the hegemony game is now a loser and not worth playing.

Political control of "other" people may have become less realistic, but domination or hegemony continue to be the prime movers of the foreign policies of major nations. Hegemony is especially strong in Soviet thinking, derived from both the Russian past and Marxist-Leninist ideology. But the Soviets are not alone. The distinction between "vital interests" and hegemony is often blurred in world politics. These notions also mistakenly provide the starting point of those who associate the global spread of business with the imperialistic ambitions of governments. For much of the seventeenth, eighteenth, and nineteenth centuries business was indeed used as an extension of national purpose, as an arm of government to extend its influence. The slogan was well-known; the pound, the franc, the guilder followed the flag—a nice way of saying that after military subjugation, the field was safe for business.

What an anomaly that this projection of yesterday's thought should so deeply influence political policy in the twentieth century. The carnage of World War II is said to have resulted from the distortions left from World War I. The tragedy of 1914 is felt by many to have resulted largely from the failure of the Central Powers to have joined the colonial game in time to get their share. But the realities of the world have now changed. After World War II, it was thought to be retribution to deprive the defeated nations of the colonies they had possessed and to deny them the military establishments to win them back. Retribution indeed! The most robust recoveries were those of Germany and Japan. True, they were assisted to serve as buffers against the Soviets and China, but the fact remains that those who were denied colonies and raw materials, and the military muscle to acquire them, have had the best of things in the postwar economy. Those that retained colonies or hegemony over others found it to be an unrewarding drain.

The use of military muscle by the former Allies to prevent change has been unsuccessful and costly. Neither the well-being of the people of Britain, France, and the United States nor the benefits to Russia in Eastern Europe have been enhanced by the use of military power. In fact, it has been counterproductive. Hegemony over others is no longer an asset.

Japan provides a dramatic example. That nation's military effort to create an "Asian Co-Prosperity Sphere" in the 1930s was a late example of nineteenth-century business following the flag; it was a failure. And yet after World War II, without military power or control of the raw materials of the Far East, Japan's prosperity has been the most robust of all nations. Other nations have also enjoyed good times without hegemony over others or political control of raw materials, for instance, Singapore and Hong Kong. They have prospered with no visible resources apart from the resourcefulness of their people. The political game of extending hegemony, or resisting the extension of hegemony, is no longer rewarding, but that fact is yet to be recognized in the foreign offices of the major nations.

It begins to appear that in recent years the foreign policies of nations have been, and are now, motivated by an enormous illusion. With the arrival of instant communication, accelerated transportation, and intermingled production and commercial relationships, the world has changed. Only a few wise leaders have found ways to challenge the inherited conviction that territory or its domination is directly related to the well-being of people. In most cases the notion has had just the opposite result. It can impair well-being.

Under the guise of territorial security and defense, global military ambitions impose an enormous drain on the resources of all nations. They compel tax burdens, the resistance to which induces huge deficits. They drain away foreign exchange to finance distant military installations. Military outlays are a major contributor to the miasma of inflation. They are a sponge that absorbs resources that otherwise would be available to achieve an improved quality of life to which all aspire. As President Dwight D. Eisenhower said in 1953:

> Every gun that is made, every warship launched, every rocket fired signifies, in the final sense, a theft from those who hunger and are not fed, those who are cold and are not clothed. This world in arms is not spending money alone. It is spending the sweat of its laborers, the genius of its scientists, the hopes of its children. . . . This is not a way of life at all in any true sense. Under the cloud of threatening war, it is humanity hanging from a cross of iron.

A century or more ago political control of physical assets was all-important. In some situations it still is today, as demonstrated by the example of petroleum for the OPEC nations, an unusual case because petroleum is a resource that impinges on most phases of production and on consumer life. And the need for access to other critical materials varies with perceived political purposes. But supplies of the world's production of most raw materials, finished products, and technical and financial services are more likely to be available as a result of business incentives. The emergence of the transnational corporation and instant communication has played a major role in this regard. Witness again the dramatic experience of Japan. An Asian co-prosperity sphere in the post-World-War-II period has been created without military muscle and without the possession of national resources other than social commitment and business initiative.

Aggression rising from cultural differences may or may not be associated with territorial ambitions. Cultural differences can express themselves in contrasting forms of government or religious beliefs and practices. Indeed, before the arrival of the nation-state as we know it today, cultural aggression was the basis of such exploits as those of Alexander the Great, the Crusaders, and the Moorish conquerors of the Mediterranean Basin. Conflict based on religious differences can be the most violent, and belief in a political system may become almost a kind of religion. Opponents become "evil empires" or "imperial capitalists."

But it need not always be so. Except for Indo-China, accommodation among the political, religious, and economic differences in the Far East has been remarkable in the postwar period. Even the extreme differences with China have been largely mitigated. But not so with Eastern Europe and the U.S.S.R. With the latter, territorial control is not so much the issue as is hegemony. It is the extension of cultural, political, and economic dominance. All are believed to be issues of grave importance. But seldom is the question asked, what and where are the benefits of achieving hegemony? When it involves the cost of maintaining a military occupation abroad or the loss of trading and cultural exchange opportunities in the world community, the net advantages are doubtful indeed.

If the current foreign policies of nations are of such questionable merit, why do their leaders wish to impose on their peoples the heavy burdens involved—and, in a nuclear age, such great risks, perhaps total risks. The tyranny of tradition is one reason. That has always been the way of the world. Aggressive strength has always been thought to be the best defense. But another and more subtle answer is available from the earliest times. Domestic political leadership has been strengthened by the existence of an external enemy. If one is not available, it may have to be created. It was true with primitive tribes and medieval principalities, and has continued to be true for modern nations. The external enemy will be most useful if it can be convincingly presented as an aggressor, whether territorial, cultural, or religious. Few leaders in history seem to have survived without this disingenuous prop. There are exceptions—but those who have invoked an external enemy usually are the ones who have been able to retain a domestic constituency. It has been the behavioral pattern for centuries.

Thus the territorial imperative and cultural aggression in the search for hegemony provide an intractable source of reverberating turbulence. Public conviction that one's neighbors have benign intent is unlikely to be encouraged unless a convenient and perhaps more distant enemy is available. The roots of conflict are deeply embedded in past practice and in inherited tradition. They are unlikely to be eradicated unless the utter horror of our capacity to obliterate provides a shock wave of universal revulsion. Perhaps the sheer magnitude of our mutually destructive power will compel a rethinking of the assumptions of the world's foreign policies.

Maximum Economic Growth and the Inflation Syndrome

At one time in the history of attitudes about growth, it was felt that a nation's wealth was measured by its stock of gold. Later, the French Physiocrats, followed shortly by Adam Smith in England, identified the wealth of nations with physical production: agricultural products by the Physiocrats, all production to satisfy life's needs by Smith. Although the Philosophical Radicals never abandoned their interest in growth, primary attention to it lasted only several decades. Early in the nineteenth century, David Ricardo diverted concern from growth to the laws governing the distribution of wealth: who gets what part and why. The neoclassical economists throughout the nineteenth century elaborated what came to be called "distribution analysis."

It was not until the third decade of the twentieth century that the idea of growth returned dramatically to center stage. The theoretical work of John Maynard Keynes and the development of national income accounting by Simon Kuznets and others were powerful influences in redirecting the focus. Very quickly, economists became enraptured with growth. With the concomitant objective of full employment, it proved to be a commanding idea—so pervasive that even the questions of growth *for what* and *for whom* were often relegated to secondary status. The problems that had so concerned the distribution theorists were alleviated, but not eliminated, by the interest in growth.

But questions are now beginning to reappear: growth for whom? growth for what? Some now qualify their enthusiasm for maximum growth by asking whether it is compatible with achieving the best quality of life for the greatest number. Does it exact too high a price in its residuals of personal stress, and in depletion and pollution—in what economists call "opportunity costs" levied against the quality of life? Is there a point at which the populations of the more-developed nations can maximize their satisfactions only through an optimal rate of economic growth, that is, a rate subjectively believed to be the most favorable for the most concerned?

Setting aside the special case of the lesser-developed countries, several questions are pertinent for the more-developed ones. Is maximum economic growth the only means of providing job opportunities to all who wish to work, together with the amenities of income to enjoy the fruits of production? Would moderate growth, in contrast to maximum growth, impose relative benefits or penalties on the disadvantaged, both within nations and internationally? Is maximum growth compatible with, or is it debilitating to, maintaining a nation's strength, security, and leadership in a turbulent world?

The most difficult of these questions is how to correlate economic growth with the human desire to be usefully employed. Since it is inhumane to challenge the concept of full employment for willing workers, it has come to be assumed that it is antisocial to question the desirability of maximum economic growth. But this assumed connection obfuscates the issue. A more fruitful inquiry would explore alternatives that are more compatible with less than the full employment budget as it is now theoretically computed.

Growth is now measured by the national production of goods and services, or Gross National Product (GNP). But it is difficult to keep pace with the production of services. Some fifty to seventy-five years ago the work force in the United States moved from a predominantly agricultural to an industrial base. In more recent years, a further shift has made service activities predominant. Many of these, including cultural, educational, and travel activities, are not fully subsumed in the current calibration of the national product, but they are activities that provide jobs, and very attractive ones. Even a significant part of the manufacturers of material goods escape the record taker. Thus, the rate of economic growth and job formation are not precisely correlated. With a slower rate of increase in the work force resulting from a diminished birthrate and a plateauing of the rate at which women are joining the work force, the difficulty of finding jobs by those who wish to work may be expected to diminish over an extended period.

Other influences may mitigate the future employment problem and make it more compatible with optimal economic growth. Thus, there are long-term trends toward shorter workweeks and shorter work careers, accompanied by expanding provisions for post-work security. The greater importance given in recent labor negotiations in the United States to job security relative to wages recognizes these trends. This increased concern with job security is making U.S. labor relations more compatible with those in the economies of nations with which we compete. The shift from agriculture to manufacturing and then to services has been accompanied by a gradual moving of activities with high routine labor content to the lesser-developed nations. The best jobs will remain with the more developed countries, but their number may be relatively fewer. All of these adjustments in the job market should occur gradually if optimal growth replaces maximum growth as a national purpose.

For recent generations, maximum growth has been the target and the major determinant of public policy, except for the unintended restraints imposed by the politics of compassion and redistribution. A shift of policy to moderate growth would represent a major change. The appearance of a gap between a theoretical full employment budget and the measured level of employment has resulted in governmental efforts to stimulate additional employment. In the United States, it has been decreed by legislation since 1946. This "forced feeding" has resulted in a bias in labor practices and wages that has lifted unit costs faster than compensating productivity improvement. If unit costs of labor increase to some 75 percent of total costs, there is no way to maintain an approximation of full employment without resorting to easy money and government deficits. For a half-century the result has required additional money and deficits to avoid a profit squeeze and a contraction of employment and total activity. The ultimate penalty has been sustained inflation—sometimes more, sometimes less—but sustained inflation. As John Kenneth Galbraith has noted:

> The belief that macroeconomic measures can reconcile high employment with price stability, a belief asserted against all the force of both experience and logic, will be counted without question the most unforgivable error of the present generation. . . .[1]

Current discussion does not challenge the desirability or undesirability of inflation, but rather questions only the degree of inflation. Seldom does one hear of the benefits of stable prices. The idea of declining prices has the ring of unreality—or is associated with a contraction of activity or depression. It has long been forgotten that, except for periods of war, during all of the nineteenth century, the United States had a sustained real growth of income per capita with gradually declining prices.

The lowest point for prices was reached at the end of the century. A sharp elbow break upward occurred after World War II, coincident with the revival of a primary interest in growth. Since then, the United States has experienced a persistent increase in prices. The contrast between the two centuries has been dramatic. Dollars have been a poor investment for those who have lived throughout the period. The government has fed inflation for most of the twentieth century.

Stable or declining prices can have positive merits. The rate of growth would not be as great as in a cycle of forced draft inflation, but growth there was in the past century, and optimal growth there now could be. Equity achieved in the distribution of the national product could then be realized without the pressure tactics of the countervailing group politics that are characteristic of the present. Most importantly, stable prices would eliminate the present discrimination against the unprotected and the disadvantaged, an inevitable accompaniment of inflation. Stable prices distribute the benefits of improving productivity to all by making personal incomes more valuable in the marketplace. Additional benefits accrue to the nation in its trading relations with others.

Apart from its inflationary aspects, maximal growth has other seriously debilitating consequences. Depletion of some of the world's resources has begun to alarm geologists. Global production levels have concerned the ecologists. Progressively higher levels of production require more energy, which means more pollution, given present technology. Simply because of the limitations imposed by geology and ecology, the more developed nations may face a future stabilization or a lower per capita real income if the world is to become a more hospitable place in which to live. In "Innovations: Scientific, Technological, and Social," Dennis Gabor, a 1971 Nobel Laureate in Physics, observed:

> Unfortunately all our drive and optimism are bound up with continuous growth: growth addiction is the unwritten and unconfessed religion of our times. In industry and also for nations, growth has become synonymous with hope. Undoubtedly, quantitative growth will have to go on for many more years, but unless we prepare for the turning point well before the end of the century, it may then be too late.

Moreover, gaps are widening. Growth has been progressively more uneven, both within nations and among nations—especially among nations. If gaps are to be narrowed by an acceleration of growth in the lesser-developed nations in pursuit of a continuing rapid growth of the more-developed, the projected result simply becomes intolerable. It is doubtful that the environment of the globe could endure it. The more-developed world in these circumstances will have difficulty maintaining its affluence and its democratic institutions next door to 80 percent of the globe's population struggling in poverty.

It is unfortunate that the slogan most heard in today's milieu of cupidity is "more, more, more." It is time again to ask the question, more of what? Of inflation, and for many, illusory increments of income? Of accelerating growth accompanied by concern for depletion and pollution? Of a turbulent society of contentious group politics? Of discrimination against pensioners, the disabled, and the disadvantaged? Of impoverishment of cultural and educational institutions? Of increased stress and tensions of daily living? It is becoming more evident that everywhere rising population, overcrowding, and pollution are resulting in greater social strife.

The Search for a Consensus

Contemplation of other values and ways to improve the quality of life must seriously question the casual acceptance of our public policies since World War II. Based as they have been on (1) the encouragement, with little restraint, of self-seeking organizations, (2) of ever-growing military strength, (3) and of maximum economic growth with its accompanying inflation, those policies are seriously flawed. Other values are beginning to contest with material abundance and military power as the prime objectives of public policy. A reappraisal and rebalancing of some of the values that have long underpinned national purposes is overdue.

A fundamental choice of future directions is yet to be made. Public policy in recent decades has oscillated between quality of life considerations and what might be called reindustrialization. Ecological and environmental control, and the alleviation of the disadvantaged have vied with maximal economic growth and military security for public approval. Although the choice has not been clearly made, we seem to like rising activity and money incomes the more. For most that spells prosperity. It is fed by the three forms of growth described. The slogan is: ever more prosperity as individuals and as members of organizations. "More, more, more."

The consensus is now unbalanced. There is little wonder that public policy is confused. Exponential growth in the West is incompatible with many of the requirements of achieving a better quality of life. It creates serious problems for the natural as well as the social environment. On the other hand, moderate growth in the West is entirely consistent with the dual aspirations for a materially and psychologically better life in a society of improved well-being. A new consensus, if one is to be found, would require the moderation of public enthusiasm for unlimited growth in several of its forms. Unfortunately, that would be a distasteful program for politicians to embrace because it would confront several cherished traditions that have become subtly tyrannical.

Notes

*Previously unpublished, 1985-86.

1. John Kenneth Galbraith. *Economic Growth Reassessed* (Ottawa: University of Ottawa Press, 1972), p. 50.

A Corporate Dilemma: Materialism vs. Humanism*

WESTERN CIVILIZATION IS IN THE MIDST of a fundamental and historic shift of value orientation. In our speeded up world, the old is barely interred before the new is fully upon us. In dozens of matters of human concern new values make themselves felt. Nor are these great shifts of value without precedent, even if the rapidity of change is new. When these changes have happened in the past, they have had enormous impact. Such a change was the emergence of secular values over religious values and authority during a period that extended over the sixteenth, seventeenth, and eighteenth centuries. In the nineteenth and early twentieth centuries the spread of secular ideas became triumphant. Adaptation was imposed on large sectors of society throughout these centuries, not without sacrifice of established ways of life. Power centers changed. Princes of the Church first gave way to princes of land, who in turn gave way to princes of industrial, commercial, and financial wealth. Even though the process of social change then was sluggish by our current pace, it was inevitable; the glacial pressures could not be denied. Societal institutions and the most firmly established organizations were forced to conform or to disappear with the passage of time.

Public Challenge - Business Response

Many now sense a similar rearrangement of societal values going on in the United States. The values that have been inherited from the Age of Science and Reason are no longer accepted without qualification. They are deemed to be too lacking in solicitude for the public welfare, and in compassion for the disadvantaged. The business corporation became, in the late nineteenth and early twentieth centuries, an organizational form expressing the high values society had come to place on rationality, efficiency, competition, and growth. The unqualified validity of those values is now being challenged by a reaffirmation of the contrasting attitudes and behavioral patterns associated with an earlier humanism. To the extent this is so, the business community would be well advised to give thought to the traditional and accepted purposes of the business corporation with a view to

48

their possible modification—and enlargement. Adaptation to a changing environment is an elementary principle of survival. Adaptation of the governance of corporations to facilitate a harmonious response to changing public expectations, and to the prospective circumstances of the future, will require perceptive identification of the influences now molding public attitudes. It will involve structural change as well as attitudinal change within the corporation.

Unfortunately, most analyses of corporate difficulties are now cast in traditional legal or commercial terms. These fail to provide adequate insights into the problem at hand. The public debate, for the most part, has dealt with minor issues of form and procedures rather than penetrating to the substantive issues of purpose and goals. Nor has it been fruitful for business spokesmen to point an accusing finger at various elements in the community as uninformed or irrational critics of business. Government, the mass media, academics, self-appointed representatives of consumers, environmentalists, conservationists, yes, and even dissident stockholders, have all shared that spotlight. Large sums and much executive time and talent have been assigned to persuade "the public" and discredit critics, all with few discernible results. In fact, the effort on balance may have been counterproductive in that it has placed business in a defensive posture, seeking, in the opinion of far too many, to protect privileged and entrenched positions.

The real values of business—and they are very real—will be restored to credibility in the present climate of opinion only when business spokesmen are able to articulate a set of guiding principles that relate the conduct of business to the whole range of human aspirations, not just to material abundance alone. The impact of business corporations on society has become too ubiquitous to be limited to the latter. To put the matter succinctly, businessmen must learn to think, talk about, and operate on a broader platform than is provided by purely economic considerations. There are admitted dangers in doing so. The career of a typical businessman provides limited opportunity to develop perceptive understanding of non-business considerations. There is an implied threat to efficiency and profitability when decisions are, in part, based on matters additional to those of an economic nature. But there may be no alternative if the relatively unentangled conduct of business is to be preserved.

Concepts that Shaped the Corporation

A brief historical review of concepts that have led to the evolution of the modern business corporation, as we now know it, is a good place to start. The strong light of historical perspective can be very useful in understanding some of the now troublesome issues that appear to be so intractable—especially the issues of why the public holds the business corporation in such relatively low esteem and why government increasingly appears in the role of adversary to business rather than its sponsor.

Reflection on the nature of attitudes and concepts that have given rise to the modern corporation provides an interesting intellectual exercise. In Western Europe, they reach back into the Middle Ages, the Renaissance, the Reformation, the rise of the national state and Mercantilism, and most particularly into the seventeenth and eighteenth century Age of Science and Reason. Conversely, some of the more humanistic attitudes inherited from these early periods are now revived to support criticism of the corporation when it shows itself reluctant to depart from what are regarded by its detractors to be too narrowly conceived commercial purposes.

Orderliness and a passion for certainty, so important for effective corporate management, were sanctified in the Middle Ages. Obedience and correct belief in the authoritative doctrine of an organization, then the Medieval Church, was accepted as a cardinal virtue. Wealth for its own sake was disapproved of but justified as a stewardship—somewhat the same image and posture claimed for the professional manager today. Other characteristics of that ancient period are less supportive of life in the modern corporation; for example, charitable service to mankind, a burning compassion for the disadvantaged, and a reverence for nature as an awesome and wonderful gift of God, the use of which should be limited.

The Renaissance awakened the specious lethargy of the earlier period. Medieval rejection of pride and excellence shifted into an acceptance of thrift and productive labor as commendable means of personal development. The Reformation went a step further in releasing the emerging middle class from the bondage of the Church to support the growth of strong monarchies, whose principal function was to assure the prosperity of newly formed national states. Puritanism, a derivative of the Reformation, elevated the purposes and aims of business society by exalting personal responsibility, discipline, punctuality, honesty, and commitment.

The then newly established monarchies promoted business with enthusiasm within the limits of their understanding. Mercantilism was the result. The art of government, according to Machiavelli, was simply three things: power, expansion, and national prosperity. The corporation emerged as a favored vehicle to achieve all three. Governments granted monopolistic favors and bounty, especially in parts of the newly discovered world, and took over from the medieval guilds the regulation of market sharing, prices, and product quality. National prosperity was sought by helping particular private ventures to succeed. What has been known in recent decades as macroeconomics, namely the stimulation of total activity through fiscal and monetary policy, was then unknown. The whole national effort was directed toward the accumulation of gold and precious metals, then conceived to be the measure of a nation's wealth.

It would be hard to exaggerate the influence of the emergence of preoccupation with the natural sciences. As the seventeenth century turned into the eighteenth century, the developing interest in natural science made two major contributions to public attitudes despite the disdain held for the new methods of science by the traditional, and still reigning, humanists. Allying mathematics and experimental observations, Isaac Newton and his predecessors found an orderliness in nature, the processes of which could be discovered and adapted to man's use. Nature was no longer something to be revered and preserved. Rather, it was a bountiful treasure to be exploited. The idea of an all-embracing natural order led to the second contribution. Instead of seeking reasons for or attributing occult purposes to nature, the direction was to let every man be free to adjust himself to what is natural. Nature and the natural became the ideal, interpreted as reason and the reasonable.

The effect on political structures and social science was profound. Absolute monarchies and the elaborate controls of Mercantilism became irksome, even though they were initially supported by the rising commercial interests. If natural science prescribed freedom for the activities of man in his relation to nature, should not the same hold true in his relations to his fellow men? To limit the power of the monarch, the ancient idea of the Social Contract was revived from Roman law and from the mutual obligations feudal lords had with their serfs. Ultimate power, it was held, rests with the people. Those powers and rights not specifically delegated remain with the people, a basic principle of political federalism. The writings of John Locke opened a path toward constitutional monarchy and away from political absolutism. The individualism and self-reliance initiated in the Reformation, and given further expression in Puritanism, displaced collectivism as a social ideal.

In economic science, then called political economy, revision of thought also occurred. Adam Smith, in particular, corrected several of the false assumptions that had characterized Mercantilism. The wealth of a nation is in its productive capability, not in its store of gold and other precious metals. Domestic trade and commerce as well as manufacturing and production added to economic value. Business, unlike politics, was not what is now called a zero-sum game, where one's gain is another's loss. Both parties to a transaction could gain. Price, if left alone, would adjust to a point that will clear markets. Price controls, whether based on tradition, fairness, or other criteria, would simply get in the way. Set the broad rules of the game that would protect property and contract; let each seek his or her enlightened self-interest in a competitive world and the greatest good for the greatest number would result: the unseen hand of nature! Competition was part of the basic laws of nature. As Charles Darwin later observed, those that were better adapted to the environment would survive; the rest would die out. Competition to survive may be cruel but the laws of nature prescribe it to be essential to the development of strength, both of animate and inanimate beings.

Centuries of Explosive Growth

Thus, by the beginning of the eighteenth century, in the three major areas of intellectual interest—natural science, political science, and economic science—the broad sweep of thought was in the direction of an open society. The corporation had had its adolescence under the tight controls of Mercantilism. It was not merely encouraged, it was supported by government. The favor was reciprocated. Under the libertarianism of the eighteenth century it flowered. In the early nineteenth century it became a legal person. It matured in the industrial environment of the late nineteenth century. The concept of material growth, which played no significant part in intellectual life until the Age of Science, began to take its place alongside the newly identified laws of nature and the ancient religious traditions in its influence on mankind.

The arrival of the eighteenth century was truly an auspicious time for the Western World. With the onrush of science, with government acceptance of the commitment to facilitate national prosperity, and with the acceptance of nature as something to be exploited rather than revered, the stage was set for an explosive growth of material wealth. The corporation was the primary vehicle. It reconciled the widely held ideal of private property and the reality of industrial concentration mandated by technology and the economics of scale. It was inevitable that the conduct of the corporation should harmonize with the values and orderly laws of natural science, and a basic law of nature was survival of the fittest by virtue of being the strongest and most efficient in the competition of life.

The Corporate Dilemma

When Leonardo da Vinci, an early scientist as well as a great artist, observed that "Whoever appeals to authority applies not his intellect but his memory," he referred to the authority of the Church and the ancient moral philosophers. He was not referring to the laws of natural science, the discovery of which was then challengingly incipient. Objective inquiry and rigorous analytical procedures became the rational means to seek truth. Successive discoveries required adaptive and flexible adjustment to new facts and circumstances, especially in the field of technology. Two major consequences ensued for the corporation. The opportunity that was involved in its development attracted men of intelligence, imagination, courage, and action to its leadership; the ability to adapt without excessive restraint became a matter of increasing importance. External political regulation became more onerous. The invocation of natural liberty was used to support, and still supports, the corporation's challenge to external political restraints.

The natural desire of corporate leadership to function without undue external hindrance, however, has provided something of a continuing contrast to the expectation of loyalty to internal corporate authority from those associated within the organization. Performance of the individual is judged by results consistent with concurred purposes. Good or bad intentions are of less relevance. Compassion is seldom an enduring sentiment, which is quite understandable when concurred purposes are focused on low costs and efficiency to support continuous growth. Growth has long been such a dominant purpose, it has become the corporate equivalent of a gospel.

Efficient and effective use of the resources marshalled under the convenient corporate form has been the principal generator of success in creating additional material wealth, in providing more jobs and, indeed, in acquiring still more capital. But the means of achieving efficiency, that is, low unit production costs, tend to make a protracted program related to humanistic consideration difficult and, in some situations, competitively prohibitive. This does not mean there is a one for one tradeoff. In certain types of situations, short-term cost may result in a long-term profit improvement, such as employee medical benefits for example. But management careers are typically developed by reference to the "bottom line" over short periods of time. The emerging humanistic tasks that public expectations are assigning to corporations generally make a poor fit with the pattern of the corporation's traditional activities and purposes in which they have so spectacularly succeeded. Yet, despite two hundred years of enormous material success, there is now an insistent questioning of whether an economic system that is so much a part of the total society should be judged alone by the abundant commodities and services it creates. Equal interest is currently evident in how the economic system exerts its influence—for better or worse—on human personality. Once again the thinking and the societal institutions

and organizations now rooted in the attitudes and methods of natural science, just as they were when they first appeared, are confronted by those
whose primary commitment is to the attitudes and to the values of the
humanist tradition. The business corporation is only one, but indeed the
principle organization, so confronted. That, in essence, is the corporate
dilemma.

The Shifting Role of National Government

The rearrangement several centuries ago of religious and secular values
also found its reflection in changes in the objects of public veneration. The
attribution of divine guidance which had given absolute authority to the
princes of the Medieval Church was transmuted to the kings of the newly
emerging nations as the divine right to rule. A fervent public enthusiasm
that translated into impassioned and patriotic allegiance to the quickly developing nation had characteristics of an acquired religious commitment;
and the king was the personification of the nation. The nation to a significant degree replaced the Church as the central object of devotion. Initially
supported in part to encourage and protect the rapidly expanding creators
of wealth, the nation in turn shed a part of its acquired respect on the businessman. As viewed by Harold R. Isaacs, it is ". . . quite possible, even reasonable, to interpret the whole process as one of identifying the interest of
God with those of the creators of the new capitalist system. . . ."[1] The
Calvinists believed that the accumulation of capital was a fulfillment of
God's work.

The gradual reversal of attitudes of government toward business that
has occurred since the eighteenth century has been persistent; ultimately it
has been nothing short of dramatic. As the ideas of the Social Contract and
ultimate power in the people led away from the divine right of kings and
toward constitutional government, government was increasingly regarded
as the representative and protector of the people. For many years, the concept of economic competition has competed with the regulatory authority
of government to play the role of protector of the public against exploitation by business; and the concept of competition has steadily lost ground.
A shift has occurred, gradual but nevertheless insistent, from government
as supporter and promoter of business to government as a restraint or as
an adversary of business, a role now widely assumed to be necessary to
protect the public. The enthusiasm for this role by many employees of government has led one observer to the view that government is now used as a
kind of secular church to make business good and virtuous.

The premise is now widely believed that business is essentially exploitative, that if left alone it will serve only itself, and that economic competition has been so greatly weakened that it can no longer be relied upon to provide protection for the public. Gone is the premise that, acting in enlightened self-interest in a competitive situation, the greatest good for the greatest number will be served. This adversary position of government is perhaps more accepted today in the United States than elsewhere. It presents a sharp contrast, for example, to Japan where the Ministry of International Trade and Industry (MITI) expends large sums and provides other benefits and favors in the encouragement of specific businesses, not unlike the posture of governments in the early days of the corporation.

Two tests are usually used by most economists to measure the alleged decline of competition: the growing size of firms, and the share of a loosely defined market held by one or several firms. The secular or long-term trend of the return on invested capital less often appears in publication. Yet the return on invested capital is the true measure of the effectiveness of competition as a balancing restraint on profits. The confusion in the public mind, in part, may be the result of an overly defensive response by business, answering the charge of monopoly power in terms in which it is made. It is, in addition, perhaps the result of the common practice by businesses of emphasising a percentage change from a previous period of current profits as a residual "bottom line" rather than focusing public attention on the rate of return on invested capital. As some scholars have found after careful research on the rate of return that adjusts for inflation, there has been no significant imparment overall of the ability of competition to protect the public against excessive profits. Quite the contrary, rates of return so measured have tended to decline alarmingly in the recent decades, thus threatening the adequacy of capital formation. But the government's case for expanding regulatory activity must necessarily rest on the failure of economic competition to do its work, or on the inability of the public to identify and reject products and services that lack integrity, both of which are dubious assumptions if the public is adequately informed. Integrity of communication is the important matter.

Moreover, the concept that profits, regardless of their level, have work to do in the service of the public seems to have been lost in the debate of whether they are too high or too low. The point of reference is against some inherited notion of fairness rather than public need or lack of need for production among a wide variety of goods and services. The energy program of the nation is currently suffering and losing valuable time from this confusion. When there is a pressing public need or desire for more of a product or service, profits should increase to attract additional capital to the activity to induce an increase of supply. When the public need or desire for an economic good or service is diminishing, profits should contract to induce a removal of capital from the activity. The mobility of capital among different types of production is of concurrent importance to the formation of capital if the business community is to serve effectively the public interest. The intervention of government has demonstrated limited awareness of this fact. Unfortunately, the business response to its critics regarding profits has frequently been in terms of the fairness of profits rather than of their function. Profits as an economic function are good for the public, not bad, yet business spokesmen have at times felt so defensive they have avoided use of the term altogether.

The business community is right in resisting the many governmental encroachments on pricing in free and open markets, whether they be capital markets, commodity markets, product markets, or service markets. Prices, just as profits, have work to do. They register changes in public needs and desires and thus serve as guides in the allocation of productive resources, including human effort. But business leaders, unfortunately, seem more aware of the debilitating results of governmental interference with price behavior than of their own restraints on uninhibited price movement in the free market system. Interference with the free adjustment of prices, whether by government or by business, constitutes a limiting qualification of the terms on which a libertarian and open society was built. A case, of course, can be made for such interference in a variety of specific situations but the burden of proof for such intervention should be respectively on government or on business in each instance.

There is a difference between protecting and preserving competition and protecting and preserving competitors. Both business and government, particularly the latter, have been guilty of confusing the two. Protection of competition is in harmony with the laws of nature on which the corporation built its spectacular successes in the expansion of material abundance. Protection of competitors through intervention in the movement of prices in free markets, while it may be in harmony with the principles of humanism, is the antithesis of the principle of survival of the fittest. Paul Weaver was perceptive when he wrote the businessman's opinion that "government intervention in the marketplace is not just a lapse from principle, but an irrational attempt to repeal the laws of nature."[2]

But business itself cannot claim title to purism as libertarian free enterprisers. It may be that the endorsement by business of direct or indirect subsidies or of regulatory procedures that diminish the sharp edge of competition represents too great a readiness to qualify the principles on which the corporation as an institution has prospered; or it could be that the implications of doing so are not fully apprehended. Intervention is not a matter of absolute right or wrong; its rightness or wrongness depends on the circumstances. But its significance should be understood. As Weaver continues in his article, "The only job of economic education facing American businessmen is the one they have to do on themselves by themselves."

The adversary posture of government toward business, unfortunately, now has deep roots. If the voice of business is to be heard and is to earn credibility among those involved with government, the public press, the electronic communications, and in the halls of academe, it must demonstrate convincingly, in free and open markets that competition is still effective in the role of public protector. Additionally, business by action and work must convey an awareness of the essential services business has provided and can provide on a broadening scale to the public. Conversely, it is a mistake for business to adopt the posture of being the custodian of economic sophistication with a desire to share that knowledge with the public.

More importantly, business must articulate more clearly its opportunities and its commitment to respond to the changing nature of public aspirations. Those usually identified as intellectuals engaged in the mass media and in academe, to quote the late Lionel Trilling, ". . . take virtually for granted the adversary intention, the actual subversive intention, . . . of detaching the reader from the habits of thought and feeling that the larger culture imposes, of giving him a ground and vantage point from which to judge and condemn. . . ."[3] This is also a characteristic of many now associated in government who may have reached their present assignment by way of the press or the campus. This pattern of behavior is more a matter of the individuals involved than of the organizations with which they are associated; witness the often strained relationships between those who speak for government and those who tear them apart in the mass media.

There is little, if anything, that business can say of a defensive nature to ameliorate the adversary attitudes of many government officials. But if this condition can be improved through reproachment or otherwise, it will be the result of informed and enlightened practice by business rather than by large expenditures to "educate" the public about business. It may not be possible fully to recapture the eighteenth and nineteenth century status of government as a sponsor of business but a public good would be served by limiting the enthusiasm for adversary activities by governmental officers in the business community.

An Expanding Range of Corporate Concerns

A recitation of various types of activities is the usual means of illustrating the new directions for corporations that public expectations now prescribe. This is useful, but an alleviation of the business corporation's disfavor will require more than that. It will require an attitudinal change that puts societal purposes and goals on an equal footing with the economic aim. That is not an easy shift to make, given the tradition and the career training of most corporate executives. There are some extraordinarily complex problems looming for the future that will fall within the orbit of corporate interest, problems that extend beyond the issues now typically listed under the rubric of social responsibility of corporations. The currently expanded range of corporate concerns are destined to expand still further. Pollution control and environmental protection, conservation, agreeable and safe work conditions, nondiscrimination, employment training and stability, support of not-for-profit activities are all very much alive in public discussions and are part of the social responsibility package. Adaptation of corporate policy and practice to accommodate these now recognized and accepted purposes is in process, and has been for some years, in part self-imposed, and in part imposed by governmental constraints and public demands. There is much yet to be done in these matters but progress has been made.

It must be said, however, that the adjustment of corporate thinking and practice to deal with these now recognized socially responsible activities has not been a comfortable one. The introduction of social performance into business organizations is a genuine innovation. Part of executive management's difficulty to respond is that there is no organized market to register these public desires and needs. Emerging societal demands are expressed through the political processes of the nation rather than through the movement of relative prices in the marketplace. They are unlikely to be sensitively perceived by the business executive with adequate lead time to avoid public condemnation. Failure to have moved more rapidly in concert as a business community in pollution control is a classic example. The real failure was in not initiating a request for and in supporting legislation, in the formulation of which business would have had a participatory role.

Yet significant, even though reluctant, adjustment has already occurred in the habits and traditions inherited from two centuries of dramatically successful expansion of material abundance, habits rooted in the values of the Age of Science. Some social costs previously borne by the public at large have been shifted to the corporation's accounts. Real unit costs of producing goods and services have risen, contrary to the results expected from progress in technology and competition in efficiency. Among other things, incremental costs of job training, the provision of personal security and the ballooning costs of record keeping associated with growing regulatory procedures have added significantly to real unit costs.

There is little prospect that these tendencies will be reversed; rather, they may be accentuated as new problems become more clearly apparent in the years ahead. Adaptation and flexibility will be required as the cardinal virtues of business leadership if the business corporation is to maintain its independence. Business leadership must imaginatively appraise the future and rely less on the past. It must understand social needs as well as business concerns. To requote the sage observation of Leonardo da Vinci, so helpful when the early corporation was adjusting to the then new field of natural science, "Whoever appeals to authority (of the past) applies not his intellect but his memory."[4] Then it was natural science encroaching on the humanities. Now it is the humanities encroaching on natural science.

Perhaps the most difficult operating problem of the future will be related to people. It will involve the adjustments required by population trends and peoples' attitudes toward work, in combination with changing rates of economic growth. In recent years there has been a diminution in the rate of total population increase in the United States, but concurrently there has occurred a remarkable increase in the size of the nation's labor force. A quarter of a century ago one third of all women of working age were employed; now the figure is closer to one half. Those born in the post-war baby boom have now reached working age. They have doubled the number in the labor force under twenty-five. Thus, while the labor force as a percentage of total population has grown remarkably, the number of the unemployed as a percentage of the total labor force has proved to be a difficult figure to reduce. Business, as the principal employer of the nation, cannot escape the resentment associated with unemployment. Comprehensive data on underemployment are not available, but the frustration from less work time than desired, or from jobs that fail to make full use of abilities and training cannot fail to be widespread.

A more rapid rate of economic growth would alleviate most of these difficulties, but many question whether future growth rates will equal those of the past. Diminishing supplies, and higher real costs of raw materials, particularly sources of energy, and the prospective inadequate accumulation of new capital, both imply a slower rate of growth. Conservation and recycling will become matters of increasing importance. In some consumer product markets there may be incipient signs of satiation, wearing apparel for example. Nonmaterial desires appear to be working changes in the psychology of some material needs.

The postwar baby boom has now reached maturity and is beginning to influence economic growth. The attitudes among this younger generation are not reliable guides as to how they may feel in later years, but as personal security arrangements have increased, savings or acquisition now seem to have less interest for them. Individualistic self-reliance has been largely submerged into a search for personal security through collective group action. The rich are disdained by many and zeal for the disadvantaged and concern for humanity tend to exceed personal interest in achievement. After basic needs are met, leisure is prized often above work. A sense of commitment to the job or to the corporation is limited. Some of these characteristics are not unlike the attitudes that go far back into the humanism of the Middle Ages. They are the antithesis of the attitudes of the Age of Science or, somewhat earlier, of the Puritans during the Reformation.

A further perspective is thrown on these contemporary attitudes by scholars working in the field of psychology. The interesting characterization is made that it was "public man" who epitomized the ancient world, the "religious man" who dominated the medieval period, the "creative man" who typified the Renaissance, and the "economic man" who moved to the center stage in the age of industrialization. Our day, it is observed, has produced the "psychological man"—an inner directed person, deeply aware of himself, and seeking fulfillment that may not be immediately related to income or status. There is some evidence that the contemporary consumption or fulfillment ethic has replaced the Puritan work ethic, that the idea of thrift and sacrifice has lost some of its potency, and that personal security is sought more through group association or governmental action than through self-reliance. Despite these radical changes in attitudes toward work and personal value systems, innovative changes in personnel practices in the corporation have been slow to develop.

Apart from the bulge of postwar babies the population is aging with lower birthrates and deaths at older ages. The effect this will have on the working career, on product quality and on productivity, is uncertain. In the absence of a higher rate of future economic growth than now seems in prospect, it does imply less upward mobility in personal careers, adding an element of discontent. It also presents a serious question of retirement policy. Should the normal retirement age continue to decline as at present or should mandatory retirement be made illegal before age seventy, as now enacted in federal legislation with minor exceptions? The latter would relieve some discontent among a growing population of retirees. It would also clearly limit the opportunities for oncoming generations and would probably drain some of the vitality and flexibility from the operations of corporations. That could not fail to be damaging to the ability to adapt to the changing circumstances of the future.

There is a paradox lurking in these personnel concerns of business that could be troublesome. Work is still regarded by most as a means of self-expression and personal fulfillment. Yet the opportunity to work may diminish for an increasing segment of the population at the same time as the quality of life takes higher priority in public attention. It is anything but clear how the humanistic values of justice, compassion, and mutual service will impact on a situation of chronic unemployment if indeed that should develop. One thing only seems clear; the purposes and values that so successfully harmonized the corporation with natural science and the libertarian society for more than two centuries can be preserved only if ways can be found to supplement the corporation's traditional purposes without excessive impairment of the values on which its success has been built. The values and ethics of humanism need a fresh reconciliation with those related to the natural sciences, and that is a fusion that has always been difficult to accomplish.

Some of the corporate adjustments that lie ahead will be of an organizational nature; others will involve a shift of resources to other activities, manufacturing to service, for example; or the development of joint ventures with governmental agencies; or the extension of operations to a global basis where there may be different, but less intractable, problems. These will all require imaginative and innovative leadership and, above all, flexibility and adaptability in the corporate structure and personnel. These qualities can be preserved in the environment of a libertarian political climate. That is more likely to be assured if the business community fully understands the requirements and meanings of libertarianism. It is quite different from the present liberal society, which has come largely to mean financial outlays to alleviate public distress and political pressures, accompanied by various types of controls.

It may be that the business community is the only one that can effectively serve as the custodian of a libertarian and open society. The political world has become excessively committed to liberality and controls, which is the antithesis of a liberal society as it was known when the restraints of Mercantilism were being shed. But business leadership can qualify for the exalted role of custodian of libertarianism only if it understands the damage that is done the open society by its own pleas for political relief when the competitive situation becomes difficult. There are penalties as well as rewards in the free economy. As Carl A. Gerstacher said recently, "When things get so bad we welcome government controls, we perform an act somewhat akin to Cleopatra's clasping the viper to her bosom."[5]

Corporate Governance for the Future

The structure for governing the business corporation probably must be modified if it is to continue to perform its valuable traditional function of providing material abundance and jobs and additionally to fulfill the new requirements of our evolving society. Change should be deliberate, undertaken only after careful consideration of each step. Excessive speed could be disruptive. But delay in setting directions of change risks further public disaffection and encroachment of misinformed and misdirected governmental action. Under the existing corporate administrative system of incentives, motivations, and objectives through which concepts are translated into operations, two assignments are in conflict. On the one hand, there is the need to preserve the efficiency criterion and incentives for growth. On the other, is the need to satisfy new social criteria, many of which call for incurring costs and investing resources in purposes now regarded as economically nonproductive.

Managers, conditioned by careers geared to "bottom line" criteria, rarely possess and do not easily acquire the values and perceptions essential for guiding the corporation through a successful adaptive response to public insistence on including quality-of-life concerns in corporate practice. Yet it is clearly preferable, for the corporation and for society as a whole, that the reconciliation of the values of economic efficiency and the newly assertive humanism occur to the maximum possible extent through voluntary initiative within the corporation. To the extent that the terms and procedures of the reconciliation are imposed on the corporation by external coercion, the results can be, and have been, debilitating. The dynamic flexibility of the market system will be contaminated with irrational rigidities. The efficient and effective use of resources will be diminished. Corporations and their managers will be perceived as adversaries of the public will. The current low-confidence rating of private institutions will be further impaired.

Some of the required business rule changes must necessarily come from government, to be sure, to prevent excessive disturbance of competitive relationships. Some of the inducements for corporate initiatives must also come from government, although there are significant opportunities for corporate managers to give technical and administrative counsel. But to the extent that the public's expectations of "responsible" corporate behavior can be satisfied by voluntary business initiative—either by individual companies or through cooperative arrangements—the society as a whole, and the business system within the society, will preserve important values.

The typical corporate organization comprises a system of substructures called departments that fit into a pyramidal type of organization that peaks at the chief executive office. A system of line and staff departments has evolved through trial and error over many years. It is a structure that has been particularly effective in maximizing efficiency in routine and repetitive kinds of operations. In an environment that is competitive above all, this is a predictable, probably a necessary, arrangement, but the control and incentive systems embedded in it tend to inhibit rather than encourage imaginative change and initiative within the organization.

The task of running the traditional business activities of a corporation will become more complex, not easier. Rapid change in production methods and in product composition associated with evolving technology will require new and distinctive executive abilities in the years ahead. Additional ingenuity will be needed to assure supplies, to develop appropriate personnel management in the context of changing population dynamics, and to adapt marketing to global dimensions in a period of changing worldwide life styles.

Maintaining efficiency will be made even more difficult by the new initiatives and incentives required to make the corporation adequately responsive to the emerging environment. Redesign of the present pattern of rewards and career development within the corporate organization to include a recognition of social performance considerations unquestionably risks diverting management attention from maximizing net return on invested capital, the ultimate measure of efficiency. Yet without such a thoroughgoing revision of individual incentives and corporate policy, the effort to respond to the revised nature of public expectations could be frustrated.

What is required is a fresh examination of the complete system of corporate governance. Among other things, new and fresh points of view will be needed in the decision-making processes of business. Only through trial and error can a harmonious combination or blend of economic and humanistic considerations emerge, and a corporate structure that provides for checks and balances would best assure that viable result.

Current efforts to achieve change in the corporation's governance through so-called stockholder democracy, or to force what is thought to be responsible behavior through group proxy pressures, may not have the potential to be very meaningful, or even to have the results sought by their sponsors. The "new and fresh point of view of stockholders" could plausibly be a narrow insistence on strict attention to "hard-nosed" business matters and higher dividends rather than the injection of humanistic considerations into corporate conduct. The organization of church, academic, and other pressure groups formed to influence policy and practice through proxies and at annual meetings of stockholders has had the merit of bringing to public attention issues that are better ventilated than left submerged. It cannot be said, however, that the activity has resulted in significant change in corporate practice.

More substantial progress has been made to enlist the shop floor employee in decision processes as they relate to his or her job. No doubt further experiments will be made with worker participation in shop decisions, both in the interest of worker satisfaction and of productivity. But these programs and practices, so much in the public awareness, are inadequate to satisfy the fundamental modifications required in the governance of corporations if their goals are to be harmonized with the changing goals of society at large. Nor is it likely that the European experiments of including constituency representation, particularly labor, on governing boards of business corporations will be a promising possibility. It has been effective only to a limited extent in Europe and the traditions and practice, both of management and labor in the United States, would probably assure its failure here.

Putting the Corporate Board to Work

The board of directors, the highest level of authority in the organization, is the best place to start, however, in refocusing the goals and purposes of the business corporation. The board has functions that are different from those of executive management, and to the extent it is staffed by outsiders, different personnel from executive management. It is unreasonable to expect executive management, whose success is measured by the return on investment, continuously to set policy and to take actions that increase cost and lessen profits, even if only in the short run. To do so requires the encouragement and initiative of a board with broad perspective. Conversely, it would be less than meaningful to assign an initiating role in societal matters to the board without a concurrent strengthening of its present involvement with management in the internal decision-making of the corporation. If the chairman of the board and his fellow board members are to be effective in guiding the corporation's goals in matters of social concern, or if they are to relieve executive management of the chore of representing the company to its several publics, there must be a public recognition that the board does, in collaboration with management, determine the organization's policy and appraise executive personnel and performance. The board is the appropriate unit for the establishment of broad policies and procedures, and for the review of performance; management is the agency delegated by the board to make these policies and procedures effective subject to board review of performance.

Credibility is hard for the business community to earn and retain. A board of directors charged with initiating responsibilities for guiding the external relations of a corporation and manned by persons with diverse

talents and backgrounds, including—but not limited to—those with business experience and acumen, is much better positioned to win that credibility. Business has long needed articulate spokesmen who can convey the
reality of business to the world of ideas in a manner that will be confident-
ly convincing; who can make clear that an open society in the world of
work and in the world of politics are one and inseparable, that the degree
of openness will increase or diminish in both together. There is no more
natural or effective place to develop the required intellectual leadership for
business than in the governing boards of its major institutions.

The implications of these suggested changes in present corporate purposes, policies and practices, and in the relationships between executive
management and the board of directors, will no doubt alarm those whose
careers have been conditioned by past and present successes in a relatively
unchanging corporate world. It is the basic thesis of this essay that the corporation is now confronted with more than a temporary decline in public
approval, that this is accompanied by the growth of a labyrinth of government controls, that there is evidence of a groundswell of revision occurring
in the value structure of contemporary society not unlike the rearrangement of values that have happened before in the history of Western civilization, and that the peril of failure to adapt innovatively the policies and
practices of the corporation to the changes in public aspirations exceeds
the recognized risks of doing so.

Two things must happen before the board of directors can be prepared
to accept and discharge a complex and far more demanding set of assignments: (1) a clarification and an organizationally accepted identification of
the board's functions as monitor, but not manager, of the executive operation of the company; and (2) the recruitment of a diversity of board members, some of whom would have distinguished themselves in careers
peripheral to or even outside the business community. Neither of these
steps will be easy.

Recent federal court cases have so increased the personal liability risks
of board members that some feel that the present ambiguity of the functions of boards may be advantageous, more positive than negative. Indeed,
highly regarded legal firms have counselled against the development of a
formally adopted set of board functions, presumably because it would provide a convenient legal reference against which to test board performance.
Failure to do so, however, enervates the usefulness of the board and denies
the opportunity, perhaps the only really effective opportunity, to adapt the
corporation to the changing nature of public expectations. The precise
nature of board functions depends on numerous things: the traditions of
the company, the personalities involved, the nature of the business, and the

size of the company, among other things. There are several observations of a general nature that can usefully be made, however.

The board is a monitoring body, not an executive one. The operating tasks of executive management are assigned by the board to the full-time officers of the company. There are four broad areas of interest in the company's activities that are of special interest to and fall within the monitoring competence of the board: (1) the determination of *policy*, in collaboration with executive management, with regard to both internal operations and external matters, particularly of a societal nature; (2) the audit or review of management's *performance*; (3) the overview of *procedures* for assuring effective operations and communications; and finally (4) the appraisal of *personnel*, particularly in the senior echelons of the company. These areas of monitoring interest might be called the four "Ps": policy, performance, procedures, and personnel.

A board that is effectively functioning in this manner will be recognized as a major influence, indeed, the major influence in the conduct of the corporation. It will then have the credibility perhaps, but not necessarily, through its chairman to represent the company and speak for it; and speak for business in general, in political, academic, literary, and communication circles. This range of activities promises to become increasingly demanding with the passage of time and should be removed from the duties of executive management, to the extent feasible, without delay. Too much executive time is now assigned to these external activities at the cost of effective administration.

The second requirement is more difficult than it might at first appear, namely the recruitment of a balanced board that would include, in addition to those familiar with the company and the business or businesses in which it operates, those who have achieved distinction in various careers. The composition of boards now typically consists of senior officers of the company, including members of the chief executive's office, senior officers of other corporations, investment and commercial bankers, law partners of leading firms which probably include the firm on retainer to the company, and in some instances, substantial stockholders. In recent years an effort has been made to obtain a broadening of background by adding one or more women and one or more members of the black community. Occasionally, an academic is included. As boards now function, there is not an excessive demand made on the time of a member. Those few women, blacks, and academics who have been identified as "board material" have often become quickly overcommitted, and it is doubtful that their influence is very great.

A balanced board of working members discharging the complex set of assignments necessary to move the corporation into closer harmony with the changing goals of society, yet mindful of the requirements of efficiency and profitability, will require a greater diversity of fresh points of view than has yet been achieved, greater commitment of time and attention, and a greater degree of independence of thought and action. That does not mean that the company interest should be secondary to the public interest, rather, it means that a board of thoughtful minds with a variety of successful career experiences, some of which would be associated with the humanities, is best equipped to find solutions to problems that harmonize the long-range interest of the company with the public interest. Obviously, more time and thought must be committed to the board's work. A sense of meaningful participation and appropriate adjustments of compensation can provide strong inducements for qualified people to provide that time.

A start has been made to move boards of directors in this direction, but it is only a start. In addition to the usual talents and career experiences now represented on boards, new ones must be found to assure a balanced consideration of the complex issues confronting the corporation, now and in the future. This should not be interpreted to mean that the board should consist of individuals, some of whom would have separately identified constituencies. Nor does it mean that legislative compulsions should be imposed to shape the composition of the board of directors. All board members should have as their first concern the interests of the company. Their differing backgrounds would simply be a means of bringing a variety of points of view to bear on corporate issues that impinge on society at large. Talents and experiences now typically present on boards include administrative, scientific and engineering, financial, marketing, legal, and in appropriate cases, medical. Not now often found on boards, but much needed, are those thoroughly familiar with politics and its processes, historians with the perspective of traditions and past societal transitions, writers and publishers knowledgeable about leading personalities in the field, yes, even a religionist or a philosopher with roots in the working world.

In contemplating a board so constituted and designed to achieve a socially, as well as economically, balanced appraisal of corporate policy it should be recognized that its discussions would differ significantly from the characteristic consensus that now usually prevails in the board room. An individual to serve as a catalyst would be essential. Logically, that would be the chairman. As the senior officer of the board, his encouragement of free and open discussion followed by his guidance of the full board to a consensus—it need not be a unanimous conclusion—would require a unique skill that should be a major consideration in his election to the post. The chairman's tasks of organizing the work of the board, preparing the agenda for and chairing its meetings, and serving as the company's spokesman to its several publics are likely to require the major part of his available time. These assignments require talents that may or may not coincide with those possessed by a successful executive manager.

It is not often that both talents can be conspicuously found in a single individual, even if the respective demands of serving as chairman and CEO in a large organization permitted time to do both tasks thoroughly. More importantly, the tasks are different. That of the executive officer is, above all, to keep the company efficient, profitable, and growing, if possible. He is the epitome of the value structure of the Age of Science on which the corporation was built. The task of the chairman and his board is to help guide the company to policy positions that will assure its public approval and secure its survival as a healthy and developing organization through time. He is, or should be, the influence that assures a blending of the humanistic values with those of science. Through this dichotomy of function and purpose the corporation can find the strengths to adapt to the changing public aspirations imposed by a growing humanism and, at the same time, preserve most of the great inherited values that have made it such an eminent contemporary institution.

What is needed is a new realization of all the factors of both a negative and a positive nature that must be taken into consideration when planning for maximum return on invested capital—the new, long-range factors as well as the short-range ones. As this knowledge becomes available to the corporation through experience, and by bringing into its decision processes a wider range of informed points of view, the ancient motivation of self-interest will best assure its adaptation to public aspirations. But this happy result will be difficult without a governance structure that provides for checks and balances. For the business corporation of the future this is as important as its counterpart in the political structure of the nation.

Notes

*The Future of Business: Global Issues in the 80s and 90s, Max Ways, ed. (New York: Pergamon Press, 1978), pp. 1–18.

1. Harold R. Isaacs, "Nationality: End of the Road," Foreign Affairs, April 1975, p. 440.

2. Paul Weaver, "Corporations Are Defending Themselves with the Wrong Weapon," Fortune, June 1977, pp. 186–87.

3. Lionel Trilling, Columbia University Today.

4. Parenthesis added.

5. Stockholder's Communication, Dow Chemical Co.

II
Corporate Governance: The Role of the Board of Directors and the CEO

Are Governing Boards Necessary?*

SOME YEARS AGO A DELIGHTFUL BOOK WAS PUBLISHED with the improbable title, *How to Manage a Bassoon Factory*.[1] Its first page gave away the theme: the managing director was the director who knew where the factory was. For those familiar with the operations of many corporate boards, this charming comment on managing directors makes a point that is more than whimsical.

The old adage has it that "directors direct and managers manage." What then can a "managing director" be? The pervasive point that will be made in this book will be that he is very likely the unhappy blending of the two quite distinct functions of managing and directing, of operating and evaluating. At least, that is what the managing directors of large corporations in business, academe, and other areas seem to have become in contemporary practice. This emergence of the managing director has in general meant that the independent role of the board of directors has been greatly reduced, and this has happened without most of us quite realizing it or reflectively comprehending its full implications. Our purpose here will be to examine the changes that have reduced the role of the board of directors in corporate life and to suggest changes that might be made both for the advantage of business as well as of society.

According to the laws that establish them, all corporations—profit-seeking and not-for-profit—are structured with a governing board and, through their by-laws, with a managing group. Positive values can be achieved when the division of functions and responsibilities between the board and management, irrespective of the purposes for which a corporation exists, is clearly and collaboratively identified. A word about the place of the corporate form of organization in contemporary society may serve to emphasize the importance of clarifying the internal relationships between governing boards and those who are charged with the responsibility for management.

The Role of the Corporation

The corporation is by no means the only type of organization available to do the work of society, but in the more developed democracies it is the

71

major type. There are currently three major types of organizational group-ings that do the work of mankind: the family, the state, and the corpora-tion.

The family is the smallest unit, and in many lesser developed societies it is to this day the typical grouping that possesses the loyalty necessary for mutual commitment and effort. Because it is a relatively small grouping and the tasks of society require a wide range of abilities and interests, the family does not achieve the efficiency of more rationally organized groups. Seniority, the usual principle of leadership in a family, does not always pro-duce the most effective direction of its activities.

At the other extreme of the spectrum is government—of the tribe, of the state, or of the nation. Here, the coercive power of the political struc-ture, in addition to providing justice and security, becomes involved in man-aging economic activity. State ownership of resources and direction of com-munity effort has appealed to many of the world's people as rational and desirable, but the balancing of contending parties which is so characteristic of the political process has not proven itself to be the most effective means of organizing the economic activity of a nation.

Between the family and the state, there is a vast array of voluntary associations, of which those in the form of corporations are the most important and most enduring. People in the developed democracies have turned predominantly to corporations rather than to family or to govern-ment organizations for the achievement of economic as well as many other purposes of society. They have found the voluntarily assembled association, i.e., the corporation, focused on the accomplishment of consistent goals in a rationally organized manner, in practice, to be by far the most efficient use of human resources.

The results of this choice have not been disappointing. Indeed, the achievement of substantial material abundance, together with educational and cultural development in an open society, would have been unlikely and might have been impossible without the voluntary associations organized as corporations, ranging in their activities from the running of businesses to the management of colleges and museums. In this sense, the corporation, possibly more than any other influence, is the organizational form that conditions the nature and the quality of our individual lives, whether or not we actually work for a corporation.

Social Criticism and the Corporation

It has become commonplace to observe that the structure and atti-tudes of contemporary society are undergoing radical changes. The corporation, particularly the business corporation, can adapt to those changes, or it can resist them, but it cannot avoid being either a positive or a negative influence in reciprocally conditioning these changes. It cannot avoid being a decisive force—perhaps the most decisive force—in determining the character of our society today and tomorrow. "If we and our institutions are not responsive and adaptable, there is really no alternative to some of the suggestions and recommendations being made by the critics in the fringe radical groups on our campuses," Ernest C. Arbuckle, formerly Dean of the Stanford Graduate School of Business and now Chairman of Wells Fargo Trust, has said.[2]

With its own self-preservation in mind, the corporation must respond constructively to social criticism and challenge. No institution of society can maintain its vitality if it violates over extended periods the community's sense of appropriate behavior. The alternative is likely to be the imposition of additional governmental controls over corporate performance, with the ultimate probability of government ownership. This is reason enough to think very seriously about designing the corporation's internal structure and relationships in a manner to assure that it will optimally serve the public interest, which in the long run is synonymous with its own interest.

Clarification of the role of the governing board and of the desirable attributes and qualities of its members must necessarily provide the foundation on which the internal structure is built. But that foundation now is anything but a firm one. A well-known corporate officer recently observed in public discussion, "Most boards of directors I have been on don't know exactly what they are supposed to do."

Should Boards Be Eliminated?

Some current opinion would disagree with the proposition that it is important to clarify and strengthen the role of the governing board. It is alleged that in many organizations the board has, in fact, been deposed by management or administrators and has been reduced to a legal fiction. As organizations grow in size and complexity, as the information requirements increase simply to maintain awareness of ongoing operations, these observers believe that the relative power of the board must necessarily shrink. Serious proposals have been made to complete the atrophy of the board, to terminate the pretense, by dissolving the board, with full responsibility and authority turned over in law to the management, as it is now, allegedly, turned over in fact. A variation of this proposal is to devise a legal way to divest the board of authority and responsibility in favor of management, except in certain clearly defined critical circumstances. But this half-way solution, because of its ambiguity, would simply shield management from the full consequences of the problems it may have caused.

Why Corporations Need Boards

There are several difficulties with these positions. First, it is simply untrue that boards in general have been deposed by management. Few boards are as inert, as supine, or as uninformed as the proposals imply. The "mushroom concept of a 'good' director," according to John T. Connor, Chairman of the Board of Allied Chemical, is a thing of the past. While a few chief executive officers still treat a good director as a mushroom, that is, "Put him in a damp dark place, feed him plenty of horse manure, and when his head rises up through the pile to get attention or ask a question cut it off quickly and decisively,"[3] most observers of the corporate scene would agree that very little of this sort of thing still exists, if indeed it ever did. Yet, many of the same observers would agree that there is a need to clarify the role of the board, and, in fact, would provide it with greater muscle.

Another reason to reject the notion of abandoning the board or reducing its influence to near-zero is that there is a potentially rewarding opportunity to achieve the positive values of a system of checks and balances through a more effective working relationship between the board and management. The board is concerned with the broad view and the long perspective more than management. Consensus decision making is most successful when a variety of points of view are represented. The major problems of today have social and political overtones; more than the experiences of a career in a single field of activity is required to cope with them. More immediate rather than long-term results are the main concern of management. Improved working procedures can and should be designed to provide better decision making by the interaction between board and management, especially with respect to what have come to be called "the externalities" of corporate organizations.

The Board and the Social Role of the Corporation

The broadening interest and activities of most organizations, particularly business corporations, in many kinds of societal affairs will require a parallel enlargement and adaptation of the range of concerns of governing boards. Management, historically and primarily held accountable for an efficient and profitable operation, increasingly will require support and guidance from a board with interests in a growing array of concerns dealing with the external environment: community improvement, charitable giving, employee benefits, employee health and safety, minority and female hiring and promotion, environmental protection, shareholder democracy, and even the determination of where to do business in a world of political and social tensions. "The present attack upon the incestuous cloister of corporate board rooms is the result of the confluence of all of these movements," said Patricia Roberts Harris at a November, 1971, symposium of the Conference Board: ". . . an individual who spends his or her life solely in the pursuit of greater corporate efficiency and maximizing the profits of the stockholders is somewhat removed from the day-to-day ferment of political life."[4]

The future opportunities of all types of corporations, both for-profit and not-for-profit, as institutions of societal significance can and probably should be strengthened by an attempt to identify all of the interest groups affected by corporate conduct. Of course, it will never be possible to foresee all of the consequences of the activities of major corporations any more than it will ever be possible to foresee all of the consequences of the actions of governments. Many of such consequences extend beyond the intentions or the powers of the initiators to control. But a better appraisal of probable results can be made when decisions emerge from discussion of varying points of view, and this an effectively constituted board of directors is ideally suited to do.

The Board and the Legitimacy of the Corporation

There is another reason why the governing board should be strengthened rather than permitted to atrophy. The very legitimacy of the corporation would become increasingly vulnerable to serious challenge if self-perpetuating management had no reference for continuing accountability. The central challenge now faced by corporations and their managers is the question of their legitimacy:

> The danger is that business managers don't have social legitimacy and don't know it, warns [Peter] Drucker.
> Legitimacy in this context means the corporation's right to go on doing what it has been doing for decades. , . . .
> . . . business' right to set prices has been controlled by government. . . . advertising is more strictly regulated. Consumer groups have become more articulate and better organized. . . . subsidiaries of multi-

national concerns have been taken over by local, right wing governments. Even professional groups normally allied with the corporation are acting up.[5]

Public sanction is built on public confidence. Despite enormous corporate expenditures for "telling the story," the public withholds its full approval. The level of public criticism of the corporation seems to run in cycles. As would be expected, it was high during the great depression of the 1930s, diminished with the demonstration of corporate effectiveness during World War II and subsequently through the 1950s, and over the last decade or so has again increased conspicuously. Just a few years ago a new and relatively adequate conception of the role of the large corporation in society was developing. Today that has been reversed, and some perceive the corporation to be an economic and political threat to democracy. Tomorrow is unpredictable, but it could emerge as an uncomfortable period for the large corporation if, as now seems probable, the tensions of a slower rate of total economic growth are experienced.

In view of this, it would be prudent for the corporation to prepare itself now to make a more convincing case that its internal structures and procedures are designed in a manner to assure consideration of a wide spectrum of "publics" in its decision making. On the other hand, a further atrophy of the position of the board of directors would be the antithesis of prudence. It would leave the corporation exposed to political and public attack, to a challenge of its legitimacy that would be hard to defend against.

A Different Reason for Strengthening the Board

There is still another reason why it is now timely to clarify the responsibilities and opportunities of board members of various types of corporations. The present status of directors and trustees with respect to their personal liabilities is at best ambiguous; some think it to be ominous.

The typical dictum in state charters provides that "the business of a corporation shall be managed by its board of directors." If taken literally, there is no board member of a large organization in the nation who could feel secure. Fortunately, *state* legislatures and judges have accepted the reality that management responsibility must necessarily be delegated to full-time corporate officers. The states have been much criticized for permissive regulations of board members' responsibilities, improperly in my view, for it is doubtful that the development of what is now called professional management would have been possible if a different position had prevailed.

The forfeit of the board's chartered responsibility to manage the day-to-day affairs of the company is no fault; it is realistic and desirable. A similar forfeit of the board's obligation and responsibility to guide, supervise, and evaluate is quite another matter. The first forfeit would seem to involve no measurable personal risk. The second involves large personal risks as evidenced by the rendering of numerous judgments in recent years by *federal* courts in cases brought under the federal securities laws.[6] Strict standards have been promulgated for accurate disclosure in key public documents such as press releases, proxy statements, annual reports, and registration statements. If the material signed by a director turns out to be inaccurate or fraudulent, he can be held accountable even though he may have relied on assurances of the organization's executive personnel. Or he may find himself guilty of negligence even though care is taken to be fully aware of the facts if he fails to make unfavorable information publicly known. These are risks that have begun to emerge that are beyond those of participation in fraud, transactions involving conflicts of interests, and "inside trading."

The governing board can protect itself from these hazards only if it participates more fully than at present in the background development of the organization's activities and care is exercised in supplying directors with operating information that is adequate in quality and quantity. As things stand, the liabilities of directors weigh more heavily than their influence on the running of the corporation. Redressing the balance could not fail to be constructive, both for the board member and for the corporation.

Governing Boards *Are* Necessary

Proposals to diminish still further the role of the board are based in part on the false notion that governing boards now have a minor role to play. That is simply not so and, indeed, the trend in recent years has been toward a greater assertiveness by boards of directors. The need for the board's participation, moreover, is increasing as corporations become more complex and their activities affect larger numbers of people. A clarification of the board's role and responsibilities is necessary for numerous reasons, of which a clear understanding of personal liabilities is only one, even though an important one. Instead of a further weakening of the board's position in the corporate structure, a substantial strengthening is desirable to provide the benefits of checks and balances, an optimal blending of harmony and challenge, as well as a commingling of specialized expertise with broad understanding and social perception in the organization's decision making.

Yes, an unqualified yes, is the answer to the title of this chapter. Governing boards *are* necessary.

Notes

Putting the Corporate Board to Work (New York: Macmillan, 1976), pp. 1–11.

1. Nigel Balchin [Mark Spade], *How to Run a Bassoon Factory* (London: Hamish Hamilton, 1950).

2. Ernest C. Arbuckle, "Chairman's Opening Remarks," *The Board of Directors: New Challenges, New Directions,* A Conference Report of the Conference Board, November 18, 1971 (New York: The Conference Board, 1972), p. 2.

3. John T. Connor, "An Alternative to the Goldberg Prescription," Remarks before the American Society of Corporate Secretaries, March 14, 1973, p. 4.

4. Patricia Roberts Harris, Esq., "New Constituencies for the Board," *The Board of Directors: New Challenges, New Directions* (New York: The Conference Board, 1972), pp. 10, 11.

5. Peter Drucker, cited in *Du Pont Context,* #1 (Wilmington, Del.: Du Pont, 1974).

6. *Securities and Exchange Commission v. Texas Gulf Sulphur Company; Escott v. Bar Chris Construction Corporation;* and *Securities and Exchange Commission v. Mattel.*

Governing Boards of Business Corporations*

DIRECTORS OF BUSINESS CORPORATIONS NOW LIVE in a world of ambiguity—some have said of myth—with regard to their legal status. For example, the relationship between a chief executive and his fellow board members—for rarely is the former not a director—is determined only in part by legalities; it is also a matter of personalities, of organization history, and of intermittently changing situations, which may include the redistribution of share ownership in a stock company. The relationship differs from company to company and from time to time, and is conditioned by the size of the organization and the nature of the business or activity in which it is engaged.

Likewise the organizational structures and procedures of boards are almost never identical. A full description of the variations would simply be confusing. What we will do here is identify certain basic principles, practices, and problems of the boards of large non-financial stock corporations as a background to offering a number of suggestions for improving corporate performance through a strengthened governing board. Some of these suggested modifications to current board structure and practice should provide a bench mark from which adaptations may be considered.

It will not be easy to describe these modifications without bruising sensibilities, for any substantive change in existing patterns would involve reassignments at the highest levels of corporate officialdom. Yet, in the long run, clarification and strengthening of the role of the board of directors as an institution may be crucial for the continued healthy development of the corporation as a major constructive influence in an open society. Mr. Roger M. Blough has expressed it very succinctly:

> . . . the search for a better way of conducting every aspect of corporate activity is never ending. There is no reason, therefore, why improvement in the work, protection, and general usefulness of outside directors should not be an integral part of this search. Like everything else, the functioning of boards is not beyond examination or above reproach and possible improvement.[1]

Just as no two boards are exactly alike in their traditions, procedures, and practices, the processes by which change can be achieved most effectively will differ from board to board. Personalities will no doubt dominate some situations. Some will prefer to invoke grandfather clauses and make changes only with a changing of the guard. Others, less satisfied perhaps, may feel it imperative to seek improvement of a board's structure and function without delay. As early as 1966, the Chairman of the Board of Texas Instruments urged a "deliberate structuring of our board and its operating procedures [to provide] a badly needed coupling between the rapidly changing external and internal environments."[2] Still others would prefer a deliberate period of reflection and contemplation before revising the board's work. The latter would, of course, be the least painful. Even those who now oppose any change might find a period of reexamination useful.

There may be, however, some peril in excessive delay. Those campaigning for the conversion of the corporation from a private to a public or quasi-public institution hang their case in part on what they perceive to be the "unrepresentativeness" of the board of directors. The board, it is alleged, represents only itself, not even the stockholders of the company. Since it is dependent on management's favor for the selection of its members, the board is in no position to function as an independent agent. The challenge to its legitimacy is frequent among reformers, who hold that a basic change in the allocation of power within the corporation is required to correct the situation.

Some of the suggested remedies, such as electing public, government, or special interest representatives to the board, conceivably could simply create internal political conflict to a degree that would make the board's function even more ambiguous, and by delay, indecision, and inaction, make it even less effective than it is at the present. Some allege that interest group representation cannot impair board effectiveness since they believe that most boards are already ineffective. A certain amount of divisiveness may, conceivably, make the board more visible, but by its nature, the board is not and cannot become a full-blown legislative body without destroying the capacity of the corporation to fulfill its traditional functions effectively.

One-Man versus Consensus Management

Probably the basic reason why boards have been exposed to the charge of a lack of independence is that their functions have not been clearly defined and kept separate from those of management. The rational way to restore a sense and, ultimately, a tradition of independence to board members is to strengthen the position and role of the board by distinguishing it from management, both in function and in membership. To be meaningful this would have to start at the very top with the chairman of the board and the chief executive officer.

In recent years the practice has grown of electing a single individual to serve the posts of chairman of the board, president, and chief executive officer, thus making a single individual the senior officer of both the board and of the company. A variation is to elect one person chairman of the board and chief executive officer, and another, president and chief operating officer. In both cases the head man is confronted with the difficulty of separating out his functions and responsibilities as the chairman of the board from those he holds as the chief executive of the company. *The ambiguity of the role of the total board begins right here.*

The merits of this concentration of authority, however, should not go unnoted. It does focus in one individual ultimate authority for policy determination and for the initiation and administration of a program of action. This arrangement streamlines and expedites decision making and helps to assure prompt implementation. When a single individual is the senior officer of the board *and* of the company, it becomes virtually certain that the program and the tone of the organization will become an expression of his attitudes and aspirations. The resulting effectiveness has given wide currency to the belief that a successful company can have but one head man. And, indeed, this arrangement can be beneficial to the company, and through the company, beneficial to society at large. . . .

The advantages of concentrated authority are more likely to be realized in the young and rapidly developing business, especially if the leader is a person of capacity, imagination, courage, and energy. The same is true in situations that have deteriorated to a point where they need the resuscitation that can be supplied only by a strong new hand at the helm. In both of these general cases, the justification for one-man control stems directly from particular circumstances, one the initial development of a business, the other the reestablishment of the healthy condition of a business. Readiness to take great risks and the capacity for quick and decisive action are important to success in both cases, although even here it should be recognized that there is the possibility that these risks can also result in disaster.

The large mature corporation, on the other hand, presents quite a different set of circumstances. The processes of decision making have come, of necessity, to involve large numbers of people. The impact of the decisions made in the large established corporation cannot but affect both those within and those outside of the company. Indeed, what have come to be called the "externalities" of the business corporation have now begun to appropriate the time and energies of executive management of the large corporation to a point that the operation of an efficient and growing business can be jeopardized. Managing the mature modern corporation in a complex and rapidly changing world involves a task that is getting beyond the capacity of a single mortal. The chief executive officer, especially of the mature corporation, is entitled to guidelines prescribed by the board that extend beyond simple "bottom-line accounting" and that reflect the total, widely based experience of a carefully selected board of directors.

As we examine this issue of whether individual management or consensus management is the more suitable for the mature corporation, a distinction must be made between the authority over *all* the affairs of the large corporation and the authority over the operating functions of the business. It is now common practice to lodge all authority of running the business, both internally and externally, in a chief executive officer who in turn delegates the responsibility and the authority that goes with it to designated officers throughout the organization. The extent of the delegation depends on the nature of the activity and the disposition of the chief executive officer involved. Where authority for all affairs of the company are delegated to the chief executive officer, the board of directors then acts more like an advisory committee than a body of ultimate authority. Consensus management, on the other hand, would involve identifying those authorities delegated to the chief executive officer and those retained by the board, just as the chief executive officer now identifies those delegated by him throughout the organization from those he retains in his own office.

The issue of concentrated versus distributed authority is characteristic of all organized groups. It is not a matter of one pattern being bad and the other being good in some absolute sense. Rather the issue should be resolved pragmatically in terms of the purposes in view. In the case of the government of the United States, Americans identify distributed authority with democracy, and hence call it good. Other peoples, in different stages of development or with different traditions, reject this aspect of the democratic process in the United States. On the other hand, in another area of activity, such as a football game, authority to call the signals is given to the quarterback, or to the coach on the bench acting through the quarterback. The point is, whether in government or football, the authority structure followed is that judged best to achieve the goals of the group. There must be a recognized and accepted method to initiate decisions on behalf of the group, transmit decisions to the group, and finally make the decisions effective through group effort.

In the case of the U.S. government, initiatives leading to decisions may originate in the House of Representatives or the Senate (depending on their

nature), in the executive office of the President, or in the executive departments. The legislative and executive branches check and balance each other,
and the final arbiter is the judiciary. The system is a bit clumsy and there
are those who question its capacity to cope with the complex and rapidly
changing circumstances of the present, even though it has recently demonstrated impressive resiliency.

Similarly, many will doubt that the authority to make the complex
decisions required of a large modern corporation should, or can, be distributed *between* the board of directors and the management. The question is
whether there are significant types of decisions that can be identified and
segregated, decisions for which the board and the management, respectively, would have the *initiating* responsibility.

True, there are not clear and distinct breakpoints in the continuous and
interrelated progression of purchasing, processing, transporting, warehousing, and marketing; and the business skills of financing and accounting
affect all of these activities. Price determinations are involved at every
stage. A business is an integrated and continuous whole. Unless consciously
guided, its operations from day to day probably do as much—and possibly
more—to mold a company's policy as do the governing board's efforts to
provide a prior blueprint for the direction of the company's development.
In other words, a case can be made for keeping or placing the locus of all
final decision making in one place, in the office of the chief executive officer who may happen also to be the chairman of the board. But a case can
also be made—and in the instance of the large corporation perhaps a better
one—for identifying types of decisions, and for distributing authority for
their initiation between management and the board.

The strength of our form of political democracy is in its system of
checks and balances more than in the rule of the majority. As the modern
corporation confronts the progressively more complex problems of what
has been called the post-industrial era, it will stand in progressively greater
need of the advantages of a system of checks and balances within its own
operations. Technology is changing rapidly, the scarcity of raw materials
and their rising real costs foreshadow a slower rate of economic growth,
corporations are spreading their interests around the globe, labor is changing in its attitudes and aspirations, and the public at large is expecting corporations to participate in, if not spearhead, the community search for a
better quality of life. The capabilities needed to guide the business corporation henceforth must be social and political as well as technical and economic. This is an agenda of interests that involves more than the continuous and integrated processes of a traditional business operation. Indeed, an
attempt by a corporation to accept an expanded range of responsibilities

without internally modifying its organization to deal with them could be counterproductive and frustrate the ability of the corporation to perform its traditional functions.

Efficiency and productivity improvement have been the great strength of the corporation. They are and must remain the distinctive task of management. This is a task properly delegated by the board and, apart from appraising results, should be left entirely to management. But it is too much to expect management to be all things to all people. Management watches—and is judged by—the "bottom line," which measures the return on investment. Actions expressing the social responsibility of corporations most frequently—although perhaps not always—involve a departure from this principle of maximizing the return on investment; and this departure cannot reasonably be expected from executive management, at least to any great extent or on a continuing basis.

When the Founding Fathers incorporated the idea of the separation of powers into the Constitution, they defied the conventional wisdom of the day that accepted the divine right of a king. We may now be at a stage in the development of corporate purposes and governance that requires the same level of imagination and courage to assure the future healthy development of an institution that has been the major builder, and now stands at the center, of our industrial society. It may be time to separate the "legislative" functions of the board from the "executive" functions of management and to establish a clear demarcation of the membership of the two groups. The ability of the corporation to adapt to the larger public expectations of the future may depend on it.

In summary, the long-term development of the corporation can be secured better by designing procedures for checks and balances between management and the board in their determination of the major directions of its internal activities. This will require a strengthening of the board in its participation and collaboration with management in certain identified functions. The exercise of a guiding role by the board in the external relationships of the corporation can be meaningful only if the board possesses the influence and prestige derived from a stronger position in overseeing the internal affairs of the corporation. Great care must be exercised, however, to preserve management's opportunity to maintain executive initiatives, flexibility, and control within predetermined guidelines.

The Legalities of Transition

There are no legal impediments to strengthening the position of the board. The dictum in state charters that the corporation "shall be managed by a board of directors" can only mean that general control and direction of corporate affairs and the supervision of the corporate officers, to whom the day-to-day management is delegated, belongs to the board. Technically, directors are elected by the voting stockholders of the company to represent the interests of stockholders with due diligence and prudence. Even though it is not typically by a conscious action, the board then collectively reserves certain types of decisions to itself and delegates other types to management. Legally, it is that simple.

The public now generally assumes that, after election by stockholders, the major tasks of a director are to participate in the selection of competent people to manage the company, including the chief executive officer or officers, and to make a reasonably continuous and comprehensive review of its operations. Another responsibility that is generally expected of a director is that of participating in establishing broad guidelines for administering the assets of the enterprise in a manner to serve the interests of the stockholders and the public at large. Not so generally recognized is the responsibility to guide the company's course into channels that will provide future fruitful development and profitable operations. Such long-term considerations may, in some circumstances, stand in contrast with management's interest in maximizing profits in a given year or years; thus, it should especially be the business for the board. . . .

The "Four Ps" Identify the Board's Concerns

Policy, personnel, procedures, and *performance* have been called the "four Ps" for the proper attention of board members. Together, they constitute the hard core of the governing board's responsibility to stockholders, who, as a legal matter, elect them to board membership. In examining these responsibilities it is important to note that many authors have called attention to the disparity between myth and fact in the present functioning of boards.

The process of *policy* formation, generally assumed to be a function of the board, has now become as management controlled as the selection of board members. If policies are discussed at all, they are usually proposed by management and presented to the board for brief review and endorsement. Seldom does a member of the board propose a basic change of policy for board discussion and approval without first obtaining the informal endorsement of the chief executive officer.

The wellsprings of policy formation at present are more likely to be the successive investment and operating proposals presented by management to the board. These proposals, drafted in the various departments of the corporation, waft implicit policy from below upward to the board for its approval: Such operating programs are now more influential in determining the directions of an organization's development than are the more generalized statements of policy and purpose that might emerge from prior board discussion and approval.

The range of interest in *personnel* implied by the legal status of directors extends beyond its own incumbency to the selection of senior company officers. Here again, the function is now fulfilled more by management than by the board, including the senior officer's selection of his own successor. The development and monitoring of administrative *procedures* that would assure a comprehensive and detailed review of performance is usually also left to management. But this should be another responsibility of the board, at least to the extent of reviewing the procedures after they have been developed. The board's concern with a review of *performance* is a major task. This is now perhaps the most adequately fulfilled of the board's functions, but the depth, regularity, and frequency of review is not always sufficient to assure that the board is fully informed.

It should be observed, moreover, that the concerns that influence policy have been substantially broadened in recent decades. Stockholders now share with other publics the attention of both board members and management. Consumers, labor, and the communities in which investments are made and operations occur, all have interests that in the long run are recognized as being functionally intertwined with the long-range interests of stockholders. The policies and regulations of federal, state, and local governments, in general and in detail, describe standards to which the corporation's activities must reasonably conform. This widening range of corporate interest in several publics and in general public purposes has been based less on altruism than on a conviction that a balanced recognition of the impact of the company's activities on all the parties involved will best serve the future development of the enterprise.

The Board's Role in Social Responsibility

A still further enlargement of board concern, if not a yet universally felt responsibility, has been emerging in recent years, again no doubt in the conviction that it is in the future interest of the corporation. Starting several decades ago with the financial support of educational and cultural activities, boards of directors and managements of corporations have progressively extended their interests to include various means of improving the quality of life in general; their concerns have gone beyond simply providing satisfying jobs and material abundance. Indeed, they have gone beyond the stipulations required by law.

It is too soon to conclude that these relatively new expressions of "social responsibility" are fully *accepted* responsibilities, although they have been given visibility with much writing and oratory. And while there have been many instances of self-imposed restraint on profit maximization to prevent public harm or displeasure, at present, such matters as ecology and conservation, personnel development, and the alleviation of poverty and discrimination must be viewed only as tentative responsibilities, except to the degree prescribed by law.

Since executive management is held accountable primarily for profits, these responsibilities probably will become generally *accepted* in the sense of extending beyond the minimums required by law only after board members are able and willing to identify and impose a very long-range view of the company's interest. Thus another major responsibility of the board, over and above the matters of policy, personnel, procedures, and performance, which are internal to the company, is to give management encouragement and guidance in matters related to such external opportunities. Management is usually ill-equipped for the purpose.

Professor Kenneth R. Andrews has written:

> ... good works, the results of which are long term and hard to quantify, do not have a chance in an organization using conventional incentives and controls and exerting pressure for ever more impressive results.
>
> ... The internal force which stubbornly resists efforts to make the corporation compassionate ... is the incentive system forcing attention to short term quantifiable results.[3]

Still further away from the matter of legal or accepted responsibility, but nevertheless of growing interest to some directors, is the participation by businessmen in the formulation of national economic policy in collaboration with government officials; in the establishment of guidelines for prices and wages in a setting of continuous inflation; in formulating a program, for example, for the continuance of a vital service such as the northeast railroads; or in the clarification of appropriate degrees of competition and monopoly in national and international trade in an increasingly aggressive world. Participation in the political formulation of national and international economic policies, however, must be viewed as another tentative responsibility except in the case of the multinational corporation that must necessarily help in reconciling conflicting legislation in different national jurisdictions.

Perhaps as important as collaborative action with government is the opportunity for businessmen in general to participate actively and forcefully in evolving public debates on the major social and economic issues of the day. No organization that plays an important role in society, nor the representatives of such an organization, can escape that responsibility, although, admittedly, it is sometimes difficult to determine whether the individual spokesman or the organization of his affiliation is heard when he or she speaks or writes. . . .

How Much Independence?

How much independence in directors is desirable? Surely an excess of independence could become intolerable. One answer is that the extent of legally imposed responsibilities on the board and the degree of independence of board members should be more positively related. One of the reasons for the disinclination of qualified men and women to join boards is that the responsibilities imposed are now felt to be out of balance with the independence that is desired or tolerable on many boards, with the result that the exposure to personal liability is excessive.

In recent years, a number of judicial decisions have enlarged the requirement of prudence in a director. Federal courts have held that board members must now be fully informed, ultra-careful regarding possible conflicts of interests, and scrupulous not to use inside information for personal benefit. They must develop more than a cursory knowledge of the company and the field or fields in which it operates. They must confirm the accuracy of important reporting documents such as registration statements and proxy material. Self-dealing, inside trading, and conflicts of interests are subject to heavy penalty. Any one or several of these requirements, if violated, can be accompanied by large liability. The more important point, however, is that all of these requirements are also necessary if a board member is to function in a positive, objective, and independent manner, and reach intelligent conclusions.

While most chief executive officers no doubt welcome the idea of a board as advisors with different but relevant experience and points of view, not all of them could be expected to embrace a shift in the present balance of power between management and the board that has evolved over the years. Their point of view here may not be so much a desire for personal power as a conviction that committee management is poor management. They are aware that more has been learned about professional management and administrative structure, making it possible for organizations to grow in size and complexity, which has made it increasingly difficult for board members to participate meaningfully.

Yet it is doubtful, because of external and internal pressures, that the existing relationships that typify board and management can be sustained; indeed they are now and will continue to be for some time in an active stage of reexamination and modification. Failure by executive management to take a positive stance in the invigoration of the board and clarification of its functions invites a high risk. External interests are becoming increasingly assertive in their clamor for reform of the corporation as a central institution of contemporary society, and they are focusing much of their attention on the board of directors. Activists among stockholders have already made their influence felt. The federal government and the courts have not been disinterested. Indeed, case law is moving discerningly toward standards of care and awareness that cannot be attained with present practices. In theory, the federal securities laws are intended to require more complete disclosure; in practice they have become a means of giving visibility to the performance of directors.

Finally, scholars have begun to look more closely at the board of directors. What they are now writing is not flattering. It will not enhance the status of the corporation. If management can find within its own strengths the determination to devise ways to revitalize the institution of the board of directors, even at the cost of surrendering some of its own authority, the result will be far more rational and constructive than if it waits until the changes are forced on the corporation by external influences. The greatest danger facing the business community is that many businessmen fail to recognize the public's increasing appetite for government regulation, and even control.

Notes

* *Putting the Corporate Board to Work* (New York: Macmillan, 1976), pp. 12–40.

1. Roger M. Blough, "The Outside Director at Work on the Board," *The Record of the Association of the Bar of the City of New York*, Vol. 28, No. 3, March, 1973, p. 203.

2. Patrick E. Haggerty, "Remarks," *First Quarter and Stockholders Meeting Report*, April 18, 1973, Texas Instruments Incorporated.

3. Kenneth R. Andrews, "Can the Best Corporations Be Made Moral?," *Harvard Business Review*, Vol. 51, No. 3, May-June, 1973, p. 61.

A New Job for the Chairman*

THE DIVISION OF RESPONSIBILITIES between the board of directors and the management of a company advanced here implies a revision of our current concept of the role of the chairman of the board. Although in most cases he would be identified and elected by the board after a successful career in the company—but not necessarily as chief executive officer—on becoming chairman he would no longer be an officer of the company. He would then be the senior officer of the board, to which he would give his primary allegiance. Beyond this his constituency would be the management, other employees of the company, stockholders, and the whole range of external publics that now affect the corporation.

In the board proposed here, the chief executive officer of the company, that is, the president, would not report directly to the chairman of the board but rather to the collective board, of which both he and the chairman would be members. They would have equal status in the sense that neither would report to the other as a subordinate. A clear delineation of their respective functions would be the foundation upon which they would build and sustain a harmonious relationship.

The Functions of the Chairman

The chairman should have two principle functions. First, he should make certain that the board is properly discharging its responsibilities. It should be his task—not that of the chief executive officer—to guide the organization of the board and determine what the board collectively does and does not do. Among his responsibilities he should assure that all board members are adequately informed. He must be a consummate negotiator. In its broadest outline, his job should be to encourage the process, and, in the long run, the tradition, of consensus decision making by a group of independently minded board members in collaboration with management, a process in which the chief executive officer should fully share, but which he should dominate only to the extent of his more intimate knowledge.

Second, the chairman should relieve the chief executive officer of the

90

company and his operating associates of some of the excessively heavy burden of representing the company to its external publics: consumer groups, environmentalists, certain government agencies, business associations, institutional investors, even Wall Street analysts. Unlike some who have been identified in the past as "Mr. Outside," the chairman would be a spokesman with recognized internal authority and prestige; a public agent of the company with intimate knowledge of its affairs and with influence within and outside the company.

Specific Tasks of the Chairman

A simple recitation of the range of specific tasks for which the chairman of the board should have initiating responsibility is impressive. If done adequately and effectively, this work would require a major time commitment. In collaboration with the chief executive officer, he would:

1. schedule meetings of the full board and its several committees;
2. organize and present the agenda for regular or special board meetings;
3. review the adequacy of documentary materials in support of management's proposals that are sent to all board members for their study in advance of meetings. Alternatives that may have been considered should be disclosed;
4. assure adequate lead time for the effective study and discussion of the business under consideration;
5. take under continuous review the flow of information to and from board members.

Subject to the full board's review and approval, he would:

6. propose to the board for its approval a committee structure together with the assignments of fellow members as committee chairmen;
7. assign specific tasks to members of the board;
8. establish procedures to govern the board's work;
9. prepare and distribute proxy material to stockholders;
10. most importantly, in collaboration with his fellow directors, identify guidelines for the conduct of the directors and assure that each is making a significant contribution.

The board's work usually should be handled in the office of the chairman. Specific matters might originate with him, or be referred to him by the president or by a committee of the board. Occasionally, they might originate with an individual board member. . . .

When a task appropriate to the board's responsibilities has been identified by the chairman, background documentation should be developed by a designated board committee, usually with the assistance of the internal company staff and the company officers involved. The documentation would be prepared under the supervision of the chairman's office if the matter falls outside a committee's designated interest. The matter would then go on the agenda of a meeting of the full board, with or without recommendation. The submission by management or the chairman of a proposal for consideration without recommendation should not imply disapproval, but rather that, in the specific instance, a discussion without prejudice by the full board is desirable.

Informing the Board

The point is often made that business organizations are poor communicators. The development of orderly procedures to assure adequate communication between management and the board, between the board and the external publics of the company, and between the board and the company's stockholders should occupy a significant part of the chairman's time.

The main concern underlying Arthur Goldberg's proposal [that outside directors be provided with staff, budget, and unlimited access to company records] was a feeling of uncertainty about the adequacy of the flow of information from management to the board; in the words of the old saw: "It isn't what I don't know that bothers me; it's what I don't know that I don't know." He would have assigned a separate staff to an overseers committee of the board with the funds to commission outside consultants when necessary to assure a comprehensive inquiry into all major proposals and their alternatives. The infirmities of the Goldberg proposal have been exhaustively presented, including the challenge it implies to the principle of delegation based on confidence. While the Goldberg proposal has problems, there remains, nevertheless, the widespread current practice of management typically serving as both advocate and judge when a new course of action is presented to the board for approval.

A procedure developed cooperatively by the chairman and by the chief executive officer, using company staff, would be a preferable and less disturbing means than the Goldberg approach to assure that all board members are comprehensively informed of the full range of thinking and analysis, including possible alternatives, that has preceded the appearance of an item on the agenda.

There can be no doubt that interposing any procedures for more thorough information dissemination to the board than is current practice would involve some delay; how much would depend on the procedures. This may be the price paid for greater certainty. To one chief executive officer it would be unacceptable: "If you have someone other than the chief executive officer filtering everything through to the board, it would be an almost impossible situation to try to operate under." Yet one of the major difficulties that faces boards of directors today is the problem of being fully informed. Without this, the values of the board's breadth of experience and wisdom are at least partially immobilized, the strengths of checks and balances are lost, and management, acting as both advocate and judge, simply cannot escape a bias in its position even though it may be unaware of it.

Numerous other means are available to inform board members more fully. The development of a committee structure, with each committee assigned to report back to the full board on specific areas of interest, can concentrate attention on different phases of the company's activities. It is important, however, that these committees of the board be chaired by officers of the board and not by officers of the company, so that, again, operations do not dominate policy.

Company staff should be used to develop background data, after the chairman and the president have determined which staff members are available and qualified. Opportunities for a board committee to be in contact with the company's external counsel and accounting organization, however, should be recognized and encouraged as a normal procedure. The chairman of the board, of course, should be kept fully informed of the work of these committees. In turn, he should serve as a bridge to keep the chief executive officer informed.

Various other means are available to the chairman to assure that board members are familiar with company affairs. Organized plant visits, management seminars, and attendance at social functions all provide an opportunity to make the board more familiar with company personnel and the nature and nuances of the company's activities. It is a matter for judgement in each case how much time can or should be assigned to these out-of-meeting activities, but present practice no doubt assigns less time than should be the case.

The most obvious means of informing the board, of course, is through reports, letters, memoranda, bulletins, etc., delivered with adequate lead time. Their effectiveness depends on their nature. Manifestly, they should be both concise and comprehensive; only long enough to cover the pros and cons of the main points at issue succinctly. The chairman can perform a highly useful role by informing management about the types of material that board members find most useful and the types that are redundant.

The Chairman as External Communications Officer

Another type of communication that should appropriate a major share of the chairman's attention concerns the company and its several external publics: security analysts, environmentalists, leaders of minority and youth groups, consumerists, academics, and other molders of public attitudes, including officers of government. This he would do both personally and indirectly through his fellow board members. Most members of the board, with the chairman's encouragement, should participate personally in public affairs in one or more ways in order to bring to the board's deliberations a sensitive awareness of external influences that now is too often missing. The chairman should facilitate these external associations of his fellow board members in numerous ways, construing the time spent on them as "company time" when appropriate and providing normal expense allowances. In a sense, this practice could constitute an alternative to special interest representation on the board. At the same time, it would strengthen the posture of the corporation at its weakest point; specifically, it would help to maintain on the board a sensitive awareness of the social changes occurring in society.

Stockholder activities present still another area of communication about which the chairman should have a direct concern. Church related funds and the endowments of foundations and universities have put pressure on managements in recent years to follow various policies that have no direct relation to profitability, the stockholders' traditional interest. Indeed, programs have been urged that would reduce immediate profits. Procedures for presenting stockholders' proposals have been established by the Securities and Exchange Commission's regulations for proxies, but there remains an insistent pressure for the development of formal procedures for review of such proposals within the company.

Institutional investors, on the other hand, have shown little interest in influencing management, preferring to keep their position flexible so that they might liquidate a holding if dissatisfied. This posture may prove to be illusory if larger percentages of a company's total outstanding issues are accumulated, making liquidation difficult if not impossible without destroying values.

A third category of stockholders, the rank and file investor with holdings ranging from an odd lot to a thousand shares, is also typically passive with respect to pressure on management. An occasional letter to the company is usually handled with a reply prepared, and sometimes signed by a member of the secretary's office. But the growing activism of church, foundation, and university groups, and of groups specifically organized to use stock ownership to bring pressure on management, and the potential pressure of the "locked in" institutional investor, all point to the growing importance of providing a ready channel of communication from the top levels of a company. The chairman's office is the logical place to locate this activity.

The Proxy Process

Another function of the chairman should be the supervision of the proxy process in collaboration with his fellow board members, including the chief executive officer. This task should be carried out with a clear recognition that control of the proxy process by executive management has been one of the features of corporate practice most subject to criticism. It is alleged that through control of the proxy process, the chief executive officer of the company determines who will be the members of the board and thus assures himself a friendly panel of "bosses." By shifting control of the proxy procedures to a committee of the board under the general guidance of the chairman (who is not at the same time the chief executive officer), this source of attack by critics of the corporation can be substantially reduced.

The Chairman's Job

From this recitation of the chairman's assignments and activities it should be clear that they should relate to general corporate matters and to board reviews of its activities—not to operations. Indeed, the chairman's only influence on operations would derive from his membership as one individual on the board. The chief executive officer of the company would be the authorized manager of the business, subject to the policies and review of a board of directors of which he is also a member.

It goes without saying that a harmonious relationship would be an essential requirement between two individuals, each holding ultimate responsibilities in designated areas of activity that are by their nature interrelated. The achievement of harmony between two rational and intelligent individuals so situated has much precedent, however, and it is reasonable to anticipate it if the respective areas of responsibility are clearly delineated. A team approach by which decisions emerge through consensus becomes the normal pattern after the transition is completed. But if a certain amount of friction should develop during a period of transition from what has been called "one-man rule" to the procedures of consensus decision making, the cost may be a modest price to pay for the greater strength of a secure organization.

A final word should be said about the new and extended job of the chairman as it is described in this chapter. Today there is a tendency to hold the total board responsible for assuring that procedures exist for a comprehensive flow of significant information from management. Some feel that recent interpretations of the federal securities laws have created intolerable risks of civil liabilities. Practical limitations make it difficult for board members to learn of or prevent conduct that may give rise to a legal action. It is uncertain how the courts would interpret an expanded role for the chairman as a major channel of communication between the board and management. It should not be prejudged whether his exposure to liability would be greater and that of other board members lessened. It can only be observed that all board members, including the chairman, now share the exposure to civil action, and it is reasonable to expect that organizing the board better to assure an adequate flow of information for the fulfillment of its responsibilities should mitigate some of the total risks involved.

Note

Putting the Corporate Board to Work (New York: Macmillan, 1976), pp. 41-49.

A Full Job for
the Chief Executive Officer*

The Duties of a Chief Executive Officer

A SUCCINCT DESCRIPTION OF ONLY SOME OF THE DUTIES that are now involved in "managing a business" is sufficient to confirm the large demands and heavy responsibilities that are imposed on the chief executive officer of a major corporation. It is these now enormous duties that are implied by the seemingly simple stipulation of state legislatures, expressed in their corporate charters, that the board of directors shall manage the business. These duties have now, of course, been delegated by the board to management as personified by the chief executive officer—and properly so.

First and foremost, his duties include making and keeping the enterprise healthy, that is, profitable, and, if at all possible, growing through internal investment or external acquisition. This should be accomplished, along with all of the other matters involved in running a large and complicated business, within the purposes and limits determined by the board. He must develop an administrative structure that is adapted to the nature of the business and yet one that retains the flexibility to change as the business changes. Under his general supervision, personnel programs must be designed that will apply to the bench worker as well as to his immediate associates in the executive office, all geared together to achieve a harmonious meshing of human talents and skills. New employees must be selected and trained, and current employees must be shifted, advanced, or pruned from the working force.

The chief executive officer must assure supplies and secure markets. He must attend to changes in inventories and to the behavior of his receivables. When difficult situations arise, he is called upon to "put out fires." He must make certain that the company's operations are compatible with legislation and regulatory law. Only rarely can he or his executive associates escape dealing directly with labor unions. Reliability in the internal preparation of financial reports to the investment community must be one of his continuous concerns.

97

He must supervise the preparation of an annual operating budget, broken down in detail for each operating unit, to guide managers throughout the organization. Long-range planning, often in the form of a moving five-year operating target that discloses future needs for capital and other resources, must be carried on continuously and reviewed for conformity to the policies of his board. All of the company's financial resources must be made to do the maximum amount of work at all times, without standing stagnant either as float or unrequired deposits. Sound and secure financial management to assure the capability to seize opportunities for unusually favorable acquisitions when they appear is a continuing concern of the chief executive officer.

The Organizational Structure of the Corporation

The administrative structure of the company must be one that will get all of these things done. And to know whether they are done or not, the chief executive officer must create the channels for a reliable and prompt internal flow of financial and operating information, both up and down the organization. Whether the traditional hierarchical pyramid will be the most effective means of control or whether his organization must be supplemented with a system of task forces for specific purposes, or even whether decision making should be diffused among plural centers, is a matter that he must judge perceptively. . . .

A further insight into the activities of the chief executive officer is provided by a brief review of the typical organization of a business firm. It is a system of substructures, usually called departments, arranged pyramidally, peaking in the chief executive office. This structure is familiar and includes the line departments of purchasing, production, manufacturing, transportation, warehousing, and marketing, as well as the staff departments of accounting, finance, personnel, public relations, law, etc. This structure is typical of all manufacturing corporations; in other types of business organizations it is varied to adapt to one special situation or another. But, by and large, most business organizations are now fundamentally similar.

This line and staff structure has been designed over many years through trial and error; it has proven effective in maximizing efficiency in routine and repetitive operations. In an environment that is above all competitive, it is a stable and predictable arrangement. And yet this kind of a structure, and the control and incentive systems that are embedded in it, can tend to inhibit rather than encourage initiative and change within the organization. Equally important, they can tend to focus attention on short-run results. Because of this, one of the tasks of the chief executive officer is to find the means of offsetting the typical influence of "corporate bureaucracy" and instilling a sense of drive, self-reliance, and purpose throughout the organization that some call vitality, others initiative.

The Increasing Operational Demands on the Chief Executive Officer

Factors such as accelerating product obsolescence are beginning to compel more frequent modification of organizational arrangements. The importance of imaginatively introducing new products is of course increased as product life cycles become shorter. The fact that expenditures on research and development have continuously increased as a percentage of total expenditures on plant and equipment assures a continuous flow of new products. Moreover, markets are rapidly changing; some are growing, some are stabilizing, and some are contracting. And markets are becoming global.

New methods of business decision making, supported by the mathematics of operations research and the fast information retrieval and computation capability of the computer, now require a level of management sophistication previously unknown. Whether one is concerned with new products or with a logistics system of procurement, production, sales, and inventory control, these new abilities now cut across the normal departmental life of a corporation. Indeed, it has been said that formerly reliable constants used in the consideration of difficult problems have now become galloping variables.

All of this leads to the simple recognition that all the operating functions of a business are interrelated and need the close and continuous attention of the chief executive officer. Into his thinking must go prices, costs, sales, volume, profit margins, investment needs, plant capacity, consumer habits, and many other variables. Sharply drawn departmental lines and programs must necessarily be supplemented and indeed modified by the overview of senior management and, ultimately, by the chief executive officer.

This is a conclusion that is reinforced by the fact that the complexity of the corporation and its economic environment now generate an increasing number of "special projects" internal to the company. Better abilities must be developed to anticipate purely business problems as well as to resolve them after they have appeared. The organizational response to such problems will require a grasp of new technology and new analytical methods as well as a vision of new tasks and markets for the company. The need for the continuous testing of deep-rooted convictions based on past operating experience will be personal as well as corporate.

The Demands of the Corporation's External Environment

All organizations, including business organizations, respond to an external as well as an internal environment. If the demands from the internal environment are strong, even more insistent demands for adaptation derive from the changing nature in which business operates. And in this external world, the organization—whether it is a business organization or otherwise—must continually deal with new facts. It is in meeting these new demands that the chief executive officer needs—and can rightfully expect—the initiative of his board.

Economic considerations not immediately related to the internal processing, servicing, and selling of goods and services have, in recent years, appropriated a progressively larger amount of the time and attention of the chief executive officer. The quality of the local environment in which factories and offices function, typically within the cities, is deteriorating. Business is called upon to cope with these problems, and the public expects it to help solve them. Government restraints in the field of antitrust are becoming more numerous; more cases are being prosecuted. Constraints imposed by labor law and labor relations are being multiplied. Consumer and environmental groups have succeeded in obtaining new regulatory legislation. Maximum economic growth with reasonably stable prices—a government policy on which business has relied for a quarter century—has more recently become, in a period of emerging shortages and alarming inflation, a hollow incantation of bewildered economists. Consumerists and environmentalists are joined by security analysts, an array of officers from government agencies, and journalists, all claiming a share of the chief executive officer's time.

It is clear that new and distinctive corporate abilities are now needed and will be needed even more in the years to come. The means must be found for the development of new initiatives within the organizational structure of the corporation if it is to make a positive response to the changing environment that is both prompt and effective. The time and attention of the chief executive officer must not be appropriated by these external demands to the neglect of his operating responsibilities. The externalities of business, as important as they are, must not be allowed to impair the capability of the corporation to get its basic work done.

Beyond the internal activities of the corporation, these external demands now being made on business will require changes in organizational structure and new assignments of authority. The tasks that loom ahead are far too complicated for one man to grasp. As Arjay Miller, former President of Ford, now Dean of the Stanford Graduate School of Business, has said, the chief executive's job simply is becoming "too much for any man to handle."[1] Indeed, the staff of a whole department of a corporation is unlikely to possess the competence to deal with the complexity and difficulty of many of these problems.

It is little wonder that a plaintive cry is heard from the chief executive officers interviewed by *Business Week* for its May 4, 1974, issue. Let the chief executive officers speak for themselves: "The amount of work necessary to prepare yourself and keep informed about the political situation, the world situation, and how investors are reacting is terrific. And it keeps getting bigger." Twelve-hour days for chief executive officers are not uncommon. "The chief executive has switched from a long-term planner to a short-term thinker." "It is easy to go from crisis to crisis and let long-term planning slip." On the other hand, "It would be easy to spend all your life on external problems and not really get into how the organization is functioning." Yet, "The chief executive must take a position on the issues. It just isn't practical for the CEO to have a junior officer make those decisions by which a corporation affects society."[2]

Consensus Management in the Corporation

The search is on within the corporation for some form of divided responsibility or consensus management that will not lose effectiveness and efficiency. It is important to identify and sort out the personal talents that are required for dealing with both the internal and external affairs of the company, and to make certain those talents are both available and located in responsible and authoritative assignments.

One solution that has been used with increasing frequency to spread the responsibilities for *operating* matters is the device of the "Office of the Chief Executive." Here, the Office of the Chief Executive usually consists of from three to five senior officers of the company, including, of course, the chief executive officer himself. External affairs are often left to the chief executive officer, sometimes assisted by a public relations department and sometimes not. But a more logical and effective place to locate the talents, attitudes, and experience needed to relieve the chief executive officer and his executive associates of the load of *external* affairs is in a reconstituted board of directors with broad social as well as business interests.

The jobs of the chief executive officer and his executive associates, on the one hand, and of the chairman of the board and his director colleagues, on the other, are necessarily and irrevocably interrelated. Recognition of the primacy of their respective authorities, however, can help to assure that corporations will, in the future, demonstrate a responsiveness to public expectations that has not heretofore been experienced. The executive officers in management are properly the initiators in matters directly related to currently running the business, subject to review and audit by the board. The board members are properly the initiators of broad policies and programs to guide operations. In addition, they are the natural interpreters of the company to its several outside "publics" as well as the interpreters of the demands or positions of those "publics" to the executive officers of the company.

Their distribution of initiating responsibility implies that boards should include members who are broadly read, have associations in numerous communities of the public, and possess a capability for oral and written expression, as well as an intimate knowledge of the business and the company. While all of this breadth of talent and background is not likely to be found in one individual, the composition of the board, if it has been carefully selected, could reasonably be expected to provide the company with the broadly based strengths that are required.

It must be recognized that a response to public expectations more frequently than not involves an immediate expense without a compensating addition to income. The maximization of short-term profits is necessarily modified by most actions related to social responsibility, even though long-range profit may be made more secure. In such situations, it is as important for management to check and balance board initiatives that represent a response to public purposes or pressures as it is for the board to review the operating proposals of management for consistency with approved policy. It is a merit of the combination of a strong board and a strong management that the resolutions of specific issues are likely to be the most rational and, in the long run, the most desirable.

A redefinition of the job of the chief executive officer can be articulated either by specifying what he and his executive associates should do or by determining what kinds of interests and decisions the board wishes to retain or recapture for itself. The latter may be the most instructive approach. With respect to purely business affairs, the board is essentially a policy and review body that delegates current operations to management. While it may be legally responsible for fixing policy and purpose, the board would be foolish to do so without the benefit of close collaboration and consultation with management. Great care must be taken to avoid participating—i.e., interfering—in operations after purposes and programs have been discussed and adopted. Operations must be left to management.

It is in the external relations of the company that the board should identify tasks for which it is uniquely qualified and take more initiative; otherwise confusion of responsibility is most likely to occur. Governmental agencies working in the fields of competition and monopoly, labor, and taxes are logical, primary external contacts for management. All other external contacts, including even those with stockholders, can probably be handled as effectively, perhaps more effectively, by a properly organized working board. In part, the resolution of the distribution of functions between the chief executive officer and the chairman of the board would depend on the personalities involved; but, other things being equal, it is better for the sound development of the organization to adjust personnel to a rational assignment of functions than to adjust the functions to the talents of those available. However, other things are seldom equal and change from existing patterns must be careful and deliberate. In the interest of continuity and stability, basic changes will no doubt occur in part through attrition and in part through deliberate action.

Notes

* *Putting the Corporate Board to Work* (New York: Macmillan, 1976), pp. 52–61.

1. Arjay Miller, cited in "The Chief Executive Officer," *Business Week*, May 4, 1974, p. 42.

2. Cited in "The Chief Executive Officer," *Business Week*, May 4, 1974, *passim.*

The Composition of the Board*

The Supply of Competent Directors

... NUMEROUS CONSIDERATIONS NECESSARILY ENTER into an effort to estimate the total current supply of, and demand for, qualified directors. The supply of those qualified under the conditions and circumstances proposed here for the "working board" would indeed be inadequate if the transition from present practices should occur rapidly and in a large number of corporations at the same time. There is, however, little prospect of this happening; nor would it be desirable that the work patterns of boards be changed too quickly. A process of trial and error, a testing of a general direction of change, would be more appropriate.

One point should be made with emphasis, however. The size of the pool of those both capable and available is inelastic only for relatively short periods. It is flexible and would expand over reasonable periods of time as the attractiveness of board membership increased. Financial rewards would be only one element of that attractiveness. Probably more important would be the opportunity and challenge to make a significant contribution, to feel a part of a group whose decisions have ultimate meaning in the governance of the enterprise. The attractiveness of board membership would also increase if exposure to presently unclear and unidentified legal liabilities were reduced. ...

Yet it is no doubt true that, if the attractiveness of board membership were enhanced, many highly competent people would seriously consider second careers as professional directors after early retirement from a variety of first career experiences. Those who contemplated future careers as directors, knowing that such service would require a breadth of vision, interest, and understanding beyond the confines of daily operating assignments, would be encouraged, during their first career, to extend their knowledge, reading, experiences, and contacts to a variety of fields.

The possibility of a second career, involving a release from routine activities, the prospect of living with intellectually exhilarating challenges, and an opportunity to share in constructive leadership, would serve as a powerful magnet to attract experienced and talented people and, in time, enlarge the pool of those eligible for board positions in the future. The now visible trend toward an earlier retirement from daily operating responsibilities is already enlarging the number of competent and proven executives who can be called upon in selected cases, to the benefit of both the individual and the activity with which he or she joins. The International Executive Service Corps provides an interesting example of capabilities that have been rededicated after retirement.

The Supply of Director-time

The supply of directors is one thing; the supply of director-time is quite another. A greater participation in the determination of policy, procedures, personnel matters, and the review of performance implies the commitment of more time and attention than is the present practice of most directors. But even to analyze the amount of time currently spent on board activities, per se, would be difficult. First, under the current general arrangements, with strong inside director participation on the board, most board work is reduced to an aspect of the operating duties of the officers of the company. Outside directors, for the most part, spend only a few hours each month and perhaps an additional four or five days a year on board business. Many of these are members of a number of boards and divide their available time among them.

Under the proposals being made here, the extent of the assignment and performance of board work will vary among the directors, some of whom will previously have been operating officers of the company. It is probable that adequate board work for some members will require as much as a third of a normal working schedule, and some members of the board, such as the chairman, may work full-time or even overtime on the work of the board.

At present, it is often the case that an individual with high visibility, particularly someone from the financial community, will serve on as many as ten, twenty, or even more boards. This can only mean infrequent attendance at meetings, limited familiarity with the company, and the ability to serve fully only at a time of crisis. In contrast, a member of a "working board" would find that his duties would preclude membership on more than a couple of boards and their committees. If he happens also to be the chief executive officer or chairman of the board of a company of some size, he probably would not wish to accept membership on more than one working board. Indeed, it is not uncommon now for companies to permit their top officers membership on only one outside board. . . .

Other Sources and Non-Sources of Directors

The more traditional, tried, and tested sources of directorship talent have been corporate officers, both active and retired, lawyers, and investment and commercial bankers. In recent years, however, some new sources have been tried. The practice has grown of adding to boards academics—frequently administrators—women, representatives of minorities such as blacks, and, in rare instances, youth. Of late, proposals have been made with increasing frequency to add government representatives to corporate boards. Representation from consumers and labor also have their advocates. Demands are even heard that that amorphous constituency, "the public," be represented.

Special group representation on boards has been much debated and, to a degree, has been accepted. The argument has been made that all the major groups in society that are affected by a corporation should have representation on its board and that it is actually to the advantage of a corporation to have firsthand access to representatives of the major currents of contemporary society. Indeed, public pressure for greater independence in board members seems to have been the influence that has led some companies to accept the notion of the specialized representation of groups such as women, ethnic minorities, consumers, *et al.*

But it is not clear how the interests of multiple, sometimes political, and even opposing constituencies can, in the long run, be reconciled with the best interests of the company as basically an economic institution. Granted that the public's sanction of the corporation as an economic entity depends ultimately upon the approval of the other interest groups in the community, it is still not called upon to become a legislative assembly. In its own interests, it should be more concerned with the general community than it has been, but the corporation cannot be effective if it becomes quasi-political.

No doubt some of the demands for interest group representation stem from a certain lethargy among many boards of directors in dealing with the social and moral aspects of their corporate activities. There is a reluctance to challenge established positions and practices or to respond to changing expectations and the adoption of different values in our dynamic contemporary society. Unless, under the chairman's encouragement, a spirit and tradition of facing up to these problems can be activated among board members, it may be desirable and necessary to add interest group representatives to serve for a period as "catfish in the herring tank." In the long run, however, a board consisting predominantly of members serving specialized interests could not be expected to maximize the development of the total enterprise.

Effective specialized representation by its nature would result in political conflict in the board and make action in the general interest more difficult. Indeed, effective service to a particular group may constitute a conflict of interests with the institution a board member is elected to help govern. Over time, all the interests of the separate parties directly or indirectly affected by the enterprise will be best served by its balanced and healthy total development. The chairman of the board can do much to provide that unifying influence.

This is not to say that specialized interests should go unsponsored. With an appropriate degree of independence, all members of the board could be expected to espouse special causes from time to time, and not just the causes of their own socioeconomic group. All who are worthy of board membership should do this, regardless of their sex, race, religion, or ethnic background. The intelligence, knowledge, and character of the director should be paramount in board work. And it is the task of the chairman to encourage the free expression of those qualities in the interest of the total enterprise. Positive encouragement of such qualities by a chairman can provide better solutions to the problems confronting the company than the device of selecting directors simply because they represent a particular constituency.

The notion of selecting members of the board to represent consumers, the community at large, or the "public" seems even less promising. A basic difficulty, of course, is the matter of selection. Everyone is a consumer and a member of the public. The consumer and public community can become very large indeed in the case of the corporation whose activities cover the nation or the world. In this connection, it is interesting to note that the mutual insurance companies and savings institutions have boards that represent primarily the consumers of their services, but little difference has been noted between the attitudes or characteristic performance of their trustees and the boards of directors of stock companies.

The growing practice of having one or more foreign representatives on the boards of multinational corporations is the most promising of the special interest proposals. This is not because of unique or special attitudes and talents brought to the board so much as because multinational participation may mitigate somewhat sharp penalties imposed on the global company by excessive chauvinism. There can also be a significant value in having on the board a perceptive interpreter of the different cultural traditions and commercial practices of other nations. . . .

Interest Group Directors Evaluated

One can logically ask, moreover, whether special interest directors, including labor representatives, would more likely be concerned than others with the impact of the corporation on the community at large. The assertion of the group self-interest of each specialized representative is the more probable. The result could be seriously debilitating to the corporation. In the opinion of Professor Phillip I. Blumberg, it

> . . . would transform the board into a political institution, a microcosm of the community. All the directors would become, in effect, special interest representatives (whether for an outside group or simply for the stockholders), working to satisfy their particular constituency. The problem of conflict of interest for the individual board members would be replaced by the problem of conflict among the directors. It is extremely doubtful that such a board could manage a corporation effectively. Board decisions would involve shifting alliances between constituent groups, with log rolling deals (for the exchange of support for respective proposals), all of which would lead to a condition described by Beardsley Ruml decades ago as "gangsterism."[1]

The present preoccupation with specialized representation on corporate boards may prove, in time, to be more a force that brings about recognition of the need for greater independence among all board members than an actual springboard for bringing very many representatives of special interest groups onto boards of directors. From the standpoint of the company, its operations, and relations to society, it is more important to have a rigorous and informed review of initiatives and proposals that reach the agenda than to have contending and specialized individuals on the board to represent limited constituencies. . . .

The Potential of Non-Business Directors

At the present, only rarely have those representing blacks, women, government, etc., on boards of directors had significant business experience in their backgrounds. That does not necessarily destroy their usefulness as board members. If they are able to relate to the needs of the company and if their perception of external influences that will affect its future is sharp, they may make very important contributions. People with quite different backgrounds can bring a useful perspective to board deliberations, especially if they place the interests of the organization ahead of the specialized interests derived from those backgrounds.

Other non-business persons who have been added to boards with increasing frequency have been from the fields of education, usually academic administrators, and occasionally, the military, medicine, journalism, or professional writing, and, even more rarely, the ministry. Although it is not a good reason by itself, adding non-business people to boards can have a public relations value to a corporation. There is a widespread public skepticism of the ability of corporate management to understand the needs, or even be aware of the aspirations, of politically potent elements in society. Additions to the board from such groups may help to forestall mandated representation from such groups. . . .

Former Corporate Officers

The most promising of all directions to look for an expansion of the pool of qualified directors, however, is to those who have had successful careers as corporate officers—and not necessarily in the company seeking board members. There is substance in the notion that business management has now acquired many of the characteristics of a profession. True, it has no commonly accepted entrance requirements, no formal certification examination, no organized apprenticeship or internship. But each of these preparatory stages of the other professions is administered in its own way by the business organizations in which management careers are incubated. Pre-career preparation frequently involves four years of liberal arts education and perhaps one or two years in a broadly based program of graduate business study at a university. Institutions of higher learning, and many companies also, offer non-degree refresher periods of intensive study of management for corporate officers who are relieved of their daily assignments for the duration of this experience. There is now, "in the pipeline" of junior and middle management, a better prepared and larger number of potential senior executives, and eventually of board members, than at any previous time in the nation's history.

Few, if any, are now contemplating early retirement with the possibility of a second career as corporate directors. As a career objective it would be thought presumptuous and of doubtful attainability; and the limited appeal of the assignment under present circumstances could not be expected to call it to the attention of bright young men and women as a major goal to achieve, as a capstone to their careers. Yet as business corporations accept an enlarged participation in the common task to improve the quality of daily living, and as boards of directors acquire a more meaningful role in the guidance of corporations, a business career that progresses through the ranks to retirement as a senior corporate officer at fifty or fifty-five, with the potential of further service as a corporate director of one or several corporations, would have great appeal. It is completely natural that the professional manager should top off a career by serving as a professional director if his or her level of perception, knowledge of business, and breadth of vision qualifies for that position. . . .

Notes

Putting the Corporate Board to Work (New York: Macmillan, 1976), pp. 88-103.

1 Phillip I. Blumberg, "Who Belongs on Corporate Boards?," *Business & Society Review,* No. 5, Spring 1973, pp. 40-47.

Future Prospects of
the Board of Directors*

... WHAT IS INVOLVED HERE IS A PARTIAL SHIFT in authority within the governance of the corporation, an identification and division of functions between management and the board, and a progressive separation of management personnel from board personnel. More particularly, it has been proposed here that the respective assignments of the chairman and the chief executive officer be differentiated and assigned to different individuals. Without such changes, it is difficult to see how the board of the future can be organized to discharge fully the complex responsibilities required for the healthy development of the corporation and the security of board members from excessive liability. ...

The Transition to Separate Membership
of the Board and Management

So that there will not be prolonged confusion about board and management functions, the objective of working toward a separation between membership on the board and membership in management should be established. At the present, people who have been and are intimately associated as executives with the activities of a large organization are often included on its board. This does have a good justification, for the activities of the large organization in business, in education, in medical care, and in philanthropy, including the financial aspects, are very complex. Considerable firsthand knowledge and experience with these aspects are indispensable. But having the executives with ongoing operating responsibilities and duties also serve as directors on the boards of these organizations is a source of ambiguity and confusion, and can operate to reduce the effectiveness of the board as an independent body. It is recognized, however, that, as a practical matter in particular cases, there must be a gradual transition of the officers involved from their operating responsibilities because of a limited availability of executive talent to man the vacated operating posts.

The common confusion between board and management can be avoided if, after joining the board, former officers of the management are relieved as rapidly as circumstances permit of all *operating* responsibilities. The one exception would be the president, whose principal function is managing the ongoing workings of the company and whose presence on the board is required both for his experience and to assure that board decisions can properly be understood, interpreted, and executed by management. A large part of the job of distinguishing the board and management can be accomplished by making sure the chairman has *no* responsibility for day-to-day management, and that his sole job is to be, completely, the chairman of the board. If this is done, the occasion for confusion of roles simply cannot arise. But, when one individual serves as both chairman of the board and chief executive officer, there is the obvious difficulty of separating out the functions and responsibilities of the chief officer of the *board* from those which he has when he acts as chief officer of the *management*. Ambiguity of the role of the total board starts here. A sequential step to cure this confusion is to make sure that other executive officers below the president drop their operating assignments as quickly as possible.

There is nothing in this dichotomy of functions to imply conflict of purposes or adversary positions between the management and the board. On the other hand, arrangements that clarify the respective and separate functions and responsibilities of both board and management, and that provide a system of checks and balances between the two, will do much to minimize mistakes and maximize successes. It would also provide a new dimension to the effort of business to respond perceptively to the enlarged expectations of the public.

A New Concept of the Board Chairman

The distinction between board and management—the clear separation of the two—does imply a new and different concept of the role of the chairman of the board. Although in most cases the chairman in a business organization would be elected by the board after a successful career in the company, the office would no longer be regarded as the reward for a job well done as chief executive officer. The talents and the interests required in the chairman's office are quite different from those of the office of chief executive, and other senior personnel in the organization may be better qualified to be a board chairman. Indeed, the chairman of not-for-profit organizations are recruited from a variety of careers in which they have demonstrated outstanding capabilities. In both cases, the chairman would become the senior officer of the *board*. The chief executive officer, that is, the president, would *not* report to the chairman directly but rather to the collective board, of which the chairman would be but one member.

The chairman's internal functions would be to organize the work of the board, which—certainly for most of our large, complex organizations—if done effectively would require a full-time or nearly full-time commitment. This would be especially true in the business corporation. In collaboration with the chief executive officer, the chairman would schedule, propose the agenda for, and organize regular and special board meetings; he would make a review of the adequacy of documentary material sent to other board members. Subject to the board's review, he would establish procedures to govern the board's work; he would keep the flow of information to board members under continuous review; he would assure adequate lead time for the effective study and discussion of matters under consideration; he would assign specific tasks to members of the board; and he would establish a committee structure to carry out the board's work.

Externally, he would serve as the principal bridge to portray the company's activities to the public at large and, conversely, to interpret the significance of the political, sociological, and economic scene for the company's activities. Clearly this would require a wide range of interests and a high level of intelligence not typically found in a single individual. For the effective discharge of such heavy responsibilities, the chairman would necessarily need the support and perspective of fellow board members with wide experience and catholic concerns, including, of course, the practical and realistic concerns of the business. The chairman's posture, in other words, should have the quality of universality. The success of the duality of board and management would depend largely on his administration of the office. In addition, he should be prepared and equipped to take his place among the leaders of business thought and participate in the development of national public policy.

Board Committees:
Their Commitments and Compensation

The legitimate functions and concerns of the board of directors of large, complex, often multinational business companies are so multifarious and difficult, and the burdens of handling them well so heavy, that special attention needs to be given to the task of setting up board committees and helping them to do their work properly without interfering with the ongoing work of management—and without being interfered with! In addition to the usual committees of finance, audit, conflicts of interests, compensation, personnel, and perhaps executive, some companies have committees concerned with technology and with public policy issues, but others feel that these are areas of interest to all members of the board. Whether or not to have these two committees or still others, is a decision that is, and can be, made only in the particular context of each company.

Generally speaking, a greater participation by governing boards in the determination of policy and procedure, and in the review of personnel and performance, implies the commitment of much more time and attention than is the present practice of most directors and trustees of large organizations. Guidance in matters of corporate social responsibility imposes an additional dimension that is likely to grow in the demands it will make.

The greater participation advocated here certainly suggests a corresponding increase in compensation for board members. Indeed, the quality of board members and their work will be enhanced with a clarification of their functions and an increase in their remuneration. Those board members recruited from careers in the organization would be expected to retire from operating responsibilities at earlier ages, perhaps in their early or middle fifties. Membership on one or more boards would become a full-time career for some and a part-time career for most. Under such a system, the provision of adequate compensation for board members becomes especially important.

Board Independence

The search for greater independence and more positive commitment of board members has led some organizations to accept the notion of special interest representation from groups such as women, ethnic minorities, consumers, labor, environmentalists, etc. But it is not clear how the conflicting interests of multiple and diverse constituencies will, in the long run, be reconciled with the basic concern of the board, which is, of course, the survival and growth of the corporation. In the long run, a board consisting predominantly of members serving special interests could not be expected to maximize the development of the total activity. Rather, the current concern for interest group representation may prove to be more of an unstated recognition of the *need* for greater *independence* among all board members than a *solution* to the problem of independence.

It is more important to have a vigorous and informed review of the proposals that come before the board from the point of view of both the company and of the general interest than it is to have contending and specialized individuals on the board trying to represent the particular interests of limited constituencies. Conflict on the board would make effective action difficult. Service to a particular group may constitute a conflict of interests with the very institution that board members are elected to govern. Over time, the concerns of the special interests involved in the enterprise will be best served by the balanced and healthy *total* development of the enterprise as a whole.

That is not to say that specialized interests should go unsponsored. With a requisite degree of independence, *all* members of the board will feel a compulsion to take initiatives and espouse special causes from time to time, and not always the same cause. This is true of all who are worthy of board membership, regardless of sex, race, religious background, or other distinction. Indeed, there is a positive advantage in having board members with diverse experiences and backgrounds, who are capable of relating them to the corporate interest. The *character* of the individual is what is really paramount.

A reconceptualization of the governing board's functions and structure is a more promising way than constituency representation of assuring independence of its posture. Especially is this true of efforts to separate clearly the "legislative" functions of the board from the "executive" functions of the management and to establish and maintain as clear a demarcation as possible between the memberships of the two groups. Such steps should provide for the technical competence required in both bodies as well as for their ability to look at themselves and each other with objectivity. Those steps, alone, should do much to assure the "legitimacy" of the business corporation, its direction, and its management. They should also improve for all forms of organizations with governing boards the effectiveness and stability of the decision process.

Numerous books and articles, critical of the effectiveness of directors and trustees in the discharge of this or that aspect of their responsibilities, have appeared in recent years. Numerous community leaders are now persuaded that revitalization of the board of directors is urgently needed to assure the continued development of the large organization as a constructive influence in contemporary society. Although there is no single prescription for that revitalization, a major contribution to that important purpose can be made by a clarification and implementation of the respective functions of board members and of management, and this can best be achieved by a separation of their respective memberships.

Note

Putting the Corporate Board to Work (New York: Macmillan, 1976), pp 107–118.

III
Corporate Social Responsibility

The Ethics of Business*

Preface

THE BASIC ATTITUDES AND ACTIONS of contemporary business are expressed most convincingly in the market place. For the most part, it is in the market place that the behavior of those responsible for our corporations is tested by the ethical standards of a free society. Conflicts of interest, matters relating to such items as expense accounts and accuracy in product representation, and even the more general affairs associated with labor relations and "social responsibility," all find the sharp edge of their expressions in the buying and selling activities of the business organization. . . .

Three propositions may contribute to the clarification of this vitally important subject. For emphasis they can be, at the outset, stated categorically. First, one does not find in philosophical scholarship any strict differentiation of ethics for the various professions, such as law, medicine, or business. Second, conformity to law and conformity to ethical norms are not necessarily synonymous. Third, the significance of a new and longer time span, which corporate decision-making must encompass when it is concerned with ultimate objectives, has largely been ignored in the reconciliation of the maximization of gain with ethical practice. Each of these propositions, implicit or made explicit in the presentations of the participants, merits elaboration.

It has been asserted that since ethics constitutes a system of moral principles which binds the fabric of the whole society, there is no distinguishable ethics as business ethics, medical ethics, or political ethics, except as business, medical, or political actions give expression to the basic social ethics. If this is a valid premise, it follows that an attempt to identify and prescribe a particular set of ethical principles for the businessman is more likely to achieve superficiality than a basic consideration of the real issues. Perhaps the real achievement will come when understanding of the contemporary nature of our business institutions and systems has reached a point where meaningful relationships with ethical principles can be readily perceived by both scholar and practitioner.

119

The second proposition asserts that conformity to existing law does not necessarily insure ethical behavior. Failure to conform to public law, of course, is reprehensible, but the law must keep abreast of developments. Even when this occurs, ethical behavior may involve acceptance of a code of conduct based on standards beyond the limits of enforceability. Compliance with the law is not enough.

If business ethics is really the basic ethics of society expressed through business institutions and actions, and if ethical business behavior may require compliance with the unenforceable, it follows that preparation for an ethical business career will require more than an examination of what is believed to be business ethics per se and more than a knowledge of business law. It will require the development of a sense of mission and service to one's fellow men and, as an absolute essential, a reconciliation of such service with the acquisitive motivations and manifestations of success in a business career. It will require a realization that, in the long run, rewards and recognition for both individuals and institutions will result from services rendered to others.

The importance of developing high moral and ethical standards is measured by the importance of business itself in contemporary Western society. The activities of business are inescapably a part of the daily lives of each of us, whether or not we are directly associated with business. The cultural characteristics of our society are conditioned for better or for worse by the impact of business. It is no exaggeration to say that the fashioning of a way of life is a by-product that has become the prime product of our business system. The corporation as the principle institution of business has become the dominant institution of our times and touches the lives of each of us in innumerable ways.

An activity of society so ubiquitous can ill afford attitudes that are narrowly based on crass cupidity or immediate advantage. Fortunately, it has not been necessary to annihilate the incentive for gain in order to bring within the orbit of corporation management the motivations of public service and ethical conduct beyond the compulsions of law.

Many insist that there is an inherent conflict between private economic goals and public interest that can be contained only by price competition or by government regulation. While short-run business considerations are often found to be contrary to public interests, the long-run corporation interests, when fully understood, appear to coincide with action that is desirable for society at large. This is particularly true in matters relating to the running of the large enterprise in which the stockholders and workers, suppliers and customers, and government are all deeply involved. Contrary to past assumptions, these several interests in the corporation have far more in common than in conflict, and the wise manager will be aware of this and transmit his conviction to the several parties. Stability and continuity built on a degree of loyalty of association of the several parties are the most certain assurance of long-run growth and mutual benefits. Such loyalty cannot be built on sharp practice or aggressive pursuit of immediate competitive advantage. . . .

Note

The Ethics of Business: Corporate Behavior in the Market Place (New York: Columbia University, Graduate School of Business, 1963), pp. vii-x.

[Corporate Giving and the Law*]

. . . ONE OF THE CHALLENGING QUESTIONS IN THE BUSINESS-SOCIETY relationship in the early 1950s was whether business might legally increase its financial support of higher education. At that time business contributions were of doubtful legality, unless the business could show that they led to a clearly reciprocal benefit. The dictum of an early English court, "Charity has no seat at the board table," still governed the attitudes of many, especially the legal counsellors to business. Corporate boards feared to go beyond fairly limited giving. A legal test case was needed to establish that a broader philanthropic role for business was permitted under the law. The Jersey Standard board, for various reasons that included the potential opportunity for numerous others to intervene, wisely declined to make the company the subject of a test case even though Frank Abrams had proposed it.

As we were puzzling out our next step, I remembered that I had a friend, Hubert O'Brien, whose plumbing and water valve company, the A. P. Smith Manufacturing Co., in New Jersey, had many of the charter characteristics of the Standard Oil Company (N.J.). After a lunch with Frank Abrams, O'Brien agreed to have his company serve as a test case if his board approved; he thought approval likely since he owned 40 percent of the stock. He announced a board resolution *proposing* a modest gift of $1,500 to Princeton "for general educational purposes," a gift that would have no direct relation to the company's business. It was arranged for a stockholder to "see" the proposal, which was published in the *New York Times*, and to bring an action in the New Jersey courts for a restraining order. We wanted a good, hard fought case, so it was arranged that the complaining stockholder would be represented by the best lawyer in New Jersey, who also happened to be counsel to Standard Oil. The A. P. Smith Company retained lawyers enlisted by the Ford and Sloan Foundations. Standard Oil and the two foundations covered the respective legal fees.

The case was assigned to an elderly judge, J. S. C. Stein. Under the guidance of Irving Olds, the Chairman of U.S. Steel and an advocate of greater corporate support, a dry run was arranged at the home of Harold Dodds, the president of Princeton. Each of us rehearsed that part of the prospective testimony about which he was best informed. On the day of the hearing, we all went to court in Newark. The judge was interested only in one man, Emerson Andrews, head of the Russell Sage Foundation, who had written books on philanthropy. His questions to Andrews convinced us that we were in trouble. It appeared that he had stopped thinking about corporate law and practice fifty years before. Shortly thereafter, the judge became ill. To our relief, the case was reassigned, and we became more hopeful. But he recovered, and the case was returned to his docket.

On the date in 1952 set for reading the opinion, Judge Stein adjourned the court, observing that no representatives of the press were present. He wanted them there. Our frustration was enormous. The next day we all returned and he read the opinion. It was not just a *right* of corporate management to use stockholders' money in the support of higher education, he said, it was a *duty* to do so. A vigorous national program of higher education, he held, was a major source of strength in the shaping of a social climate in which the business corporation could effectively function. Our elation was unbounded.

This favorable opinion by the trial judge was appealed to the highest court in New Jersey, which confirmed the opinion, and then to the U.S. Supreme Court, where jurisdiction was denied. Today, this is the basic case, the precedent giving business corporations the right—nay, in the words of the trial judge, "the duty"—to support higher education.

The A. P. Smith Manufacturing Co. case has clarified the legality of business support of higher education, but it seemed to those of us who originated the court case that additional, strong leadership was needed to stimulate a significant expansion of giving. The needs of higher education had been stated dramatically in an earlier Carnegie Commission report entitled, "Financing Higher Education in the United States." In addition to Frank Abrams' public statements, Irving Olds had made a much publicized talk at Yale on its 250th anniversary, and Alfred P. Sloan, Chairman of the General Motors Corporation, had written an article on the same subject for *Collier's Magazine.*

To explore the next step to be taken, Abrams arranged a series of luncheons with Olds and Sloan at which Clarence Faust, the president of the Fund for the Advancement of Higher Education, and I were present. Out of these luncheons emerged the concept of the Council for Financial Aid to Education (CFAE). Abrams, Olds, and Sloan were joined by Henning Prentiss, chairman of the Armstrong Cork Corporation, and Walter Paepcke, chairman of the Container Corporation of America and the developer of the Aspen Institute at Aspen, Colorado. Together, these five incorporated the Council as an educational organization under the Board of Regents of New York State. Prentiss and Paepcke had been members of the earlier Carnegie Commission. It was agreed that an annual budget of $100,000 would be shared equally by four foundations, Sloan, Ford, Carnegie, and Rockefeller.

At the outset, we established several principles. No funds would be collected for redistribution to colleges and universities. The board would have twice as many business leaders as academics, for the latter were expected to attend twice as often. And we would not get into the business of grading the academic program of colleges and universities. Our role would be to measure, endorse, and publicize the need for financial support. Even more importantly, it was recognized that endorsement by the most conspicuous leaders of the nation's business made the practice of corporate support more acceptable. My assigned task was to draft the initial papers to be approved and processed by the lawyers.

For its first ten years, the expenses of the Council continued to be financed in equal shares by those four foundations. Since then, the Council's expenses have been picked up by modest annual contributions of corporations, a project made successful by Frank Sparks, a one-time president of CFAE.

After the CFAE had been running for several years, I called on Ted Repplier, my friend from the Famine Emergency Committee days. Together with Henry Wriston, the president of Brown University and also a trustee of the Council, we arranged for the Advertising Council to promote the well-known national advertising campaign, "Give to the College of your Choice." The campaign continues to be one of the Advertising Council's most important programs, generating $31 million of advertising space in 1979-80. Support of higher education by business since the establishment of the CFAE has grown from some $35 million annually, mostly on a quid pro quo basis, to about $900 million, much of it attributable to the promotional efforts of this pilot group. With the Conference Board, it compiles data of business support of education. It also publishes pamphlets, holds luncheon meetings throughout the nation, and its travelling staff are educational counselors to corporations. . . .

Note

The Dean Meant Business (New York: Graduate School of Business, Columbia University, 1983), pp. 121-24

The Business Corporation
in Transition*

Change is Underway

. . . VERY SIGNIFICANT CHANGE IN THE BUSINESS CORPORATION is already evident; it has occurred both at home and abroad to adjust the corporation to evolving public attitudes. Thus, for example, changed public attitudes throughout the world have eroded the authoritarianism once associated with corporate executive management. In the United States, this erosion has resulted from expanded government regulation as well as more active and independent monitoring by boards of directors. In Western Europe, the weakening of executive authority is reflected in greater labor participation in decision making, from shop floors to supervisory boards. In East Asia and in much of the lesser-developed world, it has been weakened by demands for direct participation in ownership and control. Everywhere, interest has been shown in greater worker sharing in equity ownership of the corporation. Moreover, public interest and concern about a wide range of perceived impacts of the corporation on the economic, physical, and social environment, as well as various aspects of market behavior, has also worked to reduce business authoritarianism.

The important question then is not whether the business corporation has a future, but rather: What is the probable nature of that future? Can the corporation, in the modified form it is in the process of assuming, be expected to continue to produce the bountiful and ever-increasing abundance that it has provided in years past?

Change in all parts of society is moving at a rapid rate and appears in most places to be irresistible and irreversible. The status quo no longer holds fast, even though the corporation, under the guidelines that have heretofore served it, has delivered extraordinary material benefits during the centuries of its significant existence. . . .

In the transition, the simplistic purposes and guidelines that the corporation inherited from the past have become blurred. No longer sufficient is the corporate quest only for improved efficiency, competitive success, and

125

maximized profits. New tasks have been assigned by public pressures, tasks for which executive management in many cases is not prepared. . . .

The Case for the Single Purpose Corporation

Those who continue to regard the large corporation as a purely profit-making organization, in contrast to a socioeconomic institution of society, would find no inconsistency in these variable attitudes of the businessman toward government regulations. To them, the purpose of the corporation is simply to maximize profits. By making more money, the corporation, they say, performs the full range of its social obligations. If markets are effectively competitive, the corporation will provide the goods and services wanted by the public, will allocate the national resources efficiently, and create growing employment opportunities. Continuous competitive pressure for greater efficiency will assure the public an expanding flow of material goods and services at decreasing real unit costs.

And the corporation, it is held, is ill-suited to accept the newly emerging social responsibilities, which cost money—money that is not available when the competitive situation limits profits to the cost of obtaining capital from investors. In this situation, each factor of production—capital, labor, materials, and technology—earns only its own competitive rewards, and there is no surplus for good deeds. Acceptance of the costs of socially responsible action is, in this view, equivalent to a confession of guilt under antitrust laws. In a perfectly competitive situation, there would be no surplus. Moreover, corporate managers are believed to be singularly unperceptive about the nonmarketable needs of society. Why should the alleviation of those needs be turned over to what is held to be, in essence, self-selected private oligarchies?

When the corporation is conceived to have purely a profit-making purpose, a strong case can be made for adhering to traditional guidelines and the existing legal framework for the determination of its policies and practices, harsh and uncompassionate though they may at times be. It is when the business corporation is urged to exercise a major influence beyond its business functions that ambiguity of purpose and practice begins to appear. And many now feel that the corporation cannot escape the expanded social expectations of a people that now enjoys a material abundance that is the result of its own spectacular economic success. The large corporation, they believe, is not the "economic man" of the classical economists now grown up; it is rather the nexus of life in all industrially developed democracies.

The Corporation's "Quasi-Constituencies"

The basic legitimacy of the corporation has been and is grounded on stockholder ownership; stockholders are still the only constituency of a corporation's management that is recognized by corporate law. But a shadow on this legitimacy is now felt by some because of the tenuous control exercised by all but a few stockholders. The process of voting by proxy, in normal circumstances, is far from effective control.

Further, management has, in a substantive sense, acquired additional quasi-constituencies: customers, employees, suppliers, cultural and educational organizations, and environmentalists. The legal recognition of these new quasi-constituencies is found in general legislation—which is in part coercive and in part permissive—not in corporate law. The number of laws related to these quasi-constituencies' concerns is enormous. Thus, laws that constrain the corporation have been passed in the fields of labor and personnel, environment, conservation, and product integrity; other laws such as those granting tax credits for charitable contributions, have facilitated the achievement of socially desirable ends.

Hazards to the Corporation and Society

There are two major hazards involved in the transition of the corporation from a solely profit-making organization to a socioeconomic institution of society. The first is the likely dilution of the sharp-edged compulsions for continuous improvement of efficiency. The inclusion of societal considerations in strategic planning cannot fail to modify the processes of decision making. Careful consideration of administrative structure and procedures is required to preserve, to the maximum extent possible consistent with social performance, the effectiveness of the corporation in its traditional functions. . . .

The second of these hazards involves a risk to society rather than directly to the corporation. Professor Theodore Levitt of Harvard observed several years ago:

> . . . the danger is that all these things . . . will turn the corporation into a twentieth-century equivalent of the medieval church. The corporation would eventually invest itself with all-embracing duties, obligations, and finally powers, ministering to the whole man, and molding him and society in the image of the corporation's narrow ambitions and its essentially unsocial needs.[1]

The truth of the matter is that business management in general feels as uncomfortable about accepting societal functions as Professor Levitt views their possible assumption. There is a realization that, as now motivated and organized, the leadership of the corporation is ill-prepared for such a role. The concern of management is rather to find some identified limits to the socially responsible tasks assigned by public pressures. There is, nevertheless, an awareness that unless business accepts an expanded role, freedom to perform its present functions will be progressively circumscribed by the imposition of governmental regulations. There is an accompanying awareness that a broadening of corporate purposes will require the collective wisdom of personnel with a diversity of interests and experience to share in the development of corporate policy and practice.

Management's Dilemma

A dilemma is a set of circumstances in which the available courses of action are both more or less disagreeable. Corporate management is confronted with a dilemma. It would be pleasant if the rules that guided the corporation to success could be left unmolested and without the penalties of public and governmental encroachment. That is the position often taken publicly by business spokesmen. But experience has demonstrated that efforts to get public acceptance of this position have failed. The argument, cast in terms of free enterprise, that abundance has resulted from the guidelines of the past, simply has not impressed the contemporary public. Government encroachment, loss of public approbation, and the emergence of a defensive state of mind by business have been the end product of these efforts.

The other horn of the dilemma is the problems that stem from the acceptance by corporate management of a broadened range of societal concerns and activities, some of which are closely associated with business affairs and some of which are fairly tangential to business. In accepting this course, some present satisfactions are lost; a clear-cut purpose measured by quantitative results is over-laid by what appears to be a confusion of ill-defined objectives related to quality-of-life considerations. A diversity of new talents and experiences is required in the decision-making process to supplement those conditioned by careers in business. A sharing of authority is involved in either case: a sharing with the government, on the one hand, or with those brought into the orbit of decision making to supplement the purely business experience, on the other.

There is probably no fully satisfactory resolution for executive management of these deep-seated changes that are occurring in the evolution of the corporation. The best that can be hoped for is a reconciliation within the context of the corporation of the societal values of the past with those that have newly emerged.

Public Policy Alternatives

Alternatives are available for the development of future public policy. On the one hand, the past disposition to regard the corporation as a purely profit-driven entity that the public feels must be closely constrained by government can result only in further frustrations. Government regulation of business has already grown to a point where many regard it as excessively costly, ineffective, stifling, and even destructive. The continued insistence by business leaders that the non-economic values of fairness, justice, and equity are secondary to immediate stockholder interests will only assure the further encroachment of regulatory growth.

On the other hand, if corporate leaders prudently move to the acceptance of the premise that the large corporation's activities affect all groups in the community and that their interests must be seriously considered, the decisions will be made with a more perceptive awareness of the social implications involved. That could not fail to diminish the public's support of government regulation. It would serve to help assure the longevity of the private business corporation, and thereby the stockholder's interest. Business protests of government encroachment without this basic adjustment of attitude have not been effective, and are unlikely to be in the future.

Among the important questions awaiting full resolution are those concerning the extent to which various social costs should be brought within corporate accounts, costs heretofore placed on the community, in many cases quite unconsciously. Clean air, pure water, and product safety challenge efficiency and low unit costs; energy and materials conservation restrain the growth of the GNP and jobs. These are major issues that involve significant trade-offs. They require decisions as to whether, and if so how much, the real or imputed costs should be borne by the corporation—which means within the market system—or continue to be distributed to the community at large in taxes, in discomfort, or perhaps in disappointing material growth.

The achievement of equality of opportunity, a problem that starts in the community and the educational system, is now projected, with its attendant costs, into the personnel practices of the corporation. The costs cannot be wished away, only shifted. The basic adjustment will be the extent to which the corporation will become a conduit to transfer to the marketplace where they can be seen and measured, those social costs that have heretofore been hidden.

Adaptation is made more difficult by several unchallenged assumptions deeply embedded in our folklore and in our corporate law. According to a former dean of the Yale Law School, Eugene Rostow, "The law books have always said that the board of directors owes a simple-minded duty of unswerving loyalty to the stockholders, and only to the stockholders." Yet executive managers, delegated by the board of directors to operate the large modern corporation, have found it necessary and expedient to recognize other constituencies. Long-range company interests, as well as government legislation and regulation, have required it. Other groups than stockholders now share the attention, if not the loyalty of corporate boards and operating management, and, often in the case of personnel, both the attention and the loyalty.

As Professor Melvin Anshen of the Columbia Business School has said:

> Specific interest groups in our society (environmentalists, minorities, women, consumerists, etc.) are looking at specific aspects of corporate behavior and are saying, "Right here the costs of business practices outweigh the benefits; let's change the rules." No one seems to be considering the total economic implications of the aggregate of all pressures for changed behavior. This is a job for far-sighted business leaders, even business philosophers. There can be no doubt that if the corporation is to continue to generate a rising volume of economic wealth within a market system, while retaining democratic political institutions and personal freedoms, it must keep many of its traditional characteristics. Equally, there can be no doubt that if it is to survive, it must be selective and flexibly adaptive to strong and justified pressures for change.

Dual Influences of the Business Corporation

Part of the molding of public attitudes has resulted from the provision by the business corporation of an unprecedented level of material well-being. With six percent of the population, the United States, where the corporation has had its greatest expansion, currently enjoys some 30 percent of the world's production. It is common knowledge that our use of energy per capita exceeds that of most other industrialized nations.

More and more, people have been brought directly or indirectly into the orbit of the corporation's influence. It is no overstatement to say that the U.S. business corporation is the *major* institution conditioning most aspects of the daily life of every one of us—more so than political institutions, the church, or educational or cultural activities. No data have been compiled, but intuitive judgment supports the view that the man-woman hours spent in serving and thinking about the affairs of the corporation in the aggregate exceed those devoted to any other activity.

Less frequently recognized has been the influence of the corporation on the evolution of political institutions. The world's work is done by the voluntary or compulsory collaboration of groups—family, tribe, voluntary association, or government. Rejecting private business organizations as a desirable expression of voluntary association, some societies have assigned the functions of production and distribution to government. When control over production and distribution is in the hands of government, there can be no market system as we know it. The critical decisions about the types of goods produced as well as their quantity, quality, and price must be made by government officials. The result has necessarily been an authoritarian political structure that operates in a milieu of fixed prices and frozen job assignments, and an economy that may or may not conform to public desires—mostly not. Where technology and large-scale production have advanced together, the corporation has far more preserved than impaired the open market system, despite a crescendo of cries about monopoly. Without the corporation it is not possible for a complex advanced society to maintain an open market that registers public desires. Daniel P. Moynihan has put it well: ". . . the market has a lot more to do with the perpetuation of a democratic and libertarian society than you might think."[2] In an industrially developed society, the corporation makes possible the open market, and keeps it open. An open market, political democracy, and personal and intellectual freedom have an affinity that is indivisible.

By virtue of its contribution to abundance, of its provision of multiple choices, and of opportunities for self-expression through expanding the range and number of jobs, by utilization of technological advances, by its essential role in the preservation of the market system and of democratic political institutions—by all these things the business corporation has emerged as the fulcrum of a free and independent society. That does not mean that major repairs are not necessary. Quite the contrary. But the transition to new priorities has never been, is not now, and will not be a comfortable one. Nor is it likely that managing the future corporation will provide as much fun for the aggressive, hard-hitting, sometimes combative person who has done so much to build its present strength.

It is important that the corporation be preserved with its capacity for material abundance and its potential for extended public service, but in recent decades the evidence is overwhelming that it has been losing its freedom of action with alarming rapidity. The fact of the matter is that the focus of corporate purpose has necessarily come to rest on the balanced development and longevity of the corporation *per se*, and not on any one constituency, not even stockholders, although stockholders should in the long run benefit when this is more widely recognized. This is a profoundly important, but as yet not fully apprehended, shift of purposes and goals. When fully perceived inside and outside the business community, it should clarify many ambiguities associated with public attitudes toward corporations and the conceptions of business leaders about themselves. Their primary loyalty is properly to the corporation itself, and the corporate interest is best served by a balanced recognition of numerous constituencies. The essential nature of "the corporation in transition" lies in the learning experience occurring daily in corporate practice, and in the catch-up needed in corporate law, to recognize the claims of several constituencies. This constructive change is a basic requirement to the preservation of the corporation in a libertarian society.

Notes

Beyond the Bottom Line (New York: Macmillan, 1979), pp. 4-15.

1. Theodore Levitt, quoted in "Business's Stake in Education," *Change* (June-July 1978), pp. 15–16.

2. Daniel P. Moynihan in "The Social Responsibility of Business," *Business and Society in Change* (American Telephone & Telegraph Company, 1975), pp. 19–20.

Ethical Conduct in an Immoral World*

ETHICS IS A WORD OFTEN USED but less often defined. It helps to define the desirable in general without saying what the desirable may be in a particular case. Standing alone it often sets forth what is intangible, tenuous, even ethereal, except perhaps to the one who is using the term. A dictionary definition identifies ethics as that part of philosophy dealing with moral conduct, duty, and judgment. In each of the many basic ethical systems, philosophers give these three terms different meanings. Thus a hedonist and a utilitarian would have different meanings for "moral conduct," "duty," "judgment," and a wide variety of other ethical terms.

The difficulty of securing agreement on ethical matters is notorious. Even well-informed persons working from the same ethical premises frequently manage to come up with differing conclusions about what it would be right to do because different attitudes and commitments make them differently evaluate the particular circumstances within which a decision must be made. Thus, depending on the circumstances, commitments, and attitudes of an individual, his judgment may prescribe one course of action and his sense of duty may prescribe another. Witness the influence payments made to foreign government officials and the illegal domestic political contributions by leaders of American corporations. Corporate officers presumably felt that their duty to the company overruled their judgment that to make payments was wrong.

And ordinary mortals rarely think about ethical matters from a consistent ethical stance. Their ethical conclusions are usually the result of imperfect inferences drawn from assumptions taken from different ethical systems. The result is added complexity and more difficulty in securing agreement.

Another definition of ethics is conformity to formal or professional rules of right or wrong that describe a system of conduct. Several decades ago Walter Lippman made an interesting and convincing case for a code of personal behavior acceptable to society. He called it "the Public Philosophy." Codes of conduct do exist in the professions of law, medicine, and others.

Many business corporations have long had codes of conduct, and more have been added in recent years—and are still being added—to govern the activities of their members. Few such codes, however, have survived since the days of the NRA (National Recovery Act) when many were designed to cover entire industries.

In connection with the public perception of business codes, an assumption widely held for many years may be gradually weakening. Businessmen, engaged in activities for a profit, it has been believed, are more tainted with self-serving than doctors, lawyers, clergy, academics, government officials, and others in the not-for-profit sectors of society. The author's observations over many years provides convincing evidence that this is simply not so. All are self-serving to one degree or another, and businessmen not discernibly more so than those in other professions.

External restraints are required to supplement self-restraints on people in the everyday walks of life. The behavior of professionals is no exception. Examples are abundant. Until recently, doctors severely limited entry into their profession: the result was that medical fees escalated far more rapidly than other components of the cost of living. Lawyers, in a recent antitrust case, presented a legal bill in excess of $30 million that was found by the court to be too high and subsequently reduced to $8 million. The academics find their main satisfactions in activities that bring psychic income beyond financial rewards, but often follow procedures that are archaic and inefficient. The rumble resulting from an attempt to update an archaic curriculum bears witness to how highly cherished is the time that is spent on acquisitive activities, which should be devoted to keeping up with the literature in their field. Government officials work at a deliberate pace, look for ways to line their pockets, and manifest a conviction of the rightness of their use of power usually shared by few of the citizens they serve. No—businessmen as individuals are neither more nor less moral or avaricious than other professionals. Moreover, they are less contentious among themselves. For the most part, they get along very well with each other and are able to achieve consensus far more readily than those in other professions.

The image of business leaders with the public, however, is none too flattering. They are regarded as strong, hardheaded, ambitious, and unrestrained by higher moral considerations in their business relations, even though in other matters they are perceived to be as moral as the rest of society. Thus, the "off-book" payment disclosures by otherwise law-abiding corporate officers is seen by business critics as a reflection of the immorality of the business world.

At least part of the explanation can be found in the contrast between individual morality and group morality. Whether written or not, each group in society has its own code of conduct that imposes in direct and subtle ways on its members. The corporation is no exception. Even though the code of the corporation is now in a stage of transition, the conduct of most of the present leaders could not fail to have been conditioned by circumstances that existed during the period when their careers were fashioned.

The late Clarence Randall, an outspoken business leader several decades ago observed,

> Free enterprise as we practice it in the United States is authoritarian in principle. One man decides—the will of one man is the activating force—he speaks and others obey.[1]

That one man usually has been schooled in the belief that only one thing counts, the net profits of the enterprise, and that the corporation has but one constituency, the stockholders. Nothing else matters, even if law is occasionally bent or even broken to achieve the goal. Why otherwise would competent and intelligent executives have risked, and indeed lost, their careers with no prospect of significant personal gain?

The careers of most of the present generation of business leaders began with these narrow premises unquestioned. Once in the corporation and its authority accepted, reciprocity in the form of security and protection can become comfortable. Conformity and obedience to those senior in the hierarchy seem a modest price to pay for the opportunity of career progress, and a moral man or woman will only occasionally find matters that conflict with his or her personal standards of conduct. Acceptance of company goals and obedience to those who interpret them becomes a way of corporate life. Until recent years, those goals have all targeted on the single purpose of making money, as much as possible as quickly as possible. Having spent a lifetime in that environment, a present incumbent of the combined office of chairman and chief executive officer could not be expected to change the rules of the game. Public relations statements and intermittent societal programs to the contrary, basically the rules have remained the same for the devotees of "the Old School."

Will the off-book payments and similar practices be resumed, once public indignation has died down? No one knows for sure. Perhaps they will, despite the newly drawn corporate codes of conduct. Strong pressures to succeed are still in place, and typical chief executive officers are so committed to traditional expectations that they may be willing to risk a career if that seems necessary. Greater loyalty hath no one! But is it duty? Is it the right kind of loyalty to the firm? How confused and frustrated those caught in the net must feel! In any case, it is certainly bad judgment. However, if as, and when, corporations progressively abandon the authoritarian principle of one-man rule, as policies are determined on a broadened basis, the satisfactions and benefits of a business career could be still further enhanced, and such temptations could become less appealing. Business life could become more rewarding in all aspects.

Progress has already been made. The new, broadened concept of corporate purposes cannot fail to mitigate the sharp edges of bottom-line compulsions, even though they will still be felt, and properly so. A clearer, more impressive image of business and of the businessman will emerge. A recurrence of successful careers sacrificed without personal benefit would be unlikely simply because the goals of the corporation would be broadened and redirected.

Yet external restraints to supplement self-restraints will always be appropriate for the businessman, just as they are for all human beings. A corporate structure of checks and balances is the logical means of creating them. In matters relating to executive salaries, perquisites, and conflicts of interests, self-restraint is not enough. These things should not be self-determined. A strong and independently minded board of directors should be prepared to exercise jurisdiction in an objective manner after considering all the circumstances, including the competition for executive talent. In a comprehensive sense, senior executives should be protected as much as possible from excessive tension and physical strain so that they can conserve their energies to concentrate on company affairs. The control of deviant practices in salaries, perquisites, and conflicts of interests is easily accomplished by an effective board, but it should be done with both firmness and understanding of all the circumstances. It is a task better assigned to those who know the company, the personnel, and its industry, than to external governmental agencies.

In all questions having ethical aspects, such as advertising, environmental protection, the movement of manufacturing plants out of communities or overseas, or personnel discrimination, the solution is likely to be most rational if developed within a corporate structure of checks and balances. Externally imposed solutions, however, will inevitably make their appearance if the problems are not handled well internally. And those solutions will inevitably and invariably be less rational.

There is no reason to believe that personal morality is higher in government or in the professions than it is in business. The important thing is to provide within the corporate structure effective disincentives to behavior that is antisocial. Departures from what is regarded as moral conduct are found in all phases of human existence, and should be identified and penalized wherever they appear. But the building of a tradition within the corporation of integrity and ethical conduct, together with a system of internal checks and balances, provides a greater assurance of public protection than chaperonage by those external to business, many of whose personal behavior itself has failed to qualify for that role.

Notes

Beyond the Bottom Line (New York: Macmillan, 1979), pp. 56-62.

1. *Folklore of Management* (1959), p. 28.

Restructuring the Corporation*

Some General Features of Social Commitment

. . . To COPE WITH ENVIRONMENTAL, conservational, and other problems will require philosophic wisdom as well as economic understanding. The adjustments involved will present a hazard to efficiency and stability. They will cut into the traditional motivations and incentives of businessmen. To understand the adjustments, business will need wise participants with diverse points of view to help make its decisions. Solutions to environmental problems, for example, even now require that competition be commingled with collaboration within and among business organizations, as well as between business and governmental agencies.

Modifying Administrative Structure

Where should these newly emerging responsibilities be assigned in the pyramidal organization tied to maximum efficiency and minimum unit costs? There is no comfortable fit. The evident answer is that additional organizational devices are required, devices that supplement the present relationships among the traditional line and staff functions.

One obvious device is to make social considerations a major input, along with economic factors, in the discussions prior to the drafting of the annual operating budget. The directional development of the corporation, embodied in its five- or ten-year strategic plans, provides another opportunity to appraise methodically shifts in public attitudes and to evaluate their impact on resource allocation and internal administrative policies. The periodic distribution to the organization of annual operating budgets and of longer-period strategic plans, incorporating the background thinking and assumptions that went into their preparation, can be helpful in awakening an awareness of social issues throughout an organization. But there remains the difficult task of reconciling the traditional incentives and motivations at the working levels with responses to the dual economic and social influences.

138

If the corporation is to be effective in its new and strange world, responsibilities must be assigned in ways that are now novel and unfamiliar. Traditional corporate units alone cannot cope with the tasks. To be sure, the traditional pyramidal structure has neat and understandable orderliness. By successive downward delegations of responsibility, authority, and accountability, business assignments get done. There is, however, a continuous centripetal pressure to push decisions inward to the center. That is especially true with regard to anything new or novel. . . .

Of course, many day-to-day business operations have societal aspects: closing a plant or expanding one in an already crowded community; energy conservation in all phases of a company's activities; the training and best use of new entrants to the labor force from the female or minority population; the introduction of new processes or new product technology. Still other ongoing problems have induced corporations to supplement the traditional administrative structures. Separate departments have been established to design and develop pollution control equipment, to follow regulatory affairs pertaining to pollution and conservation, to test operations on employee health and teach safe product handling, and to deal with solid waste disposal. But it is when the corporation moves outside its normal business functions that it exposes itself to major new risks. It is then that the greatest impact on structure occurs.

For example, there has been much discussion of business participation in raising the quality of life in the inner cities. Some of this has already begun to occur through the return of suburbanites to the urban center. A recent study of the Committee for Economic Development, however, called

> particularly on private industry, state and local governments, and
> citizens to explore means of identifying and implementing solutions to
> urban life.[1]

A corporate commitment to participate in urban rehabilitation raises the question of who will make the investment. Who will pay the operating bill? There are numerous alternatives to choose from. If an assignment is given to a newly organized action group within the company, it could operate either for the account of the corporation—which is the least likely—or as an agent of the government for a fee, or for a joint account with the government. The group involved would differ from the characteristic study or research group. Illustrative is General Motors lead participation to refurbish, through a newly organized subsidiary, six blocks of a residential section of Detroit, financed one-third from private sources, with the rest from city, state, and federal funds. Another instance is the City Venture

Corporation, formed by Control Data Corporation with a group of partners, to revive the core of depressed cities. . . .

Many would object that it would be diversionary for a business to participate in arrangements with, or contract with, government for the provision of public services to ameliorate social problems. But there appear to be growing pressures in the country today, to do so, as our democracy searches for its public will. Governmental agencies at all levels now provide public services of many kinds that require some 30 percent or more of the nation's GNP to finance. The public may soon put a tax ceiling on that part of the national product they are willing to shift from private to public hands. Contracting out would not necessarily change the end use of total funds between social and business purposes, but it would represent a shift of activity back to private hands, thus limiting the growth of government employment, which, ratchet-like, never seems to shrink. There is also a conviction that the productivity of social services can be increased.

Some in the government no doubt dislike the very idea of a profit; and to have a business corporation make a profit on a contract as an agent for the government to provide public services or to alleviate social ills can be a sore point. Hostility among civil servants results as well from the competitive pressures placed on public agencies. But, it may be necessary to abandon such notions if the combining of government resources with business talents and incentives should prove to be the least costly way for the nation to accomplish the job of social reconstruction. And, if a massive program using corporations as agents of government should be mounted, it would compel a major restructuring of certain aspects of corporate administration.

This does not mean business organizations would rush to dissolve existing departments, but growing up alongside the traditional departments there would be new structures to accomplish new purposes. This can be very disturbing to managers who have lived only under the old and stable management habits. Such managers like to have things precise, orderly, and carefully worked out, with lines of authority clearly identified. Then one can relax with these smooth working arrangements, or so it is said. But it is not, and never has been, quite that way. Numerous *new* problems, both internal and external, in unending procession have been challenging the traditional habits. Contract work for governments will be another challenge.

The criteria for career progress must be extended to include more than a person's contribution to short-term financial results. Social criteria, hard but not impossible to measure, must be included. When an individual now is taken out of the accustomed line of career progression and out of the routine activities of the corporation, it is disquieting. One wonders what will happen to his or her career—will he or she get lost? Lines of authority become confused, and responsibilities must be clarified and reclarified. Those who have experimented with matrix or project management have found the transition is not easy. New working relationships and interpersonal skills must be developed, based more and more on consensus than authority.

These ambiguous new organizational forms require consensus and cooperation, the opposite of the traditional competition among personnel. Recall that the administrative pyramid was designed to be most effective in a competitive situation. In contrast, these task forces and action groups—if they are to be effective—must acquire an attitude of collaboration within themselves. It is not easy to measure the performance of individuals on a task force. In many cases, even the success of the group itself can be measured only over an extended period of time. These are significant, but not insurmountable, difficulties. And they can be small as compared with the advantages of the flexibility, adaptability, and initiative that such innovative organizational structure can generate. The paramount adjustment required to reconcile competitive efficiencies with social commitments will be the formation of working relationships between the pyramidal line and staff departments and these new "special task" groupings.

Experience analogous to participation in these new relationships has existed for a long time, for many traditional staff functions cut across line departments. Although it has not been easy, this reconciliation of staff and line has had the unifying advantage of an acceptance of the primacy of competition and the bottom line. Now the adjustment will be even more difficult, for the concept of collaboration will increasingly stand alongside competition as a motivation. It is evident, however, that if the corporation is to shift the focus of its purposes to encompass the dual roles of business efficiency and societal concerns, the basic changes must occur at the working level of the departments and project-assigned task forces.

In another set of activities, the interface between the corporation and government has begun to affect corporate structure. Numerous municipalities, as well as state and federal agencies, have on request received the temporary services of business executives on loan to apply corporate administrative and communications technology to governmental operations. Joint business-government task forces dealing with such diverse matters as purchasing methods, cash managements, personnel practices, records management, budgeting, and construction have often made major contributions to improved public administration. Of course, the removal of key executives from corporate operations for varying periods of time is still another disturbing element in business operations as the corporation goes out into the community. And sometimes a whole company instead of an individual manager will be commissioned to survey a particular governmental problem or department; the results in dislocation of normal activities may be very much the same. But despite the problems to business as it involves itself more deeply in the improvement of what are essentially social or socioeconomic problems, business has no real alternative but to participate in those new challenges if society is to reject an all pervasive government, with all the restrictions on traditional liberties that that implies.

Notes

Beyond the Bottom Line (New York: Macmillan, 1979), pp. 111-18.

1. Committee for Economic Development, *Social Responsibility of Business Corporations: A Statement on National Policy by the Research and Policy Committee* (New York: June 1971).

Description: Preface to Prescription*

. . . ADAPTATION TO THE EMERGING ENVIRONMENT is no easy task for business managers, trained as they are in pursuing a single purpose, the efficiency that assures a maximum return on stockholders' investment. In doing so, business managers have had extraordinary success. The result is an abundance unimagined by earlier generations. Indeed, it is an abundance that has encouraged and made possible the resurgence of the values of humanism expressed as solicitude for the whole person. An approach to material satiation among a growing proportion of the population has removed some of the alarm from a possible diminution in the rate of economic growth.

The corporation as a centrally important institution of society has made another contribution of even greater importance, though it is less well recognized. It has made possible a highly complex, technologically based society, without resort to the all-enveloping direction of the political state. Without the business corporation, the state in an advanced society must necessarily appropriate the functions of the open market in the task of marshalling large resources, allocating their use, assigning employment, and determining the level and relationship of a wide range of prices.

Experience has shown convincingly that where this has occurred it has been accompanied by political repression. The corporation's silent defense of political democracy, almost by virtue of its existence, has been more significant than the hortatory free enterprise proclamations of its leaders. It is urgently important that the corporation be preserved in its full vigor in the interest of all the people—not just for those who own and manage it. The dilemma of corporate management is not found in what the corporation may ultimately become—it is in the discomfort of the process of change and the underlying nudging compulsions to choose among unfamiliar and often displeasing alternatives.

Acceptance of a multiplicity of corporate purposes carries with it numerous consequences, some of which are little understood and yet to be tested. . . .

The assignments and functions respectively of executive management and members of the board of directors are beginning to reflect these new

143

demands on the corporation. Organizational structures for administration have been designed to supplement the traditional line and staff pyramids that have been so effective in the singular pursuit of the bottom line. But constructive revision of the interface between government and business has yet to develop in a significant manner. Sorely needed is an altered attitude that would identify and use the relative strengths of each in a manner to maximize benefits in the response to public needs.

The business corporation is a truly remarkable social invention whose accomplishments in the past have been impressive, but whose opportunities for constructive good have only begun to be realized. A greater awareness of this fact by business management, by government personnel, and by the public at large would make its passage from a single to a multiple purpose organization less alarming and painful, and, indeed, more rational. A broad vision of the nature and direction of this evolution, accompanied by continued trial and error, provides a better assurance of service to the public than the detailed prescriptions of regulations. . . .

[The corporation's]. . . future will be unlike its past. Other than that, the precise form and characteristics of its future are yet to be determined. It will be shaped more by the dominant values of the society that gives it sanction, as those values change through time, than by the conscious direction of its leaders. The optimum policies for corporate management will be to assure a sensitive response to changing public aspirations, and at the same time, preserve to the greatest extent possible, the great strengths of efficiency and capacity it now enjoys. Beyond the admonition of flexibility and adaptability, a detailed blueprint prescribing its future is of doubtful merit.

The business corporation's past contributions to material abundance have been notable. By means of its evolutionary development, it now has the great challenge of a complementary and equally auspicious career to enhance its service to the welfare of the human race.

Note

Beyond the Bottom Line (New York: Macmillan, 1979), pp. 142-45.

IV

Business Education
and
Academic Administration

Emerging Themes
in Business Education

[The Graduate Study of Business*]

TO PROCLAIM THAT THE PURPOSE of the graduate study of business is to train for potential business leadership is not particularly informative. Leadership for *what* in business is the obvious and essential question.

The requirements made upon the business leader have been enlarged in recent decades by the growing complexity of business. The greater size of administrative units made possible by accelerated change in production and control technology; the progressive emergence of human factors in the operation of a business; the ideological as well as the production role played by business in the "Cold War"—these all combine to place unprecedented demands on the personal resources of the successful business leader.

Business institutions have long played a major role in contemporary life, particularly in the Western world. Businessmen, on the other hand, have only recently begun to share the burden of intellectual and cultural leadership with politicians, generals and admirals, churchmen, scientists, academicians, and other professionally trained members of the community. Without ceremony, without extensive recognition by himself or others, the business leader has been catapulted into a key role in the conditioning of Western society.

It is not enough that he knows the skills of his business or the nuances of the markets in which he operates. These he must have, but specialized job interest alone is inadequate. The issues he faces in his administrative activities involve conflicting human value judgments as well as the arithmetic of the accounting office. Individuality must be reconciled with conformity, creativity with organizational chain-of-command; these are typical of the contradictions he must continuously resolve within himself and within his organization.

It is not an exaggeration to say that today we lack an adequate theory of business enterprise. Even the languages of economic theory, of business law, and of accountancy have been unable to keep pace with the dramatic twentieth century changes that have placed the business leader in this socially responsible position. Accordingly, he has no time-tested and clear bench mark against which to measure many of the decisions he must make each day. Yet, if he defers decision, he makes decision by default. For business is a kaleidoscopic and dynamic process. It moves on.

These are serious deficiencies, for the extent of a clear and consistent understanding of the business system by the leaders of community thought will ultimately measure that system's opportunity for useful development and growth. A major task of a graduate faculty of business is to seek that understanding and provide an accurate restatement of the essential characteristics and influences that underlie the contemporary business scene.

The institutions within which the business leader functions have themselves changed to such a degree that the change has become a difference of kind. The modern corporation has fulfilled the promise contained in nineteenth-century textbooks to mobilize capital and other resources and to enlarge the base of material well-being. It has, however, done much more. It has provided the means to spread beneficial ownership, directly through stockholdings and indirectly through savings accounts, insurance, and pension funds. Quite inadvertently, beneficial ownership has been separated from operating control, thus qualifying the concept of property. The result has been beneficial, however, for this feature of the corporation has provided the setting in which has emerged a group known as professional managers with a sense of stewardship that dominates their sense of proprietorship. It is a major part of the task of a graduate school of business to study professional management and prepare its students for potential participation as managers.

The motivations of professional managers as stewards are exceedingly complex; they are not generally or clearly understood. The simple profit motive that provides the keystone for the construction of traditional economic theory is but one among many motives. There is a lack of reality in an image of the businessman who bases each transaction on the singular goal of maximum profit. This was the image assigned many years ago to the classical "economic man." A stable flow of supplies, production, inventories, and sales is far more important; it is essential if the business organization is to prosper and develop. Long-term growth, assured supplies and outlets, and financial strength take precedence over, and may be incompatible with, a maximum net return on individual transactions. Approval of the community, and of the organization itself, cannot be earned or retained through sharp or haggling practices. Profits will always be a major factor in the motivations of the business manager, but they are gradually becoming more a means to an end than the end itself; a measure of success in pursuing the larger end which is a reasonably contented, financially strong, and publicly approved business organization.

One sees or hears with increasing frequency reference to the modern business corporation as a quasi-political state. It is certainly political in that most of the hierarchical relationships of people in a political state with each other, and with those outside the political state, are duplicated in the corporation. Happily, it differs from the political state in several important respects. The association of those attached to the corporation is the result of a voluntary and reversible act. There is no such thing as compulsory corporate citizenship. This being so, the element of consent must necessarily loom large in administrative action. The society of the corporation is a free society whose members possess a range of alternative choices. This is one of the great contributions, perhaps the greatest, made by the corporation to contemporary life. It has provided a means of abundance in an era of great technological complexity without government ownership and without excessive control by the political state, which even in a republic has the reserve power of compulsion. It has thus helped preserve our libertarian way of life in all of its phases.

A more subtle difference between the corporation and the state illustrates the kinds of rich intellectual materials available to a graduate faculty of business and to the serious graduate student bent on a business career.

Those who accept employment in the corporation accept a set of responsibilities by the voluntary act of association. Citizens of a republic, on the other hand, involuntarily associated by birth, are endowed with a set of guaranteed constitutional rights. The subject of "corporate constitutionality," carrying the implication of inalienable personal rights received from the corporation, is just beginning to emerge in discussions of business administration. Conversely, the citizens of the republic are frequently admonished to accept voluntarily an expanding range of personal responsibilities. Conceivably the corporation could become more like the state and the state more like the corporation, perhaps to the detriment of both, since each has quite different functions to perform in our pluralistic society. It is one of the strengths of our way of life that we are organized in a pluralistic manner to achieve multiple and different purposes, and it is important to clarify and understand the respective functions and characteristics of different types of institutions.

There can be no doubt that the proper graduate study of business is more than the study of business skills. It is more than applied economic theory. It is more than training in the art of making decisions, which is a daily requirement of all business leaders. It is all of these, but graduate business education must also draw discriminately from the disciplines of many of the natural sciences and of all the related social sciences if it is to make its maximum contribution to the business environment. It must include the study of improved ways of making expeditious, imaginative, and effective group decisions. It must enlist the mathematician's skills in linear programming, probability formulae, and other features of "operations research" to facilitate stable production and inventory control. It must help to provide the means of nurturing individuality and creativity in an organizational setting. It must additionally be rooted in those branches of philosophy called ethics and politics. This is indeed a large order for any faculty to master and transmit to its students. By the same token, however, it provides a setting for almost limitless intellectual stimulation.

The range of opportunities for the study of business at the undergraduate level is perhaps more circumscribed by the less mature student. It is true, nevertheless, that education for business has become the largest and most rapidly growing field of professional education in this country; and substantially all of the growth in recent years has occurred in undergraduate schools. The increased number of students throughout the nation that will reach graduate age in the immediate years ahead indicates a prospective comparable growth in advanced business education. . . .

Notes

*Graduate School of Business, Columbia University, *Report of the Dean for 1953–54 through 1957–58*, Columbia University Bulletin, Series 58, No. 38 (September 20, 1958), pp. 3–6.

Emerging Themes in Business Education*

EDUCATION FOR BUSINESS has been appropriately described as a restless giant thrashing about in the halls of academe. Starting less than a century ago, it has become a major force in the world of higher education in the United States. Moreover, there are evidences of accelerating interest in business education in both the developed and lesser-developed areas of the world. As faculties and students increase in numbers, the number of seeming ambiguities and contradictions in the content of business education increases also. The full story of the search for the ideal curriculum would fill a large book; and the book would be incomplete, for the quest is still very active indeed. At the risk of oversimplification, it may be useful to record some of the major themes that have emerged during this brief but significant phase of academic history and to offer some conjectures with regard to future developments. For a full understanding of some of the nuances of the story, it may be helpful to begin some two centuries before business education as we now know it was conceived.

As the Industrial Revolution in the eighteenth century gathered momentum, increased opportunities were presented for enterprise. The time-honored restraints of the mercantilism of the Middle Ages became increasingly oppressive. A new interpretation and rationale of the place of enterprise in the structure of society was required. It was provided successively by such leaders of thought as John Locke, David Hume, and Adam Smith in England, and to a lesser extent by the physiocrats in France. These early interpreters of the advantages of liberation, including liberation of the business system, quite properly made the individual operating in the market place the nexus of their analysis of commerce and industry. Economic man was personified, and indeed, in the course of time, nearly became deified.

During the past two centuries the academic discipline of economics, rooted in the appraisal of the individual and his business behavior, has

151

become highly developed. At one time it was accepted by most scholars as the main, if not sole, means of studying and understanding the nature of the business system.

Strangely, when business education was initiated in the United States during the last decades of the nineteenth century, the typical curriculum was not closely related to the discipline of economics. Some of the most famous faculties of business of the last half century openly expressed disdain for the contributions economics might make to the understanding of business and its management. There may have been some justification for this lack of affinity, even though the net result has been unfortunate. The implications and conclusions of economic analysis, despite the rigor of their development, have not always provided a good fit to observable fact. One reason, perhaps, for this failure, is that the principal initiator of business action changed at about the turn of the century. It ceased to be the individual and shifted to the corporation—a development deplored by popular authors of the time and even frowned upon by federal legislation. Economic man could be understood, or at least this was the belief. His motivations were thought to have been identified and described. Moreover, his actions in the market as an individual were unlikely to be of a magnitude to impair the only reliable protector of the public—rugged and vigorous competition.

In the course of time, it became increasingly clear that the corporation was far more complex than economic man. It was more than economic man on a larger scale. Skeptics on early faculties of business properly questioned whether the academic discipline of economics, built on the assumptions of motivations and behavior attributed to the individual was, by itself, adequate to provide comprehensive and penetrating insights into the nature of the modern business system. Not having an established academic discipline on which they felt they could build with confidence, or not being willing to accept economics for such a role, these early faculties initially developed their curricula as one might expect. They observed the totality of business, found it segmented in numerous identifiable activities—or "industries"—and constructed course materials relating to them. This segmenting of the curriculum into advertising, banking, retailing, insurance, transportation, real estate, and others, was not only plausible but appealed to the practitioners involved in these activities. Moreover, it provided a degree of specialization that encouraged scholars to explore in depth all of the characteristics and processes of a specific area of the business community. The results were not wholly successful. Course materials tended to be more descriptive than analytical. Since faculties of business tended to devote themselves to specialized fields of interest, their individual members in turn tended to become segmented in their respective interests and in their work.

Concomitantly with the development of so-called industry studies among faculties of business, other materials relating to the functions of business were developed that were more unifying in nature. There are only five basic functions of business: production, distribution, financing, the personnel function, and accounting (which includes both auditing and the development of administrative control and tax data). The course materials relating to these functions, instead of dividing the totality of business activities into numerous vertical segments, tend to cut horizontally across all businesses.

The curricula of business faculties for the past half century have been characterized by an admixture of courses dealing with both industry studies and functional studies. Faculty members, for the most part, have been able to accept and adapt themselves to some overlap and ambiguity inherent in this admixture.

Another unifying influence was introduced following World War II, particularly by the Harvard Business School faculty, when attention began to focus on the single purpose of preparation for decision-making in the corporation. The case method of instruction lent itself admirably to exploration of the practices and processes of group decision-making, permitting the simulation in the classroom of the task force that is so often recruited in a business organization to cope with a problem which requires the talents of numerous specialists. During the last two decades most faculties of business have added to the admixture of industry and functional studies a preoccupation with the processes of group decision-making. The terms "administration" and "management" have been assigned to these studies. It is proper to have done so, for they involve all of the phases of getting things done through people: (1) the development of policy, (2) the detailed description of a specific program, (3) the plan and schedule of action, and (4) the recording and appraisal of results.

Many scholarly observers, however, have long felt something lacking in each of these three themes in the development of business education. More particularly, they have felt that business education has been handicapped by limited contact with relevant and related academic disciplines. Building on the premise that the discipline of economics could not provide adequate insight into contemporary business problems or adequate preparation for business administration, the study of business has tended to emphasize descriptive materials, role playing, and case discussions. Valuable though these have been, they have resulted in de-emphasizing concept and theory and the methodologies that underpin disciplined analysis.

. . . The structure and processes of business itself have increased in complexity, thus making more obvious the inadequacies of description derived chiefly from yesterday's observed experience. Simple assumptions of motivation, of effective organization structure and practice, and of business purpose, have become increasingly difficult to reconcile with observed fact. The second set of circumstances is that while the growing complexity of business has made research more urgent and inviting, the livelier intellects both in and peripheral to faculties of business have by progressive stages eagerly accepted the challenge of more comprehensive inquiry. There is no area of human existence more fruitful for research than that provided by business and its multifarious interests and activities.

In retrospect, the initial assault by researchers on the ramparts of business education seems to have been made by the historians. Encouraged by the influence of the great German historical school before the turn of the century and, subsequently, by the institutionalists in this country, the historians have quietly but insistently contributed to a deeper perception of the nature of business development. Still more significantly, the historians have provided understanding of the intellectual and conceptual influences that have given business communities different characteristics in different cultures.

It was in the decades between the two World Wars that the economists began successfully to demonstrate the fallacy of the initial assumption on which business education was established. As research in economics began to broaden and qualify its own classical postulates, the polemics between the "vocationalists" and the "theoreticians" that had occupied many campuses began to subside. Economists were frequently added to business faculties, with no visible impairment to either the faculty or the man. Indeed there were numerous instances where both seem to have benefited. Today no self-respecting faculty of business could contemplate the lack of a strong contingent of qualified economists among its members.

The same thing has become true since World War II with respect to those qualified in the methodologies of mathematics and the behavioral sciences.

Business faculties have always had a conspicuous place in their curricula for the quantitative "tools" of business, accounting and statistics. In recent decades, however, a newer and, for many purposes, more powerful set of tools, popularly subsumed under the rubric of operations research, has developed with dramatic speed. This progress has been encouraged and facilitated by the availability of the electronic computer, a device that seems to have no visible limit for rapid computation and for storage and retrieval of quantitative information.

Why people behave as they do, individually and in groups, is a question that has become more and more interesting to all scholars and particularly students of business and of its organizations. Some progress has been made in quantitative measurement of human behavior—enough to invalidate the simple formulas of yesterday. Careful observation, coupled with rigorous and disciplined analysis, has to date provided more confirmation of complexity than prescription for it, but the reward of understanding behavior is great and the challenge enticing. Anthropologists, sociologists, and social psychologists are now contributing significantly to the study of business and—of equal importance—are revealing to colleagues on the faculties of business their methods of observing social variables and their analytic disciplines.

Now that these several related academic disciplines are becoming fully integrated into the business curriculum, the study of business itself may be approaching its maturity as a study of major social significance. It is interesting to reflect that over the ages the characteristic preoccupation of an epoch has been expressed in the establishment of fields of academic interest and of faculties to serve as their custodians. The faculties of theology and philosophy emerged out of the churchly, early Middle Ages; of law out of the codifications of the late Middle Ages; of medicine, of science, and of engineering out of the shifting preoccupations of their respective times. Contemporary society is concerned with material development and the security, physical comfort, and cultural opportunities it is expected to bring. Business and its organizations, whether private, quasi-private or public, are the instruments through which the realization of these aspirations is sought. In an age so preoccupied it is plausible that the study of business, and of qualified faculties to give it development and expression, should emerge as a major academic activity. . . .

There is one final thought about the emerging themes of business education that should be recorded. At best, and indeed probably, the study of business will become more interdisciplinary in nature. Not infrequently one hears the historian talk of institutional development; the economist of a theory of the firm; the mathematician of management science; the behavioral scientist of organizational theory. All of these disciplines are contributing new insights; none of them alone has fulfilled the need for a comprehensive rearticulation of the contemporary business system, or for an adequate understanding of the corporation and its several functions. A major business faculty, possessed of the opportunity of interdisciplinary inquiry and stimulated by the sharp minds and questions of carefully selected graduate students, may one day succeed. It will do so if its interdisciplinary interests result in the fusion of practice and theory in a manner to strengthen both.

Note

*Graduate School of Business, Columbia University, "Emerging Themes in Business Education," *Report for the Year 1964-1965*, pp. 1-6.

[What Is To Be
Taught in Business School?*]

. . . WITH THE TRULY EDUCATED, the process of learning is never-ending. The taste of knowledge has so kindled curiosity in the educated man that inner compulsions assure his continued intellectual development throughout life. It is the essence of formal education to light and nurture the sparks of learning until the resulting fires of interest are self-sustaining.

The range of knowledge, however, spreads at an accelerating rate. Knowledge and ignorance have been compared to an expanding balloon. The dimensions of the inner sphere, knowledge, can never be so great as the outer space, ignorance. The more we know, the more we realize what we do not know. That is the fascination of the quest for knowledge. But it is quite impossible for the most avid scholar to keep abreast of more than a fraction of the accretions to knowledge. He feels impelled to focus on progressively smaller segments of total knowledge. This seems to be true in all the established academic disciplines, in the professional fields of medicine, engineering, law, and business as well as in the nonprofessional.

There are both advantages and disadvantages to a high degree of concentration during formal education. The disadvantages are conspicuous in education for business. The opportunity may never again be so favorable to become familiar with, and to think about, the many features of business, their interrelationships, and their significance to the society in which we live; to develop that interest and curiosity about all phases of business that will make one a continuous student of the whole of business throughout a business career. The need to concentrate will be felt quickly enough after initial entry into a business assignment. If these premises are true, it follows that the program of a business school, and particularly of a graduate business faculty, should be integrated and comprehensive if it is to succeed in helping its graduates become balanced and effective members of the business community. Formal education for business should be as much concerned with preparation for the unpredictable business problems of tomorrow as with the complex problems of today.

Changes in the business world during the past quarter of a century have greatly increased the demand for the graduates of business schools. In every direction businesses have grown in their dimensions and total volume, in the complexity of their processes, and in the size of their units.

Some of today's common business practices were virtually unknown twenty-five years ago. In many industries automation is in full flower, with possible consequences which intrigue management and, conversely, alarm labor. Organized labor has acquired unprecedented power with a decline in some phases of management's authority. Big government has an impact on and significance for the economy in ways that are now widely accepted, but from yesterday's vantage point were viewed as alien and hostile to a healthy business environment. Social security provisions and other structural modifications have created rigidities which raise doubts about the responsiveness and adaptability of the economy to basic changes. Corporation management has moved perceptibly from the older proprietary concepts to a kind of stewardship that seeks maximum long-range profits by recognizing a wide range of interests. These interests include, but certainly do not concentrate exclusively on, the short-range interests of owners. The modern corporation, with its impingement on practically every sector of organized human activity, has a crucial relevance to the cultural, as well as to the material, characteristics of contemporary society. . . .

Note

*Graduate School of Business, Columbia University, *Report of the Dean [for 1958–59],* Columbia University Bulletin, Series 59, No. 31 (August 1, 1959).

[Education for Large Business— and Small*]

IT HAS BEEN SAID THAT THE BUSINESS SCHOOLS of the nation, particularly the graduate business schools, have focused attention too much on the task of preparing their students for careers in large corporations. The rewarding opportunities in small business or in self-employment, it is held, are unduly neglected.

The admonition carries some truth. It was only natural that this should have been so for those years when the business schools accepted as their principal task the preparation of staff specialists. Statisticians, market researchers, economists, even personnel officers and tax experts find the chief outlets for their business talents in large organizations. But now, even though business schools to a degree are giving greater emphasis to the methods of administration or management—in contrast to preoccupation with staff skills—the admonition still seems to be valid. Curricula continue to be oriented toward large organizations and most of the business schools' graduates take initial jobs in large organizations. Indeed, the better of the nation's business schools may be emerging as a major source, perhaps the major source, of candidates for the future management of large corporations.

The contribution of these schools to the spirit of adventure, the enterprise, and the initiative that encourage self-employment or careers in small business is less impressive. It is interesting to contemplate why this is so. It is true that these same qualities, within limits, are assets to a career in large business, and it is desirable that they be given greater emphasis for all students irrespective of career intention. There is a difference, however, in that they are utterly essential qualities for success in self-employment.

The difference between the large corporation and the small business is more than a difference of size. In the former, managerial control is less likely to coincide with the benefits and penalties of ownership. The motivations of the corporation manager are more related to those of the custodian or steward than to those of the promoter or proprietor. Profit is his main consideration, but it is profit as a measure of success over a prolonged period

159

of operations, not on a single or even a short series of transactions. The need for a continuous and stable flow of business during a cycle of growth is too great to jeopardize, for temporary advantage, the good will of workers, of important suppliers, or of essential outlets. The corporation has brought a longer time dimension into the process of business decision-making than the economist has envisaged for the single enterpriser.

The large corporation has also by its sheer size complicated the task of internal communications and of group and personal adjustment thereby enhancing the importance of collaborative attitudes and activities. By virtue of its expanded influence, it has imposed on its managers the necessity of considering the non-business repercussions of the business decisions.

There are other differences of degree and kind between the large and the small business organization, but perhaps this succinct account is sufficient to suggest the possibility that preparation for one or the other may involve corresponding differences. For example, the involvement of the corporation manager with a wide range of human problems, as well as with the market place, has resulted in the so-called "behavioral sciences" assuming a place alongside economics as a basic discipline in the advanced business-school curriculum. The increase in the number of variables involved in corporate decisions puts a premium on mathematical knowledge and computer use. The study of the corporation as a major sociological institution of our time, in contrast to the study of management, has directed attention to the perspectives of history and philosophy.

Needless to say, the purposes of such breadth in a program of business preparation extend beyond the mere acquisition of business skills and of money-making ability. The management of a major corporation today is not only a skilled exercise in policy, decision, and action, but is also a public trust involving stockholders, employees, labor unions, consumers, government officials, community groups, and that less tangible entity called public opinion. The modern corporation, with its impingement on practically every sector of organized human activity, has a crucial relevance to cultural, as well as to the material, characteristics of contemporary society.

Education for business is in that stage of its development where the extent of the task has been largely recognized, but there is still much uncertainty regarding the best means of successful preparation for careers either in small business or large corporations. In the circumstances, there is little wonder that the business schools have gravitated toward programs that promise to be most fruitful to the growing numbers of students that arrive with predeveloped interests in careers in large business. Such programs most certainly must encourage the development of disciplined analytical abilities, of the capacity to understand specific business situations in the context of their larger setting, and of a sense of business mission that extends beyond personal enrichment. Apart from this, perhaps the most that should be expected of the schools at this stage in their progress is that the importance to all business careers of imagination, individuality, and initiative be stated and reiterated throughout the student's period of study. Excessive conformity among its personnel may be the greatest danger to the fulfillment of a corporation's opportunities as an institution, as well as to an individual's career.

It is doubtful that much thought has been given to the design of a curriculum to emphasize preparation for small business. Attention has been focused rather on the preparation of staff skills and on the administration of large organizations. It would be interesting to examine the possibilities of a curriculum designed to prepare the students for self-employment; one day some faculty may try it despite the ambiguities involved. The important thing, however, is that the objectives of each faculty of business be clearly articulated and accepted by those involved. The development of precise purposes is a necessary prerequisite to the achievement of excellence, and education for business can be validated only in terms of excellence. . . .

It is much too early to draw conclusions [about new course materials being developed at the Columbia Graduate School of Business], but there is the hope by some who have worked with these comprehensive study materials that eventually there may emerge from them a coordinated theory of the corporation that would fall between the economists' development of the theories of business enterprise focused chiefly on the individual and his market behavior, and the theories of government as developed by the political scientists.

Perhaps one reason it has been so difficult to comprehend the full implications, the opportunities, and the limitations of the corporation is our habit of applying to it the principles derived from the individualistic-market economy on the one hand and from the study of government on the other. An example is the disposition to impose on the corporation the conditions that would make for perfectly competitive price behavior in the markets in which the corporation operates. The effort, it might be added, has had singularly little success. Another example, one that promises to disappoint its sponsors on the other side, is the current interest in the applicability of the political principles of due process and constitutionalism to the internal administration of corporations.

The corporation is a voluntary association of people. Its characteristics are neither individualistic or compulsory. It deserves a comprehensive theory of its own. Without such a theory, the attempt to articulate the business system of the West—a system that has the publicly owned corporation as its nexus—will continue to be ambiguous and less than convincing. In the present world of tense ideological conflict, this is indeed a serious indictment. . . .

Notes

*Graduate School of Business, Columbia University, *Report of the Dean [for 1959-60]*, Columbia University Bulletin, Series 60, No. 42, October 15, 1960, pp. 3–6.

Management Capabilities—
How Transferable?*

DISCUSSION OF THE FUTURE DIRECTIONS of development for business education frequently concludes with the thought that the principles, methods, and structures that have proved so successful in business management have applicability in other fields of human effort; that the business schools in years to come will prepare their graduates for management careers with organizations operating in such diverse activities as the fine and performing arts, in public service, in eleemosynary activities—yes, even in education—as well as in the business community. A business school would thus serve, in a sense, as a bridge or a conduit to transmit some of the means of success of the business community to other organizational activities that are becoming increasingly important to the quality of contemporary life.

This is a fascinating idea that has much to commend it. But the transfer of management skills from one environment to another cannot be made without disturbing many cherished preconceptions and privileges; that is to say, without threatening the comfortable security of established practice. A test of this thesis of effective transferability is conveniently at hand in a contrast of the purposes and the management methods generally found in institutions of higher education with those that characterize business organizations. There is today much interest in, and dissatisfaction with, the administration of higher education and much thought is being given on and off the campus to administrative restructuring.

There has been a bewildering variety of responses by administrators and faculties to turbulence among students throughout the world. This turbulence is generally recognized as a protest against certain features of our society, bequeathed to oncoming generations by their elders. It is suspected that some of the protest may also be against the academic community itself, the ambiguity of its purposes, practices, and administrative methods.

Despite the deficiencies apparent on every hand, there can be no doubt that both the business and academic communities share a dedication to improvement of the quality of life. Business is more concerned with the flow of material things that will provide security and a measure of leisure for cultural development; academe has been more committed to the direct achievement of intellectual amenities. Business is "result" oriented; the accomplishment of predetermined constructive purposes counts as much if not more than the methods and procedures used to reach the result. The academic community, on the other hand, has less capacity precisely to measure results and is more concerned with processes and procedures as well as theory. It lives in a subjective world, whereas business is quantitatively accountable for its actions.

While business organizations throughout the world seem to be moving toward a more democratic form of management—in the sense of obtaining organizational concurrence and consent to proposed activities—the presence of authority remains far more visible in the business organization than in the academy. The academy is an open society. In it, individualism and independence are carried to the ultimate. Persuasion, disputation, mediation, and discussion typically take the place of the ubiquitous use of material rewards to obtain concurrence.

These differences do not provide a full catalogue of the comparative characteristics of management in academic and business organizations. They do, however, serve to explain why the respective administrative structures of organizations operating in these fields differ markedly in their patterns and practices. The interesting questions are: (1) can each learn something from the other? and (2) has each achieved an optimum structure for the fulfillment of its purposes?

There are three major parties at interest in the college and university: students, faculty, and administrators. In one sense the students are the customers, or at least should be. In fact, they are far more than customers; they are full-time participants in the life of the academy and feel very much a part of it while in residence and in later life as alumni. Down through history there have been periods of student unrest, sometimes of violence. By and large, however, the prevailing pattern of behavior has been one of study, play, and relative passivity, except in Latin America where student activism has a long tradition. In recent years student turbulence has been general throughout the world.

Students look to their college or university to personify their youthful ideals and are quick to resent a failure to do so. Their youth, inexperience, and immaturity are inherent disabilities which limit their effort to participate in the determination of the policies and administrative processes of their institutions, but this by no means discourages the attempt to do so when they have become dissatisfied. Part of that dissatisfaction has resulted from failure to design channels through which student aspirations can be informally expressed, and from the absence of responsiveness when they have become known. There are many matters relating to the quality of their educational experience on which students have every reason to express themselves.

It has been said by members of the faculties that "the faculty is the university." Perhaps nothing can better describe the position of preferment that many faculties have come to expect. The precious value of maintaining high faculty morale is recognized by everyone as necessary for a constructive relationship between faculty and students. Equally accepted is the principle of free inquiry and opportunity for self-expression without inhibition. Out of these two postulates has emerged the concept of academic freedom protected by the practice of tenure—designed to provide careers without fear of reprisal for unconventional statement and writing. The scholar may, indeed must, seek new knowledge and its elaboration, even though it may disturb the conventional wisdom of his time.

Members of the faculty are in essence the channels through which the two purposes of the academy are fulfilled: teaching and research. The organizational structure of the academy is thus built around the faculty, usually in departments that are coterminous with an academic discipline—such as mathematics, sociology, history, romance languages, etc. A faculty of business is more likely to be structured into departments or divisions analogous to those of a business organization—such as marketing, finance, production, personnel, etc.

Usually the chairman or coordinator of any department is a scholar, a member of the faculty who spends part of his time in administration and part in research and/or teaching. Inevitably, he exercises a major influence, if not final authority, on new appointments to the faculty in the field of his scholarly interest, on promotions, and on budget recommendations related to the work of his department.

These arrangements, which began to take clear form in the United States about a century ago, have served to strengthen the interest of scholars in a specific area of learning and have no doubt contributed to advancing the frontiers of knowledge in many fields of human interest. They have had, however, some unanticipated consequences that may have impaired the ability of the college or university to respond to changing needs and to cope with the difficult administrative problems associated with recent student turbulence.

Since the department chairman is typically a scholar, deeply interested in the field of learning to which he has devoted his career, his appraisal of his junior associates is more related to their capacity for original research and publication than it is to teaching. The faculty in the junior as well as senior ranks, knowing this to be so, too frequently downgrade teaching and out-of-classroom work with students in favor of a greater commitment to the development and preparation of manuscripts for academic journals and for other evidence of their research capacities. The consequence for students is apparent. Since the department chairman and the senior men in an academic discipline usually concur on the assignments of the junior members, and since the focus of interest is on research and publication as a means of professional recognition, there is a tendency for the senior men to assign the teaching duties to the junior staff and to neglect their contacts with students. One often hears the complaint of a student that he has never even seen the most distinguished professor in the field of his studies.

Moreover, these departmental arrangements have given impetus to preoccupation with specialized materials and knowledge. Whether commitment to specialization is a response to the needs of a complex society, or whether it represents a personal satisfaction and search for scholarly recognition is a matter on which few agree. Both motivations are no doubt involved, but one is reminded of the cliché of the scholar who knows more and more about less and less, until he knows everything about nothing! Perhaps the complaint by students that much of their academic work is of little relevance is not unrelated to this administrative pattern in the academic community.

Finally, and perhaps most damaging to the ability of the college or university to cope with difficult administrative situations, is the tendency of the departmental structure to develop faculty loyalties to their respective disciplines rather than to the institution with which they are associated. The old image of Mr. Chips with his tweed coat and pipe as a fixture on the campus of Ivy-Covered College is gone forever. Today's faculty man is peripatetic, a frequenter of conventions of his scholarly associations, a lecturer at a wide variety of occasions, often treating his scheduled classes as a lesser commitment. One even begins to hear of occasional joint appointments of one man by several colleges and universities—requiring commutation by air to his various campuses.

One may begin to wonder in this recitation where the academic administrator might fit. There are those who would "assign him the task of counting the paper clips and keeping the grass green," but that is the extreme view. Most academic administrators have emerged from previous assignments as members of the faculty; they bring to their task many of the attitudes and practices associated with the departmental administration of the academic program. As a result, most administrators in the academic community look upon their assignment as one of mediation, of reconciling opposing points of view, rather than of initiating thoughtful proposals of change on their own. The result gives the appearance of passivity rather than of positive leadership.

In this setting there is little opportunity to develop that perception which anticipates difficulties as a preface to corrective action *before* the difficulties arise. Moreover, there is too little awareness that corrective action can sometimes take the form of a firm but reasoned *no*, before the issues have crystallized. Academic administration has become too much a belated response to protest and an attempt to reconcile opposing points of view *after* the trouble has begun and the opinions have hardened.

These characteristics, coupled with the tradition of change only after concurrence sought through extended persuasion and discussion, cannot fail to result in a lack of administrative direction. Indeed, there is a built-in "foul-up factor" that makes it exceedingly difficult to move positively in an academic community. It is little wonder that the open society of a college or university appears as an awkward and helpless giant in the face of student discontent and turbulence.

Whether the academy can learn something from the administrative and management patterns of business, or whether business can learn something from the academy, either of a negative or positive nature, is itself a matter on which one finds disagreement even among businessmen-trustees of the academic community. After all, the business organization and the academic organization are different in their purposes, their concerns, their accountability, and the ability to measure results.

It seems plausible, however, if knowledge and learning are indeed the real interests of the academic faculties, that the present drift of their involvement with academic administration will inevitably deprive them of precious time and energy for scholarly work. They will have even less time for teaching than at present if their desire to participate actively in the governance and adaptation to society of their colleges and universities is realized. More plausible is the recent reaction of a senior member of the Cornell faculty: "Most faculty members are more interested in carrying on academic business as usual and don't want to be bothered with having to face up to the social problems of the day that the students are becoming more and more interested in."

The assignment of management responsibility respectively in the academy and in business is a matter that involves interesting questions that should be explored more thoughtfully than they have been to date. They should not be dismissed out of hand with the casual comment: business and academe are different. For human nature seems to respond to similar stimuli in pretty much the same manner, regardless of the environment in which those stimuli occur. In the end, academic as well as corporate management is responsible to the institution and to the community at large for the way in which the leadership carries out its mandate, and it must render an acceptable account if it is to retain its sanction. No institution of society can long be immune from the penalties of failure to conduct its affairs in a manner to win and hold public approval. The values of the campus, including the values of academic freedom, are as precious as they are subtle; if they are impaired, the impairment could be more the result of administrative inadequacies than of external disapproval of the work of scholars as such.

The faculties of business schools in our institutions of higher education are familiar with the environmental factors influencing management practice in both academe and business. They should thus be uniquely equipped to identify and correlate the practices and structures that will best serve the respective purposes of each community. If this can be done dispassionately, impersonally and with objectivity, a bridge of mutual strength can be provided to serve both communities.

Notes

*Graduate School of Business, Columbia University, "Management Capabilities–How Transferable?," *Report for the Year 1968–1969*, pp. 1-8.

[Ethics in Business: What Is To Be Taught?*]

THE PUBLIC IS PROPERLY CONCERNED with the characteristic attitudes that govern the conduct of all socially significant activities; the more significant the activity, the greater the concern. This is true whether such activity is related to politics, religion, business, or to other major facets of institutional life.

A general apprehension regarding the ethical aspects of business attitudes and activities has emerged during the past year as a result of several extensively publicized episodes involving conflicts of interest and collusive practices. These have served to underscore the crucial relevance of important business decisions by modern corporate managers to the larger ends of our free society.

It is singularly appropriate for business schools to be concerned with moral attitudes and ethical practices in business when constructing their educational programs. Indeed, teaching business facts and developing student skills in the processes of business decision-making are of secondary importance to a contribution to the development of attitudes compatible with the best long-run interests of society and business. Unfortunately, attitude-formation is a subject about which there are as many ambiguities as certainties. In this area the nation's business schools reflect the confusions of the larger society of which they are a part. The topic has been much discussed among professional business educators and enough progress is being made to give encouragement to the belief that the "fissures in our public philosophy"—to use Walter Lippman's apt phrase—are being slowly yet steadily repaired.

Three propositions may contribute to the discussion of this vitally important subject. For emphasis they are, at the outset, stated categorically. First, one does not find in philosophical scholarship any strict differentiation of ethics for the various professions, such as law, medicine, or business. Second, conformity to law and conformity to ethical norms are not necessarily synonymous. Third, the significance of a new and longer time span, which corporate decision-making must encompass when it is concerned

169

with ultimate objectives, has largely been ignored in the reconciliation of the maximization of gain with ethical practice.

It has been asserted that since ethics constitutes a system of moral principles which binds the fabric of the whole society, there is no distinguishable ethics such as business ethics, medical ethics, or political ethics, except as business, medical, or political actions give expression to the basic social ethics. If this is a valid proposition, it follows that an attempt to identify and prescribe a particular set of ethical principles for the businessman is more likely to achieve superficiality than a basic consideration of the real issues. While the analysis of business cases which are focused on ethical issues can sharpen student thought, courses organized under labels such as "Ethical Standards for Business Management," are likely to fall short of making a lasting impression: they too often appear hortatory to a student rather than analytical. Perhaps the real achievement will come when understanding of the contemporary nature of our business institutions and systems has reached a point where meaningful relationships with ethical principles can be readily perceived by both scholar and practitioner.

The second proposition asserts that conformity to existing law does not necessarily ensure ethical behavior. Failure to conform to public law, of course, is reprehensible, but the law must keep abreast of developments. Even when this occurs, ethical behavior may involve acceptance of a code of conduct based on standards beyond the limits of enforceability. Compliance with law is not enough!

If business ethics are really the basic ethics of society expressed through business institutions and actions, and if ethical business behavior may require compliance with the unenforceable, it follows that preparation for an ethical business career will require more than a study of what is believed to be business ethics per se and more than a knowledge of business law. It will require the development of a sense of mission and service to one's fellow man and, as an absolute essential, a reconciliation of such service with the acquisitive motivations and manifestations of success in a business career. It will require a realization that, in the long run, rewards and recognition for both individuals and institutions will result from services rendered to others. This is the third proposition.

The importance of developing high moral and ethical standards is measured by the importance of business itself in contemporary Western society. The activities of business are inescapably a part of the daily lives of each of us, whether or not we are directly associated with business. The cultural characteristics of our society are conditioned for better or worse by the impact of business. It is no exaggeration to say that the fashioning of a way of life is a by-product that has become the prime product of our business system. The corporation, the principal institution of business, has become the dominant institution of our times and touches the lives of each of us in innumerable ways.

An activity of society so ubiquitous can ill afford attitudes that are narrowly based on crass cupidity or immediate advantage. Fortunately, it has not been necessary to annihilate the incentive for gain in order to bring within the orbit of corporation management the motivations of public service and ethical conduct beyond the compulsions of law. There are many who insist that there is an inherent conflict between private economic goals and public interest that can be contained only by price competition or by government regulation. While short-run business considerations are often found to be contrary to public interests, the long-run corporation interests, when fully understood, appear to coincide with action that is desirable for society at large. This is particularly true in matters relating to the running of a large enterprise in which stockholders and workers, suppliers and customers, and government are all deeply involved. Contrary to past assumptions, these several interests in the corporation have far more in common than in conflict and the wise manager will be aware of this and transmit his conviction to the several parties. Stability and continuity built on a degree of loyalty of association of the several parties are the most certain assurance of long-run growth and mutual benefits. Such loyalty cannot be built on sharp practice or aggressive pursuit of immediate competitive advantage.

It is appropriate to observe that despite the emergence, in markets dominated by corporations, of conditions that increasingly fail to meet perfectly the economists' concept of competitive conditions, there has been no widespread exploitation of the public as the writers of a generation ago gloomily predicted there would be. Instead we have had the development of professional managers whose characteristic view of the corporate interest is based, not on maximizing profit on single transactions, but rather on building a strong organization in terms of personnel, technology, and finance; managers who are convinced that stability of growth in long-run profits is enhanced only through enduring and mutually beneficial relations with labor, suppliers, and customers. An "internalized ethic" of business appears when authority is exercised properly—and this is precisely the primary assignment of management. Authority in the corporation, which is a voluntary association of people, relies ultimately on reason and persuasion of all the interested parties and not on coercive power for its enduring effect.

In the area of public policy, however, it is less clear that pursuit of what are believed to be long-range business interests will harmonize with the public interest, simply because immediate penalties often are real, and the ultimate benefits of public policy may be so long-range as to lose visibility.

Income and social security taxes, initially fought by business, have distributed income and helped the growth of mass purchasing power. The regulation of securities and their markets has provided a solid base for a growth in the securities business that less stable conditions could hardly have supported. Liberal trade and tariff policies have contributed to an extension of markets throughout the world. In its early stages, legislation encouraging labor organization provided orderliness in labor relations that were then becoming increasingly chaotic. Yet these public policies, which many now agree are beneficial to business on balance and in the long run, were vigorously resisted or supported by but a small fraction of the business community when they were introduced. Pockets of resistance are still evident and are given encouragement by the excesses to which some of these public policies have been pressed, particularly in the field of labor.

The dedication of the manager is to his corporation, and it is easier to see the benefits that derive from internally developed policy than from adjustments that are externally imposed. Yet, as management becomes more sophisticated and more professional, it is reasonable to anticipate greater recognition of harmonies between the long-run corporate interests and those externally imposed public policies that intelligently serve the total public interest, even though their immediate impact may require awkward and expensive adjustments.

Within the compass of this enlarged range and extension-in-time of business motivations and purposes, there is ample room for business management to live by high moral and ethical standards. Because the business manager is a competent and intelligent member of society, he will surely translate into meaningful actions the best of society's moral and ethical postulates once he fully comprehends the real long-run interest of the corporation.

These observations, if valid, have much significance for business education. They suggest that the most fruitful study programs will be concerned with the development of a more penetrating understanding of contemporary business—its genesis, and its place in a liberal society—and particularly of an understanding of the corporation, rather than with classroom presentations of a set or code of ethical principles of business conduct or even in a more extensive study of business law.

A certain cynicism has crept into discussions of business ethics and of motivations of corporation management. Business, it is held, is a hardheaded and practical affair. To be successful, a businessman must be aggressive, pushing his advantage to the edge of legality. Failure to be guided by the singular calculus of the next due profit-and-loss account will diminish efficiency and result in a lessened contribution to society. Motivations related to social welfare, it is said, are the province of government, not of business. They are expensive and if business can afford to indulge in them, it is prima facie evidence of at least a quasi-monopolistic position in the market. What has been called "The Soulful Corporation," in this view, is inappropriately appropriating some of the proper functions of government. The effective functioning of perfect competition would mean that business could not afford to indulge its ethical and moral propensities beyond compliance with indiscriminately applied law; hence no ethical problem arises apart from knowledge of and conformity with the law.

This statement of the position has the sanction of inherited economic theory and legal doctrine, and provides a much less complex interpretation of the role of the businessman. The trouble is that it has the disadvantage of failing to conform to the facts of contemporary life. It confuses the individual businessman and his motivations with the corporation and the motivations of its management. It fails to account for the longer time factor that now characterizes business decisions.

The conditions of perfectly competitive markets do not exist for most products and there is no honest desire to "atomize" the economy to restore them. The cost in terms of abundance and well-being would be prohibitive. Mass production requires large aggregates of talent, technology, and other resources, even in socialistically directed economies. If well managed, the corporation has a continuous life, and that continuity is best assured by the long-term planning and vision of its management. Such planning is concerned with the progressive improvement of people and processes, with assurance of supplies and outlets, with financial strength; most certainly not with maximizing profit on single transactions within the limits permitted by law.

Business decisions in the corporate world have taken on a progressively longer time dimension in markets that have progressively lost attributes deemed necessary for perfectly competitive conditions. This has happened despite our antitrust laws, and we can anticipate still greater encroachments on the economists' competitive prescriptions with the rapid development of technology in the years ahead. The time has arrived when we simply must escape the imaginary world envisaged by our nineteenth-century-based theory and laws, and achieve a new clarity in our understanding of the role of the corporation and its management in contemporary society. Without valid guidelines, even high-minded managers often find it difficult to be sure of the ethical basis for their actions.

It is the highest function of a graduate faculty of business to help find some of the social and economic truths imbedded in our contemporary business system. The programs of research, study, and instruction developed by the graduate Faculty of Business of Columbia are all focused directly or indirectly on this great challenge. . . .

Note

*Graduate School of Business, Columbia University, *Report of the Dean for 1960-61,* Columbia University Bulletin, Series 61, No. 37 (September 16, 1961), pp. 3-8.

The Content of Economic Education*

IT IS WIDELY BELIEVED THAT BUSINESS is essentially exploitative, that if left alone it will serve only itself, and that economic competition has been so greatly weakened that it can no longer be relied upon to protect the public. Gone is the conviction that actions to serve enlightened self-interest in a competitive situation will result in the greatest good for the greatest number. Profits are thought to be excessive and to represent a withdrawal from the stream of national income at the expense of those who need a larger piece of the economic pie. These beliefs are consistent with the current commitment to egalitarianism.

Large sums and much executive time and talent have been expended by business to persuade "the public" of the business position and to discredit critics, all with few discernible results. Unfortunately, the effort on balance may have been counter-productive in that it has placed business in a defensive posture, seeking, in the opinion of far too many, to protect privileged and entrenched positions. The "public" to be reached has been identified as including employees, elementary and secondary school teachers, occasionally members of college faculties, and a cross section of the populace. Better understanding of the economic system and the nature of business operations, it has been held, will moderate public criticism and reduce the pressures for continuous expansion of governmental regulations and control. The content of the educational effort is elementary, designed to achieve as much popular attention as is possible using "the dismal science of economics." To carry out this effort, the number of public relations functionaries has been expanded significantly.

Part of the confusion associated with this program in the public mind may be that the program materials are overly defensive, answering the charges of monopoly and excessive profits in the terms in which they are made.

Business also has a common practice of emphasizing in its public releases a percentage change of net profits from a previous period, reported as a residual "bottom line," rather than focusing attention on the rate of return on invested capital. A 25 to 50 percent increase over the year before

175

is often confused as an exorbitant return, thus confirming the public's impression of monopolistic practices.

What needs to be conveyed to the public, in a program of economic education, about monopoly and competition is quite a different matter. Two tests are frequently used by economists to measure the alleged decline of competition; the growing size of firms and the share of an ambiguously defined market held by one or several firms. But the return earned on invested capital is a more reliable measure. As some scholars have found after careful research in which the rate of return is adjusted for inflation, there has been no significant overall impairment of the ability of the competition to protect the consumer. Quite the contrary, rates of return so adjusted have declined alarmingly in recent decades, thus threatening the adequacy of capital formation. But the government's case for expanding regulatory activity rests in large measure on the failure of economic competition to do its work, or on the inability of the public to identify and reject products and services that lack integrity. Both of these are dubious assumptions.

The operation of a workably competitive economy surrounds business with constraints that are ever present in the thinking of business management. The possibility of new competitors entering the market can never be disregarded. The broadened range and shortened time spans of mass communications assure greater public knowledge of the degree of integrity and kind of performance of a wide variety of goods and services. Consumer loyalties can and have shifted rapidly. The opportunity for alternate choices has broadened—not contracted.

Moreover, the verity that profits, regardless of their level, have work to do in the service of the public seems to have been lost in the debate on whether they are too high or too low. The point of regulatory reference is measured against some inherent notion of fairness rather than the public's desire or lack of desire for more or less production among a wide variety of goods and services. The energy program of the nation is currently suffering and losing valuable time from this confusion. When there is a pressing public need or desire for more of a product or service, profits should increase to attract additional capital to induce an increase of supply. When the public need or desire for an economic good or service is diminishing, profits should contract to induce a removal of capital from the activity; more dog collars, fewer horse collars, for example.

The mobility of capital among different types of production is of concurrent importance with the aggregate formation of capital if the business community is to serve the public interest effectively. The intervention of government has demonstrated limited awareness of this fact. Unfortunately, the business response to its critics regarding profits has frequently been in terms of the *fairness* of profits rather than of their *function.* Profits as an economic function are good for the public, not bad, yet business spokesmen have at times felt so defensive that they have avoided mention of the term altogether.

Business is right in resisting the many governmental encroachments on pricing in free and open markets, whether they be capital markets, commodity markets, product markets, or service markets. Relative prices, just as profits, have work to do. They register changes in public needs and desire, and thus serve as guides in the allocation of productive resources, including human effort. Unfortunately, business leaders seem more aware of the debilitating results of governmental interference with price behavior than of their own interference with price movement in the free market. Interference with the free adjustment of prices, whether by government or business, limits the terms on which a libertarian and open society can exist. A case, of course, can be made for such interference in a variety of specific situations, but the burden of proof for intervention should be on government and on business in each instance, especially as regards restraints on new entry into the market.

There is a difference between protecting and preserving competition, and protecting and preserving competitors. Both business and government, particularly the latter, have been guilty of confusing the two. Protection of competition is in harmony with what were taken to be the laws of nature on which the corporation built its spectacular success. Protection of competitors through intervention in the movement of prices in free markets is the antithesis of the principle of survival of the fittest. Paul Weaver was perceptive when he noted in his June 1977 *Fortune* article the businessman's opinion that "government intervention in the marketplace is not just a lapse from principle, but an irrational attempt to repeal the laws of nature."[1]

But business itself cannot claim title to purism as libertarian free enterprisers. The endorsement by business of direct or indirect subsidies, or of regulatory procedures that protect competitors, diminishes competition. Could this be the result of too great a readiness to qualify the principles on which the corporation has prospered, or could it be that the implications are not fully apprehended? Is economic regulation acceptable, but social regulation never? Intervention is not a matter of absolute right or wrong: its rightness or wrongness depends on the circumstances. But its significance should be understood. As Weaver continues in his *Fortune* article: "The only job of economic education facing American businessmen is the one they have to do on themselves by themselves."[2]

The opportunity for self-adjustment and for self-regulation can be best preserved in a libertarian political climate. That condition is more likely to be available if the business community fully understands the requirements and meaning of *libertarianism*. It is quite different from the modern so-called *liberalism*, which has largely come to mean financial outlays to alleviate public distress and political pressures, accompanied by various types of controls. It may be that the business community is the only one that can effectively serve as the custodian of a libertarian and open society. The political world has become excessively committed to free-spending *liberalism*, which is the antithesis of classical liberalism as it was known when the restraints of mercantilism were being shed by the Philosophical Radicals.

Business leadership can qualify for the exalted role of custodian of libertarianism only if it understands the damage that is done the open society by its own pleas for political and financial relief when the competitive situation becomes difficult. There are penalties as well as rewards in the free economy. . . .

. . . If the voice of business is to be heard better and earn credibility in government and media circles as well as in the halls of academe, it must demonstrate convincingly, in free and open markets, that competition is still effective in the role of public protector. And, business by action and word must convey an awareness of the societal as well as the material services it has provided and has the opportunity to provide on a broadening scale to the public. Conversely, it is a mistake for business to adopt the posture of being the custodian of economic sophistication with a desire to share that knowledge with the public.

More importantly, business must articulate more clearly its opportunities and its commitment to respond to the public's aspirations. Those usually identified as intellectuals engaged in the mass media and in academe, to quote the late Lionel Trilling,

> . . . take virtually for granted the adversary intention, the actual subversive intention . . . of detaching the reader from habits of thought and feeling that the larger culture imposes, of giving him a ground and vantage point from which to judge and condemn. . . .[3]

Notes

Beyond the Bottom Line (New York: Macmillan, 1979), pp. 38–44.

1. Paul Weaver, "Corporations are Defending with the Wrong Weapons," *Fortune* (June 1977).

2. *Ibid.*

3. Lionel Trilling, cited in *Columbia Today*.

On the Student Revolt

A Message for Business from Columbia*

MUCH THOUGHT HAS BEEN GIVEN, and will be given, to the turbulent events that occurred on the Columbia campus beginning at the end of last April [1968]. The emotions and forces that were unleashed here were perhaps more visible and violent than elsewhere in academe, but they were far from unique. Hardly a campus in the nation has escaped the impact of student protests in one form or another.

Indeed, throughout the world, students have appeared to be in revolt without having a clear articulation of the objectives of their protest. Unlike the radicalism of the 1930's, it seems to be motivated more by a protest against the way things are than by a program for the future. This has been true in Communist-controlled countries behind the Iron Curtain, in nations whose governments have been characterized as Fascist, and in the capitalist countries of the West and East. The revolt seems to have been against what is vaguely called "The Establishment," whether the establishment is represented by authoritarian or libertarian institutions.

The emergence of this worldwide youthful protest cannot fail to have meaning for the business community, and for the graduates of this and other schools who plan to spend their careers in that community. Perhaps a few observations and reflections about the Columbia experience may throw interpretive light on the global pattern of youthful protest.

There can be little doubt that at Columbia a comparatively small group, perhaps no more than one percent of the total student enrollment of the University, had become so deeply dissatisfied with contemporary society that they had committed themselves to revolutionary purposes. The specific issues on which their initial protests were based later tended to fade into the background or to be replaced as primary complaints by other issues. The issues as they sequentially emerged were: The University's association with the Institute for Defense Analyses, prohibition of demonstrations inside of campus buildings, construction of a gymnasium on land leased in

179

Morningside Park, amnesty for student demonstrators, restructuring the administration of the University to increase "participatory democracy," and finally the encroachment of the University's physical expansion on the surrounding community. Some have felt that several or all of these issues related more from a lack of understanding by all concerned than from the nature of their substance. Admittedly there had been a major failure of perceptive communication among all the parties at interest; a vast amount of misunderstanding resulted, and all of these issues served as a convenient focus for the leaders of the demonstration.

It remains, however, difficult to understand why the small group of instigators of violence were able to enlist the support of a following that became progressively larger during the initial week of turbulence. Even though one might recognize that a college or university student is and should be the personification of vitality seeking a cause, and even though, typically, he carries no great responsibilities and his actions are frequently irresponsible, the accelerating alignment during the first week of the turbulence of the University community, including many members of the University faculties, with what might be called the revolutionary core is a matter that will be a source of dispute to observers as long as the events are debated.

For plausible explanations one looks for flaws in the University community as well as in the larger world. Students have complained on many campuses about the impersonal nature and dubious relevance of their academic programs. Specifically, they have sensed a lack of faculty commitment to work in the classroom, a propensity to place other commitments ahead of classroom appearances and office hours; they have complained of classes where discussion is desirable but prevented by the size of the enrollment, and of other practices that have accompanied the growth of what has been called "academic professionalism."

In a recent review of the Jencks and Reisman book, *The Academic Revolution*, E. Z. Friedenberg observed that: "Its most conspicuous and influential index has been the increased status and prominence of the research scholar, with his ancillary skills in grantsmanship and his relatively great mobility between institutions and correspondingly great bargaining power. The professional standards of each discipline, enforced on the administration by the demands of a faculty concerned with its own claims to scholarly distinction, lead to familiar emphasis on research at the expense of teaching in the university."

These characteristics of faculty have been evident in differing degrees on most university campuses. Commitment to the institution and its students has too frequently been given second priority to a personal professional interest, with an inevitable growing reliance for classroom work on preceptors, teaching assistants, and other types of junior instruction. This has occurred at a time when the costs of education have greatly increased. The student has tended to feel short-changed. These are generalized characteristics of academe. They have not been in evidence in some of the faculties at Columbia any more than at other institutions; perhaps not as much. Although from the point of view of the student these flaws in his collegiate community have been legitimate sources of protest and complaints which too often have met with no perceptive response, it is not clear that they serve to explain the full intensity and breadth of the revolts. . . .

. . . [O]ne can perhaps find more plausible explanation [of the revolt of the young] in the flaws that have become increasingly conspicuous in the social and political environment of the student's larger world. Violence in one form or another seems to be fed to him daily. The mass media carry stories and pictures of violence in many forms. War, as an instrument of national policy, has been rejected in principle but practiced in fact. The young man's daily diet of gunplay on television, of gruesome statistics of the numbers killed in conflict in the Far East, and of group violence reported in the daily press, cannot fail subtly to condition his conviction that violence is a legitimate means to accomplish desired objectives, even if those objectives may be no more than involuntary self-identification. It is easy for him to conclude that were this not so, there would not be so much violence. The fact that he is told it is not so by the older generations who practice violence simply serves to secure him in his conviction that a certain amount of fraud is accepted as a way of life by his elders.

In addition, he hears all forms of discrimination daily deplored, and the exaltation of equal opportunity for all, which he sees intractably denied to all. The elaboration of the evils embodied in persistent pockets of poverty and in the debasement of the environment provide popular and enduring issues for the successful election and re-election of leading politicians, but being young and vital, he feels that something must be done to convert the protestations into effective programs of action, and he wants part of the action.

Additionally, his attitudes and expectations have been developed during the period in which group action has emerged as the accepted way to achieve a pre-determined purpose, a period in which individual effort has been denigrated along with the initiatives and responsibilities that have attached to each man in individualistic societies. Acceptable conduct is more determined by the behavior of the group to which one has become attached. Flexible moral and ethical standards have thus tended to replace the guidelines of personal conduct based on the verities of civilized behavior received from the great religious traditions. These are debilitations that may have become more embedded than we realize in this as well as other societies. The confluence of violence together with the acceptance of group action as a way of life cannot fail to spell group violence.

The student of today may simply be reflecting many of the things that he learned earlier in his family environment: that war is wrong and an evil; that discrimination is a blight on mankind; that the nation's constitution stipulates that all men are born equal and by implication should receive equal opportunity; that each of us to an extent is his brother's keeper and that poverty in the presence of plenty is wrong; that the environment and the resources of our nation must be preserved for future generations and not debased or excessively depleted. These things he has learned, but he does not see them as the basis of positive action so much as a means of proclamation to assuage the conscience, or as a platform for personal political aggrandizement. There is a new temper among the young to test as well as act on the values that have been handed down from older and past generations.

These are commendable even laudable ends. It is the means that have emerged to achieve them that provide the mischief. The means seem to involve a rejection of all discipline imposed by authority in any form save that of the group formed by the protestors themselves. Authority in any other form becomes identified as the Establishment in whatever organization it may be embodied and wherever it may appear, political, educational, economic, or cultural, East or West, North or South.

If these premises are correct, a plausible explanation is provided of why the universities and colleges have been the first target to feel the impact of these global forces. In a complex society discipline is imposed in numerous ways. Admittedly a gross oversimplification, three of these ways might be listed in the order in which they are typically made effective; the imposition of discipline (1) by respect for the moral and intellectual integrity of institutions and organizations that resort to compulsions only as a last resort; (2) by legislative and administrative law and the acceptance of law, or the penalties of its violation; and (3) by the police power of the state.

The extent to which the first is effective is the measure of the openness of a society, and by its very nature a university is, and should be, the most open of all societies. It is a part of the university's nature to be hospitable to dissent and to be cordial to the continuous probing of skeptical and inquiring minds. Only thus can the university fulfill its responsibility for the correction and refinement of knowledge and its transmission to successive generations.

The concomitant of this posture is that the college or university by its very nature is ill-equipped to protect its integrity from the imposition of organized group force. A retreat to the security of law or of police action must be interpreted as a defeat. The institution's only genuine defense is to prevent the necessity for such action, if at all possible, through the acceptance of its purposes and programs by the great majority of its students and faculty, and by the community in which it lives. A preferment of professional career development by faculty at the expense of attention to students in and out of classrooms, an absence of program involvement in the burning issues of the day, or the failure to make adequate arrangements for a continuous and perceptive dialogue between the academic and non-academic communities—all or any one of these are capable of alienating large segments of the constituencies so necessary to building and retaining the sanction that must underpin effective administration of an institution of higher learning.

A loss of contact with the aspirations of any major group of constituents can be, and has been on occasion, disastrous. This is not to say that the purposes and programs of the college or university should not lead in the development of thought and attitude—not at all. It does mean, however, that the institution of higher learning will fulfill its obligations and secure its own future only when its pronouncements and its actions are directed at the betterment of the human race, and are clearly recognized to be so. Put simply, a high level of idealism is the greatest security a college or university can possess.

That may be true of other organizations in our society as well, including business organizations. This essay began by asking the question of the meaning of the Columbia experience for the business community. Apart from the matters that are unique to life on campus, the broad social issues that seem to have stimulated student protests and riots are just as relevant to business organizations as they are to institutions of higher learning. They are the issues of war, of discrimination, of unequal opportunity, of poverty amid plenty, of debasement of the environment. These are issues that share a common characteristic: they all contribute to an erosion of the quality of human existence. The business community can, and has, aligned itself in the pronouncements of its leaders with an eradication of these social evils. There are those who feel that war as an instrument of foreign policy cannot be terminated by nation states determined to sanctify their sovereignty, that if war is to be eliminated as an ancient plague of mankind it will result from the mutually beneficial and multiplying associations of men through the spread of global business. More and more people are becoming convinced that discrimination and the debilitating impact of pockets of poverty will never be overcome without the positive and aggressive participation of business. The debasement of the environment associated with urban decay and pollution in its several forms can never be reversed by government acting alone; it will require the collaborative efforts of both business and government.

It remains for the actions of business to validate in conspicuous and convincing fashion the pronouncements of its leaders. It is simply good business that the deed follow the commitment. The involvement of business in social change is inescapable in any event; the leaders of business have recognized this and have increasingly taken their place in the leadership of social change.

But business has other equally challenging and even more positive opportunities. Embedded in the very fabric of business is the concept of individual initiative and personal responsibility. If the contemporary notions of mass action for personal purpose, and of group mores for personal guidance are to be modified, if the worth and dignity of the individual are to be restored to their primary place in the public philosophy, it will not be through government policies that by their nature deal with group interests; it will not even result from characteristic patterns of thought and discussion in the academic community. If the virtues of individualism, self-reliance, and personal responsibility are to be restored, this must result mainly from business policies and practices. One of the most important considerations for modern management, in its own interest as well as that of society, is the preservation and encouragement of individual initiatives in large organizations.

Business has another major opportunity of a positive nature: to accelerate the conversion of modern technology into an ever-increasing flow of goods and services, thus providing the material base for the alleviation of social ills. In a period characterized by an explosion of knowledge and by shrinking social distances, rapid changes need not be confined to technology. The quality of human existence can also be rapidly changed for the better, but only if the business community with its great capacity and resources participates in a massive manner in the common effort.

When these challenges and opportunities of the business community become more accepted and better known, increasing numbers of young people will reject the hard-core revolutionaries who have inspired their protests. They will once again seek social and economic progress through the organization of productive efforts and through the pursuit of individual careers which they now feel provide insufficient purpose or moral content. . . .

Note

*Graduate School of Business, Columbia University, "A Message for Business from Columbia," *Report for the Year 1967–1968,* pp. 1-9.

Higher Education

The Governance of Higher Education:
Drift or Direction?*

. . . PERHAPS NO ACTIVITY IS MORE ENCUMBERED than academic administration with debilitating clichés that masquerade as guides to appropriate action. For illustrative purposes it is useful to identify two attitudes toward academic administration that stand at opposite poles. One comes down from the German universities of the mid and late nineteenth century. It starts from the premise that a university is a faculty and all else is redundancy. The position is perhaps best expressed in our tradition by the story of Mark Hopkins sitting on one end of a log and the student on the other.

This attitude was expounded with more than usual vigor by John Ciardi, of the *Saturday Review*, in the March 24, 1962, issue of that journal. Reflecting on his days as a teacher he ruminated, "My nostalgic notion of the true college was of an absolute and self-determining body of scholar-teachers. They are the faculty. They are appointed for their distinction and responsibility. And they, by discussion and vote, set the college policy, which is then passed on as formulated to a variety of clerk known as a dean. The duty of such clerks is to count the paper clips and add up the totals as instructed, leaving the faculty free for the important business of gathering information, of thinking about it, and of transmitting the information, the thought, and the method of thinking to the students."

Those familiar with the academic community will quickly recognize significant omissions in this position. Faculties typically accept as important business, matters that extend far beyond information gathering and contact with students. Again, to put the point in sharp focus, a quotation is selected from the same journal: a June 16, 1962, book review of Dr. K. E. Eble's *The Profane Comedy*. "Only in a secular Paradise [a leading college or university] could one find the bitchiness which often marks faculty relationships, . . . the maneuvering for position and prestige, the grudging acceptance given outsiders, the mild corruption of human values which power and high position and rare intellect can bring."

Both quotations are recorded here not because either has general validity but because the virulence of their expression serves to raise the question: Is a faculty's propensity to administer its own affairs compatible with its capacity to do so effectively? Can it do so in a manner that will best serve its own interest, individually and collectively—in a manner to optimize the social costs of education by optimizing the man-hours expended per graduate?

The other attitude toward academic administration, which is at the opposite pole of faculty autonomy and is fortunately not too frequently found, holds that the institution is controlled by the administrators on behalf of the trustees. The faculty is hired to teach and research; and the academic program as well as the business affairs are subject to detailed as well as general review and direction. This comes perilously close to, if it is not, an infringement of academic freedom. No institution of quality would entertain such a notion despite the promise that it would provide a possible means of cost reduction. The fact that this position is an utterly unacceptable basis for the nation's program of higher education simply makes it the more urgent that greater concurrence and clarity be achieved in the relations between faculty and administration.

There are many who would agree with Dr. Eble that "the war between college faculties and administrators is one of higher education's longest inconclusive struggles." It need not be, and it must not be, for it is not in the interest of the faculties. It is not in the interest of the administrators. It is not in the interest of education. It is a barren and unnecessary struggle, a national expense that can be ill afforded in the years ahead.

The activities of higher education are a continuous spectrum in which the processes of instruction blend imperceptibly with and ultimately emerge as administrative processes. There is no sharp line that divides education and the administration of education. It may be feasible to identify functions and assign primary tasks in a manner that best serves the interests of all concerned, but it will never be possible to dispense with the need for collaboration.

A whimsical sequel to the Mark Hopkins story was recently suggested by a senior member of the graduate Faculty of Business who asked: "Could this one-man class be combined with another class and given at a different hour? Maybe the class would be more comfortable with a smoother log. Should the class be scheduled only in the pleasant weather of the summer term? Could the Ford Foundation be interested in financing further experiments along this line? Enough. Even the educational process of Mark Hopkins on the log raises administrative matters and the question of who should handle them. To what extent is it good for Dr. Hopkins to be diverted from his student by such matters? Would it serve the best interest of the student, the teacher, or education itself? Would it be better if the administrative matters were disposed of by someone else in the interest of the teacher and the student, leaving both to think, inquire, and discuss?"

The simple illustration points to a premise of profound importance. Since the administrative problems emerge out of educational matters, the competent administrator must always be perceptive of, and responsive to, the legitimate needs and desires of those educating and being educated. Legitimate needs are those that can be reconciled with the basic policies and purposes of the college or university, in the setting of which the faculties should properly have a major role. Favors received by individuals and recognition of alleged needs that fail to harmonize with these limits are simply discriminatory, and are in the long run disastrous to the morale both of those receiving and those not receiving them. It may be that skepticism of the ability of administrators to be perceptive to, and firmly consistent with, predetermined and concurred policy underlies much of the usual faculty concern with administrative matters.

Perhaps the first step toward the development of a national faculty-administrator rapprochement is that administrators recognize that most of their actions vitally affect the work in the classroom or in the study, and hence should be taken only after careful and objective appraisal. Many of the practices that have become costly and debilitating appendages of higher education are perhaps cherished even less by the faculties than by others.

Several frequently observed practices of academic administration may serve to illustrate instances of less than prudent use of resources. A faculty member may find it hard to respect an administrator who attempts to lure a "name" professor from another institution with an obviously out-of-line salary and almost nonexisting teaching duties, when those with previous appointments can expect no such favorable treatment. That is to say, the previously appointed can typically expect no comparable treatment under this pattern of administration unless they in turn receive a competitive offer from a "sister" institution. Such practices by administrators tend to confirm the suspicion that there is a lack of aggressive sponsorship for the welfare of the existing staff. On the other hand, a program of salary and status improvement without prior requests or pressures, particularly when it is based on recognition of conspicuous contributions in teaching, research, and other work with students and colleagues, cannot fail to be a tonic to morale.

Moreover, it is no service to students, and probably not to the faculty man either, to encourage a member of the staff to place his research activities ahead of his teaching responsibilities, including the meeting of his appropriate quota of classes. Productive research is the essence of scholarly development and the advancement of knowledge, and should be facilitated in every feasible manner. But, in the social sciences and humanities especially, an optimum balance between teaching and research seems to favor both scholarly development and the expansion of knowledge. There is some evidence that beyond a certain point light teaching schedules, which incidentally must be compensated for by heavier schedules for colleagues, may be more debilitating than helpful for significant and productive research.

There are occasional practices related to students that likewise suggest administrative judgment based on expediency. For example, it is hardly an expression of confidence in the attractiveness of the academic program when fellowships are offered by administrators competitively with other institutions, rather than being awarded on the basis of comparative merit.

These and similar practices cannot fail to dissipate unnecessarily the scarce resources that are available to higher education. Additionally, they subtly impair the development of healthy working relationships among faculties and administrators. Only when the actions of administrators are based on predetermined policies and carry the conviction of certainty, fairness, mature judgment, and dedication will faculty confidence be prepared to accept ungrudgingly the full participation of the administration in those phases of the academic process in which significant conservation of resources can be achieved.

The faculty's primary interest is in the development of the program of study. The curriculum must necessarily reflect the professional interests of the faculty, individually and jointly. It must be reconciled with the needs of the student, however, if a program of balance and educational integrity is to emerge. Uncoordinated development of courses of study based on the specialized interests of individual scholars can very quickly result in excessive proliferation, distorted emphasis, and excessive costs.

It is very difficult, if not impossible, for a faculty acting alone to correct such proliferation. Each course becomes the private preserve of its sponsor. There is a tradition in most cases of "live and let live." Faculty action in curriculum matters can be made more effective by administrators who merit confidence, especially if it is established that any savings which result from such action will be used, at least in part, for better salaries and conditions of work. Likewise, by proper action of administrators, class scheduling and the determination of class sizes can be prevented from becoming chaotic. The achievement of greater orderliness, and corresponding reductions in the absorption of scarce space and other resources, typically requires administrative participation. Finally, the task of faculty recruitment, to replace retirements and to provide for expanding enrollments, can be materially facilitated if a collaborative spirit between faculties and administrators has been developed.

It may be appropriate, in this report, to describe how some of these matters have been adjusted in recent years by the faculty and administration of the Graduate School of Business.

Responsibility for initial consideration of the curriculum is assigned to a Committee on Instruction, consisting of six members of the faculty elected by the Faculty of Business; the Dean, who serves as chairman; and the Assistant Dean (Student Affairs), who serves as secretary. All matters relating to the course structure and substance of the teaching program are discussed at length in this forum, after which changes are recommended to the entire faculty for approval or disapproval. It is a well-understood and accepted policy of the School, however, that each man will present in the classroom those unique contributions expected of a member of a graduate faculty in a great university.

The course materials resulting from this consideration of the curriculum constitute the offerings which must be provided with teaching staff and offered in successive academic terms of work. Since the changes are moderate in number under normal circumstances, the study program can be developed with a reasonable degree of certainty for each term over a period of two or more years ahead. The School operates on a trimester calendar, and two or three years is the equivalent of six or nine terms of academic work. Each member of the faculty is committed to teach four out of six terms (the equivalent of the normal teaching schedule of two terms a year), but may teach no more than three terms in succession. After adjustment for sabbatical and research leaves, retirement, and other considerations, the courses to be offered are matched with available faculty personnel for each of the forthcoming terms—after, of course, consultation with each man to assure a maximum convenience in his program. Classes are scheduled in a manner that reconciles to the extent possible the need of the students for a balanced study program throughout the week with the wishes of individual instructors for certain teaching periods.

After the assignment of available faculty personnel has been agreed upon, the remaining unstaffed classes provide the faculty and the administration with an indication of the additional personnel that must be recruited and the professional interests that are required. This analysis is developed by a small Manpower Analysis Group, made up of three members of the Committee on Instruction who are selected by their teaching colleagues on the committee, and two representatives of the Office of the Dean.

When needs for additional personnel have been thus determined, the Manpower Analysis Group appoints appropriate search committees to locate and recommend leading scholars in the fields involved. Each search committee consists of three faculty members and an administrator. Attention is given to the age distribution and professional status of existing personnel, and nominees are recommended in a manner to achieve a manpower progression with respect to both professional development and ages of those working in the several fields.

Each recommendation of the search committee is submitted to the entire faculty, and observations are invited. If no serious objections are encountered, the recommendation is made to the Dean, and if he in turn has no objection, it is then transmitted to the Dean of Faculties and Provost for action. Recommendations that involve tenure appointments are screened still further by a campus *ad hoc* committee, which includes members of other University graduate faculties in addition to the Faculty of Business, and are then transmitted to the Dean of Faculties.

In this way the formulation of the program of study, its translation for each academic term into a specific number of courses and sections of courses and their scheduling throughout the week, the determination of resulting manpower needs, and the finding and recommendation of new appointments, is a continuous and integrated activity in which the faculty and the administration collaborate at every stage. It is not a perfect process by any means, but additional experience should result in refinements and improvements. The important feature of the procedure is that, being clearly defined, it does facilitate the collaboration that serves to lighten the heavy demands on time and other resources. It is recorded here, not with the thought that it may provide a prototype for others, but simply as an illustration of the fact that collaborative arrangements between a faculty and an administrative group can be made to yield effective results. Obviously, the traditions of each institution condition the specific arrangements that may be most appropriate.

An attempt to accommodate the large increases of enrollment which face our colleges and universities in the years ahead would be seriously disappointing, if not positively frustrating, without prior clarification of primary functions and collaboration between faculties and administrators. Without collaboration the financial costs would rise more than proportionally, even after adjustment for possible inflation.

The problems of financing will undoubtedly present difficult tasks for higher education in the coming years. . . . The resource in shortest supply, however, will be qualified academic talent for the classroom. The nation's educational system simply cannot afford the indulgence of an excessive and unnecessary expenditure of faculty time in administrative matters, or the ambiguous and complex arrangements that typically seem to accompany the efforts of faculties to administer themselves.

These are the reasons why it is of the utmost importance that academic administrators recognize a dual necessity: to develop sound principles of academic administration, and to administer in a manner which will win the confidence of the faculty and thereby ensure full participation in common tasks. Only thus can a control of costs be achieved concomitantly with the maintenance of quality in our programs of higher education. . . .

Note

*Graduate School of Business, Columbia University, "The Governance of Higher Education: Drift or Direction?" *Report for the Year, 1961-1962*, pp. 1–8.

Notes on Governing Boards
of Not-for-Profit Corporations*

Colleges and Universities

THE BUSINESS OF INSTITUTIONS OF HIGHER LEARNING is dual in nature; to educate (i.e., to preserve and transmit knowledge) and to advance the fund of knowledge through research. Some would put the importance of these two functions in the order stated. Others would reverse it, particularly for those institutions that award advanced academic degrees. In recent years, a third function has begun to win some sponsors: participation in community action programs for the alleviation of social problems. This new job for the institutions of higher learning has by no means been fully accepted on the campus. There has been serious question in many minds whether involvement by universities and colleges in community problems may not be incompatible with the degree of objectivity required in a community of learning and research.

Colleges and universities are unique among corporate organizations in the variety of influences that bear on their activities. Centuries ago they started as clusters of scholars who individually admitted students to their classes for a fee. There was no administrative direction in those distant days, and faculties have continued to cherish the thought that their own limited legislative and administrative devices are quite adequate. On this view, the single function served by deans, vice presidents, presidents, and trustees is simply to keep the faculty nourished with adequate salaries, classrooms, offices, and research funds. Thus, it is reported that when General Eisenhower became President of Columbia University he admonished a faculty assembly to greater support of the university. "But, Mr. President," a senior professor rose to proclaim, "the faculty *is* the university."

There is much truth in the professor's statement, but it hardly implies that there is no role for academic and institutional administration. More than any other type of organization, a college or university presents two

192

quite different sets of administrative tasks: what might be called academic administration, concerned with the scholarly program, on the one hand, and institutional administration, on the other. Departmental chairmen, deans, provosts, vice presidents for academic affairs, and presidents may be conceived as being in the line of academic administrators, working closely with faculty in the development and structure of scholarly activities. Directors of buildings and grounds, of food, and of other services, the registrar and other custodians of student and institutional records, the director of the budget, the treasurer, the vice president for government and public affairs, the vice president for development, and, yes, the chairman of the board and his board colleagues, all have responsibilities that are not essentially academic, even though they must be harmonized with the academic program.

Academic Administrators

Left alone, faculty members are understandably disposed to pursue their personal professional interests. But often these are so specialized that they have little interest for students. The achievement of a balanced teaching program among the several academic disciplines, and even within departments concerned with a single discipline, would be unusual without administrative guidance. Without it, the result could readily be an extensive—and expensive—proliferation of specialized and sparsely attended course offerings.

` There is, moreover, an unfortunate tendency among many intellectuals toward what has been called "bitchiness" and professional arrogance. Faculty fights are so verbally violent, it has been said, because the stakes are so low! Administrators must be available to mediate and reconcile. It is particularly important that administrators give encouragement in numerous ways to junior faculty members, who frequently feel impelled for the purpose of winning tenure to pattern their development after that of the senior professors in their departments. When this does happen, individuality suffers. That is one of the more subtle penalties of the faculty tenure system that is now under review throughout the nation.

There are numerous other academic administrative functions that must be carried out in managing a truly qualified program of higher learning. In addition to being financed, research leaves must be scheduled so that faculty is available to staff the program of course offerings for each semester and term. Schedules are constructed after student enrollments are estimated, the number and time of course offerings established, and the number of courses to be taught by each member of the available faculty has been determined. These are all matters that must be resolved within the limits of financial budgets that have been previously determined. In a large academic institution, such budgets require a lead time of not less than a year.

If a need develops for additional faculty members due to retirements, withdrawals for other reasons, or expanded enrollments, it is only natural that those most familiar with the work in a professional field initially identify the potential candidates. Even here, however, it is good to have the benefit of checks and balances provided by faculty colleagues in adjacent disciplines and by academic administrators.

The total intermeshing of functions presents an interesting problem in continuing logistics. And all of these procedures involve a high quantity of persuasion and consent in contrast to the greater emphasis on authority in the business corporation.

This brief recitation of the thoroughly integrated functioning between faculty and academic administrators will help to identify and emphasize two unique practices in the world of academe. First, academic administrators are usually chosen from the faculties, with little or no previous administrative experience. There is no precedent for a program of careful preparation for succession to important academic administrative posts. Second, an orderly program of career progression in academic administration is more the exception than the rule.

These practices are probably defensible when the administrator is in direct contact with the faculty, but they become less so to the degree that the administrative assignments are more removed from the academic program. Many contemporary universities and colleges have become large and enormously complex corporate organizations. Their annual budgets typically run into tens or even into hundreds of millions of dollars. The acquisition of resources and the development of the physical plant, the organization of an orderly system of operating and financial record keeping, and the task of representing the institution in its external relations, all are part of what we may here call institutional administration in contrast to academic administration.

Institutional Administrators

The tasks of institutional administration in colleges and universities are now enormously varied. A major task is the preservation of resources. The annual budget cannot be unbalanced indefinitely without incurring disaster. The endowment funds, if any, must be securely invested to provide income to supplement gifts and tuition fees. Tuition fees must be adjusted to reflect changing costs. Salary levels, both for the faculty and the administration, must be maintained at competitive levels. The physical properties must be maintained in good and attractive condition. Continuing decisions must be made in the allocation of available space to approved activities, financial resources must be allocated in directions of predetermined development, and even the intellectual resources represented in the faculties may be persuaded or cajoled to devote their energies and talents to purposes desired by those responsible for the directional development of the institution.

The assignment of faculty to institutional needs must necessarily involve mutual consent. It illustrates the importance of harmonizing institutional administration with the academic program. Thus, the activities of institutional administrators must be carefully tuned to the academic program and, in turn, the academic program should be harmonized with the constrictions imposed by budgetary and other nonacademic circumstances. To the largest extent possible, academic considerations should prevail.

Many of the functions of institutional administrators are comparable to those of a business organization administrator, yet the procedures for picking most university and college administrators today are simply an extension of those used to pick members of the teaching faculties. Reasonably successful in the latter case, they are often inadequate for selecting academic administrators, and may fail completely in picking institutional administrators. It is unrealistic to expect a professor whose career has been shaped by scholarly concerns to adapt quickly to the rigors and requirements for hard decisions involved in administering a multi-million dollar enterprise. Traditional methods that require no prior preparation for appointment to posts in institutional administration are unlikely to be successful. Excessive risks are incurred even when academic administrators are selected from the ranks of scholars by search committees without extended periods of observation. . . .

Note

Putting the Corporate Board to Work (New York: Macmillan, 1976), pp. 126–31.

Academic Fund Raising:
Yesterday and Today*
A Change in the Pattern of Giving

A HALF-CENTURY AGO IT WAS CHARACTERISTIC of philanthropists to grant or bequeath substantial and unrestricted sums to their preferred university, college, hospital, or museum. This practice implied confidence in the trustees and the administrative officers of the selected institutions and provided endowment and income for the time-tested activities of the institution. The incremental resources received from the grant or bequest could be assigned by the trustees and administrators in their discretion to expand existing activities, to experiment with new activities, or even to build new buildings and add to old ones. Decisions regarding the use of the resources rested with those responsible for the development of the institution, presumably on the premise that those actively involved would be the best judges of effective use.

In more recent years the practice of direct giving has been replaced in part by that of transferring large resources to personal or public welfare foundations. These foundations, in turn, allocate their resources to purposes and institutions designated by the donors or determined by the foundation's administrative officers and trustees.

It has been said that the task of fund raising has been made harder by the disappearance of many large fortunes through progressive taxation. It is not clear that this is so. The almost startling growth of personal and public welfare foundations in recent years would suggest that the opposite may be closer to the truth. Very large resources indeed have been assigned to this channel of philanthropy. As recently as the 1930's the annual distribution of funds by foundations to all types of recipients totaled perhaps less than $200,000,000; the current figure is $800,000,000 or more. The total resources of foundations are now estimated to exceed $15,000,000,000.

Another source of substantial eleemosynary resources has appeared in the last several decades. Until recent years the dictum "Charity has no place

196

at the board (of directors') table" was widely accepted and quoted in the business community. Corporate managers, becoming more aware of their opportunities to serve the community in numerous ways, have increasingly accepted the judgment dealing with corporation contributions rendered in the now famous A. P. Smith Manufacturing Company case of 1953:

> What promotes the general good inescapably advances the corporate weal. I hold that corporation contributions to Princeton and institutions rendering the like public service are, if held within reasonable limitations, a matter of direct benefit to the giving corporations, and this without regard to the extent of sweep of the donor's business. . . . Such giving may be called an incidental power, but when it is considered in its essential character, it may well be regarded as a major, though unwritten, corporate power. It is even more than that. In the court's view of the case it amounts to a solemn duty.

The managements of many corporations now make provision in their corporate budgets and in their administrative staffs to develop and rationalize a program of annual contributions. Some have established company foundations to stabilize annual contributions by making them less dependent on fluctuations in earnings. There has been an expansion of corporate contributions to higher education alone, from perhaps $50,000,000 to $200,000,000 annually, in the decade since the A. P. Smith case clarified the legal sanctions. Corporate contributions to activities such as the Community Chest, the Red Cross, the Salvation Army, museums, and hospitals have likewise grown.

Today's Sources of Support

Administrators of academic institutions today thus must seek donations from three principal groups: individuals, foundations, and corporations. At an earlier time the task was simpler, generally involving little more than a convincing presentation of the work of the institutions to individuals of great wealth. Church-supported colleges and universities were spared even this exertion. They paid little attention to the task of fund raising, for the required support came in the normal order of their relationship to a sponsoring church affiliation.

The shift from one to three principal sources of support has had a number of consequences important to the academic community. There is less opportunity today to build endowments than there was at an earlier time. Foundations typically make few, if any, endowment grants. Indeed, the transfer of funds to a foundation rather than to an operating institution is essentially a substitute for the creation of a university, college, or hospital endowment by a donor. Corporations and foundations have on occasion made endowment grants to create a professorial chair, but they have generally preferred to limit their awards to current and specific uses by the recipient. Occasionally, large bequests or grants have been made by individuals for restricted endowment or for building purposes, but large grants for unrestricted endowment have been in recent years the exception rather than the rule.

The development of the annual alumni fund illustrates the nature of current support. Each year large numbers of donors contribute, typically, somewhat modest amounts individually. The annual fund has the security of many donors who quite appropriately acquire the habit of annual giving, thus establishing a principle of, if not a commitment to, continuity. The capitalized value of the annual income from some of the more successful annual funds would be the equivalent of a large endowment indeed.

Fellowships and other assistance grants usually have the same characteristics of modest size and continuity through repetition; they are rarely based on the annual income of invested endowment funds.

The greatest part of the increased budgets of non-tax-supported academic institutions has been supplied by raises in tuition and by gifts for current use. Increased income earned on unrestricted endowments has been less significant. This has meant that the task of fund raising by colleges and universities has had to be not only continuous but intensified, to assure an expanding volume of gifts from year to year. Many contributors, particularly foundations, are reluctant to provide continuous support for extended periods of time. In these circumstances the academic fund raiser, and that usually means the senior academic administrator, has no alternative to a daily commitment to his task. He must be a knowledgeable and authoritative interpreter of the institution's programs and aspirations if he is to convey conviction and confidence. Frequent, time-consuming, and direct personal contact with prospective donors old and new is an absolute prerequisite to success.

The Use of the Total Resources

Perhaps the most significant change that has resulted from this development of multiple sources of funds, a change that has come about so subtly that it has not yet been fully realized, is that greater restraint tends to be placed on the use of the total resources available to academic institutions. Income from endowment capital accumulated in earlier years is usually unrestricted as to use. Significantly, this income may be available for the expansion of time-tested programs of the college or university, including the enlargement of physical facilities to accommodate such programs. When a foundation or corporation contributions program is significantly large, however, a staff is employed to receive and analyze requests and to design new and imaginative programs for the use of available resources. The need of funds for existing activities of colleges and universities thus tends to fall outside the orbit of interest. Phrases such as "supplying the venture capital of social change" have long had great influence as guides to giving, particularly in foundation thinking. As the annual grants of foundations and corporations have grown both in total amounts and relative to the annual income from college and university endowments, institutions of higher learning have become more amply supplied with funds for new projects while remaining relatively starved for "bread and butter" money. There is no implication of a conscious effort by foundations or business to "control education." The situation is simply a consequence of trends that have emerged from the modified structure of philanthropy.

More particularly, it has been increasingly difficult, though not impossible, for non-tax-supported colleges and universities to find new money for the expansion of physical facilities. It is understandable that a foundation would be reluctant to make a grant for new construction for a project or program in which it is not directly and specifically interested. The need for physical expansion is so great that even the wealthiest foundations would soon find their resources exhausted by such financing. The contributions officers of business organizations share this reluctance. Yet if the non-tax-supported colleges and universities are to maintain their relative strength in the pluralistic structure of our educational system, they must expand their physical facilities in order to take their share of the enrollment growth along with the tax-supported institutions. It is encouraging that both foundations and business organizations recognize these ambiguities, and there is increasing evidence that they are trying to find ways to be helpful.

Part of the problem has been met by the development of large "capital fund" drives, the proceeds of which are applied to all of the activities of an academic institution, including the expansion of facilities to house existing programs as well as new academic ventures. Although these capital fund drives have been somewhat more successful in their appeals to large individual donors than to foundations as such, a balanced report must credit a number of large matching grants by foundations to encourage specific institutions to undertake well organized campaigns for capital funds.

The Fund-Raising Task Today

These observations, based on the Dean's experiences in seeking the financing for Uris Hall and support for other activities of the School, may serve to illustrate several features of the existing fund-raising task:

First, it is clear that fund raising is and must continue to be a major occupation of all academic administrations. Since most colleges and universities have an admixture of public and private funds in their budgets these days, this is as true of tax-supported colleges and universities as it is of those primarily privately supported, but it applies with special force to the latter.

Second, far greater reliance must be placed, now and in the future, on obtaining modest annual grants from numerous sources, with the implication if not the promise of continuity. Foundations are not fond of the principle of indefinite continuity. This means that the task of fund raising involves a constant search for new donors, and this never-ending search must be recognized as a vital part of academic administration.

Third, a larger proportion of future grants will probably be accompanied by some restrictions on their use—simply because that is the nature of foundation giving, and a larger share of total gifts is flowing through foundations than in the past.

Finally, it would appear to be desirable for all donors, particularly foundations and corporations, to continue their consideration of ways to make more adequate provision for the physical facilities required by expanding enrollments and by the numerous experimental projects that they are now constructively encouraging.

Notes

*Graduate School of Business, Columbia University, "Academic Fund Raising: Yesterday and Today," *Report for the Year, 1963-1964,* pp. 1-5.

Business School Dean
Overhaul at Columbia*

. . . [By 1954, WHEN I BECAME DEAN of the Graduate School of Business of Columbia University, the] curriculum was no longer suitable for the revised program of the School. Yet the course material that had been developed over a quarter of a century could not be lightly abandoned. While at Jersey Standard I had formed some ideas of how a graduate business program should be organized, but those thoughts had not evolved in collaboration with my new-found faculty—or with any other faculty for that matter. My thinking was somewhat fragmented and nebulous, but I did have a general sense of the direction I thought we should go. That direction was toward a study of the corporation and its role in society, a theme that had been a major part of my thinking during the Jersey Standard days. I knew that business had a large influence on the cultural, as well as the material, life of the contemporary world. On the other hand, I knew that I did not fully understand the corporation and its place in the world—but then I doubted if anyone really did.

It was pretty clear that the economists did not understand the institutional impact of the corporation. They were still living in the world of the single enterpriser and of Alfred Marshall's traditional supply and demand curves as modified by E. H. Chamberlain and Joan Robinson. Behavior in the marketplace was still interpreted in terms of the single buyer-seller transaction instead of the continuous flow of business in stabilized relationships with other businesses and customers. Accountants saw the corporation through its financial records, but missed much of the rest. Lawyers dealt with management-stockholder relations, the corporation's contracts, interpretation of regulations, and lawsuits, but hardly grasped the impact on society, if indeed many of them cared. Engineers were concerned with material processes and physical structures, but rarely thought about social structures. Sociologists were just discovering the corporation

201

as a laboratory to test their theories. And the general public was largely uninformed or misinformed.

It seemed to me that there was a wide open field and a great challenge to achieve a better understanding of the corporation and its limitations as well as its opportunities to serve society. I was especially eager to stimulate investigation of the relationship of the institutions of business to the value structure of the society that gives business its right to exist and thrive. This was the approach that, I hoped, should guide the formation of a new graduate curriculum at the Columbia Business School. We were to succeed only in part.

Faculty control of the curriculum is one of the sacred cows of the academic world. There are, of course, very good reasons for this. They come out of the long evolution of the university, institutions that started in Europe in the thirteenth and fourteenth centuries as collegiums. Clusters of scholars gathered in population centers to offer their own courses and admit their own students, from whom they would collect their fees. The faculty-student relationship was very personal. What was taught was the result of each professor's study, inquiry, and reflection.

To some extent similar attitudes guided the initial shaping of the academic program in the Columbia Business School. This made a collective revision of the curriculum no easier. Nothing is more highly prized on the campus than intellectual independence and integrity along with the opportunity to follow one's broadly informed interests and carefully derived convictions with unrestricted objectivity. A professor builds his intellectual capital in much the same way that a businessman builds his skills and productive capital.

The Columbia business faculty had been accumulating an inventory of intellectual capital for nearly four decades when the new dean arrived. Only naiveté could explain my initial intention to get right to the job of revising the curriculum. I had not at that time heard the comment attributed to Woodrow Wilson when he was at Princeton: "Reforming a college curriculum is like moving a graveyard." Had it not been for the frequent expressions of discontent from individual members of the faculty, it would have been pure bravado. What I did notice was that the expressed dissatisfaction of one faculty member about the curriculum always referred to the contents of another professor's courses, not his own. Another complaint was the lack of balance and integration in the whole instructional program.

Business education in the United States had gotten its start at the Wharton School of the University of Pennsylvania in 1898. The pattern for organizing the curriculum initiated there was still followed in the mid-1950s by most business schools, including Columbia. Indeed, many of the members of the Columbia business faculty had been recruited from Wharton during the presidency of Nicholas Murray Butler. The functional studies of accounting, statistics, personnel practices, and administration were supplemented by the study of a specialized field of business on which the student spent the largest block of time.

Harvard was the first to modify this basic pattern with its heavy use of the case method of instruction, a method appropriated from the nation's law schools. The Columbia Business School had looked at the case method and rejected its use as the dominant means of instruction, wisely in my judgment. It was, of course, deemed to have merit. In fact, it had been adopted for some of our advanced courses after the degree candidate had acquired enough knowledge to support meaningful participation in a case discussion. But the case method as the principal way of presenting instructional materials, it was felt, was too wasteful of the limited time available. The price paid in neglected subject matter was seen as too great, as well as financially costly. Rather, our faculty was dedicated to a combination of the interrupted lecture, plus the case method, and student presentations in seminars. The adoption of each method was determined by the nature of the subject matter, and to a certain extent by the propensities of the instructor.

Four or five attempts at curriculum revision had been made before my time. Professors would compare their courses for overlaps. Many were found, but curiously they were always in the other fellow's courses. Little was done to investigate significant areas of business that did not happen to coincide with a faculty member's major interest. Needless to say, the efforts of the past had not been successful. Faculty discontent with the curriculum was matched by that of the students.

It was clear that another round of attempts would be futile if the same approaches were tried. Something new had to be done. It had to be subtle, avoiding by all means the implication that the ideas of the dean were being imposed. It must avoid simply copying the efforts of others; that had also been tried before without success. Whatever was done had to derive from fresh thinking. What was required, it seemed to me, was an analytical consideration of the needs and opportunities in the current business world, arrived at from extended discussions by the faculty, individually and collectively. With only a modest bit of nudging from the dean, we decided to adopt a novel *procedure* that, so far as we were aware, had not been tried before in curriculum building.

To begin, we rejected a comparison of our course offerings with those of other business schools, regardless of their quality. We were not even interested in analyzing what we ourselves had been doing. But as a business school desiring to operate at advanced levels of instruction, we were keenly interested in what *business* was doing, what *business* was thinking, and which problems of *business* were important.

Only after a comprehensive examination of the entire business spectrum would we be ready to assign its most important parts to specific courses of study that could be further developed. The initial faculty effort was not to adopt, modify, or eliminate in-place course materials, but to accept a new *procedure*. It would start with the totality of business, then move to phases of that totality, and finally to the design and selection of specific course materials, which would be constructed as needed by members of the faculty itself. Only then would we be ready to appraise the new curriculum for balance and comprehensiveness.

It was an ambitious undertaking, and everyone felt a bit threatened. But it was a group exercise that created its own momentum, esprit de corps, and requirements as it evolved. The faculty was constituted as a committee of the whole to review the successive progress reports. With a grant from the Ford Foundation, we were able to engage several visiting scholars from other faculties to teach some of our classes. This released certain of our own scholars to do the research and writing demanded by our new project.

Three major sectors of business life were soon identified: (1) the *environment* in which business operates, (2) the organizational *arrangements* for the internal management of business, and (3) the communicating and analytical *tools* used by business. A third of the faculty was assigned to each of these sectors with a senior man as chairman. Each group made frequent and comprehensive reports that were reviewed and discussed by the entire faculty. Out of these review sessions we gradually identified the content of the three areas that were important to the business community.

Concerning the first major sector, we concluded that the environment in which business operates is conditioned by three main forces: the state of the economy, the legal concepts and social attitudes inherited from the past, and the interplay throughout the world of specific kinds of resources: physical, technological, and human. That meant that there were three basic courses that all degree candidates should take. The first was economics, including both macroeconomics (the study of economic aggregates on the national level) and microeconomics (the analysis of specific variables), which were well-established subjects with us. The other two areas of interest in the business environment would require fresh approaches and, therefore, new courses.

The second area was an unusual study of the attitudes, ideas, and cultural practices, largely inherited from England and Western Europe, that had resulted in the evolution of the modern corporation. We called it the "Conceptual Foundations of Business." It was our way of presenting the societal and ethical issues that today increasingly confront business decision making. The material has proved to be reasonably successful. I wanted very much to have Charles Malik of Lebanon and Sterling McMurrin of the University of Utah, two leading philosophical thinkers, join the faculty to help us with these materials, but, as noted earlier, the faculty found the proposal a bit too imaginative.

We gave the task of studying the third area, the several interrelated world resources, to our geographers. The results were disappointing for their training had covered physical resources and their location, rather than a comprehensive analysis of all resources including demography and technology. Ultimately, our geography division was made a department in the nonprofessional graduate faculties of the University.

We also found it necessary to build a new course in our second major sector, namely the internal organizational arrangements of business. Behavioral science was a subject much discussed in the mid-1950s by academics. We thought that in a new course we could relate this body of emerging knowledge to behavior and decision making in business. This we did, but the results were only partly successful.

Another course in this second sector, the administrative structures of business firms, had long been a part of the curriculum and fitted nicely with the study of behavioral patterns. The legal framework within which the corporation is managed, including taxation and the strengths and weaknesses of regulation, provided supplementary material for a modified course to round out this second major segment of business interests. It was agreed by the faculty that our graduate students should also be exposed to all three courses in this second sector.

The tools of business, our third sector, was already in the curriculum and presented less of a challenge to innovate. An attempt was made to blend the subjects of accounting and statistics as is frequently done in business. But we were not successful in this; the two teaching staffs had lived too long in their separate compartments. The mathematics of operations research had a fascination, however. Several members of the faculty structured a course that made extensive use of the newly emerging computer to test business assumptions and decisions with simulation models and fast computation. Comprehensive exposure to all the tools of business, the faculty concluded, was essential to graduate business study.

The study of these three major segments of business life, produced a total of nine courses. Several of these would require new syllabi, a very large task if adequately done. But the faculty was not through. It was concluded that, as a capstone in the last or fourth term of study, the student should be exposed to the processes of group decision making, based on the knowledge acquired in earlier terms. This was accomplished through a course on business policy that used the case method of instruction. In short, it was an attempt to duplicate the reality of decision making in the corporation.

Together these formed a core of ten required courses, half of the twenty stipulated for the MBA degree. Another five courses, it was decided, could be taken in a student-selected field of concentration—we did not call it a specialization—such as finance, marketing, international business, transportation, etc. International business was a newly introduced field that students could select for concentration, based on the rapidly emerging multinational corporation. The remaining five courses of the total of twenty the student could select at random from offerings of the faculty of business or of other graduate faculties.

The adoption of this program of study did several things. It achieved the integration and balance long sought by the faculty. It approached the study of business as a comprehensive activity with an emphasis on the reciprocal influences between business and society at large. It shifted the primary goal of graduate business education at Columbia from preparation for the first job to preparation for a business career. And as a significant byproduct, it made redundant many of the specialized—sometimes antiquated—course materials that had accumulated to serve different purposes. The total number of courses was reduced from 130 to 80. We had constructed an integrated program of study that had a far lower expenditure of time and money per classroom hour.

No longer was the curriculum suitable for the occasional student looking for a particular topic or two he could squeeze in at night. There is a place for such a program, but we did not think that place should be at inconveniently located Columbia. Nor was the ten-course MS degree compatible with our newly adopted curriculum. Accordingly, we no longer accepted the part-time student except in unique circumstances, we stopped the matriculation of candidates for the MS degree, and scheduled no further evening classes. The whole complexion of the School changed.

Had the dean disclosed his personal ideas of curriculum revision to the faculty, it would have been resented and properly so. We might have gone nowhere. But getting agreement on a procedure led to success. It resulted in a curriculum revision that had the intellectual integrity to attract widespread faculty and student attention throughout the nation, and we were told, abroad as well.

The experience of organizing and living through this curriculum revision was one of the most exhilarating of my life. My first five years as dean were exciting, but it cannot be said that they were serene. To use an expression often heard on the campus, "a bit of blood was left on the floor." There was a continuous chorus of dissent by a small but sincere group that protested vigorously change of any kind. I particularly felt bad about a conflict with an old friend and colleague, Haggott Beckhart, that ended in his retirement several years before he had planned. Despite the determined efforts of that small group, it bordered on the inspirational to observe a majority of mature scholars deliberately deciding to scrap, or fundamentally to modify, more than a quarter century of established course construction and venture into new and untested territory. In the end almost everyone—but not all—felt a sense of satisfaction. Numerous faculties in other colleges and university business schools have since been influenced by this Columbia business curriculum.

Moreover, the new curriculum gave greater flexibility to the University's total study program. With the provision that the five elective courses could be taken in other graduate faculties of the University, joint degree programs were worked out with Law, International Affairs, Journalism, Urban Land Use, Public Health, Teachers College, and others.

These joint programs brought to the surface the recognition that what the School of Business was teaching was basically management, an occupation by no means limited to business. Some even suggested that the School change its name to the Graduate School of Management. But the time was not yet ripe for that. . . .

Notes

The Dean Meant Business (New York: Columbia University, Graduate School of Business, 1983), pp. 156-64.

Campus Entrepreneur*

WHEN PRESIDENT KIRK ASKED ME IN 1955 to be the vice president for business, I had made it clear that I thought we had a task far more difficult and demanding than simply housekeeping; that a revised administrative structure was needed to give the University more precise knowledge of its activities, a coordinated direction, and a means of control. The casual meetings each morning of the president, the provost, and the business vice president were not enough. It seemed to me that important changes had to be made in the administration of the University's resources: the allocation of space, of talent, of money, and the procedure for strengthening one field of activity and contracting another. At that time, it seemed, the University's resources were "flying in the wind." There was limited ability to know precisely what was going on, or to determine what should be going on.

I proposed the establishment of a central policy group as well as a system for a more efficient and prompt flow of data for administrative decision making. Selected members of the University administration and operating heads of academic divisions, that is, deans and chairmen of certain departments, would determine policy and make wholesale allocations of available resources. Responsibility to administer the academic divisions of the University would be delegated to deans and chairmen, within the policy guidelines and previously determined allocations, accompanied by a system of accountability to calibrate success or failure.

I wrote many memoranda on this subject. Nothing happened. A budget director left, and I recommended expanding his job into an office of Director of Budgets and Operating Data. Nothing happened. Concerning my proposal for the delegation of administrative authority to deans and department chairmen, I found that the tradition of detailed supervision by the central administration in Low Library was too strong to change. The proposals were either misunderstood, or more likely the shift of day-to-day authority to the academic divisions was resented. Laborious and time-consuming line-by-line review of budgets in Low Library had always been and, I learned, would continue to be the approved practice. At long last, it now has been modified.

208

But Columbia had grown big and complex. Close examination of each "tree" (budget line) meant that the size and contours of the forest were obscured. In fact, the way the University was administered was painfully simplistic. Every morning Grayson Kirk, John Krout, and I—we called it the troika—would meet to discuss a short agenda of current problems and reach agreement on solutions. I found that the decisions made were frequently subject to later reversal or modification when pressures were applied. There was no doubt in my mind that this was a poor way to administer a large, intricate organization.

This failure to rationalize the administrative structure of Columbia puzzled me. It may have resulted in part because so many of the leading members of the administration had academic backgrounds in political science. Familiar with the horse-trading of politics, they tended toward solutions that usually involved placating and expensive compromises between or among contesting parties instead of hard analysis of the best solution for the institution joined to a firm intention to see it through. The loss of control was almost certain. In subsequent years, the result was accumulated deficits of some $80 million. This "political" attitude violated one of my firmly held convictions about good management: effective administration involves the occasional administration of pain, but as painlessly as possible. There is seldom a way to eliminate all pain among contesting parties, but the interests of the institution should be paramount.

In the course of time I realized that the attitudes of many academic administrators were not unlike some of those that I had observed in government. When a difficult matter arises, first thoughts often turn to solving it with additional personnel or money. Without one or the other, compromise means neither contestant gets what he or she wants. The malignancy of staff expansion may be attributed to ambition, or it may be the effort to resolve issues without imposing unwanted courses of action on those involved. Or it may be a bit of both. In any event, the merits of a lean operating organization are more often than not sacrificed to "keeping peace in the family." The end result is a multiplication of occasions for future conflict and ballooning costs.

Avoidance of confrontation sometimes leads to even greater difficulties. It is much easier to settle a problem when it first emerges than when the passage of time has invited other people to align themselves with contesting parties. It is easier to put out small fires than big ones. This is particularly true of academic disputes. Let an academic dispute become faculty-wide, even though the issue is minor, and real trouble ensues. It has been said faculty fights are so vicious because the stakes are so low.

Another observation about academic administration often has applicability. One of the joys of the campus is the relaxed atmosphere of informal discussion with colleagues. Too often, however, the practice is indulged to the point of excluding time for important matters. Assigning one's time to make the most of it has a low priority in the scale of values of many administrators.

I lasted as vice president for business about a year and a half, after which I returned full time as dean of the Business School. Our family doctor on the occasion of an annual physical examination in late 1955 had said, "Courtney, there is no chance of your getting an ulcer, but I'll bet you two to one you'll get two ulcers if you don't get rid of two of the three jobs you are now carrying." With this advice in mind, I was able to induce Henry Wriston, the retiring president of Brown University, to come to New York and take over the leadership of the American Assembly. I knew of his strong attachment to the Council on Foreign Relations, located in New York, and felt the two interests would harmonize nicely. They did.

Resigning my vice presidency was not without pain. I think that President Kirk had assumed I would surrender the deanship instead. Departure from the central administration left some scars that probably stayed with me throughout my Columbia career. Although subsequent requests were made to undertake a number of tasks, they always seemed to carry a certain quality of reserve on the part of the president's office, and even among some of the trustees. At times I had the feeling of a certain defensiveness in the central administration, a concern perhaps that the Business School and its dean were becoming more of a factor on campus than was desirable. Indeed, among the professional schools, the Business School particularly was identified by some as a fiefdom administered not by a dean but by a duke. Such an image was regrettable, but we were determined to do all we could to make the Business School strong in scholarship and financially sound. Our successes were not always greeted with unqualified enthusiasm by less fortunate divisions of the University. . . .

The business corporation is a truly remarkable social invention whose accomplishments in the past have been impressive, and whose opportunities for constructive good have only begun to be realized. While its past contributions to material abundance have been notable, it now has the great challenge of a complementary and equally auspicious career to enhance its service to the welfare of humanity.

It is a prime task of the nation's business schools to teach the procedures and techniques of business, including communications technology, but more importantly, it is to help future business leaders to appreciate their emerging opportunities for public good. The point is well made in a line of Alfred North Whitehead's that is incised in the stone of Columbia's Uris Hall: "A great society is one in which its men of business think greatly of their functions."

Note

The Dean Meant Business (New York: Columbia University, Graduate School of Business, 1983), pp. 170–74, 262.

V
The Globalization
of Business
and Culture

Innovation Abroad*

. . . MOST OF THESE INTERCHANGES OF CAPITAL, products, and services have taken place since World War II, and most have taken place through the activities of business corporations. The difficult transition experienced by domestic corporations from the single goal of profit-making to the multiple purposes of profits *and* wider participation in society becomes even more complicated when recognition must be accorded the often conflicting political purposes and differing cultures of other nations. As a result, multinational corporations have been the target of much defamatory attention, even more than domestic companies.

These attacks are not without precedent. Despite the role the multinational corporation has played for centuries in the development of the world of nation-states, it has never been conspicuously popular, either at home or abroad. The Russia Company, the Levant Company, and the East India Company, all chartered in England in the sixteenth century to find export markets for woolens and other British products, also found it profitable to export from their foreign outposts and sell in third country markets in competition with the home country. Imports into Britain were especially unwelcome. This, of course, frustrated the basic mercantile purpose of acquiring, through favorable trade balances, larger stocks of gold and silver for the home country. Later the Virginia Company and the Plymouth Company were chartered to colonize the New World, but their overseas production, it was held, in the colonies or in third countries was not supposed to compete with that of the home country. In other words, the early multinational companies were chartered to serve the interests of the home country, and that they did even though they were criticized. England, Holland, France, and Portugal, all with chartered companies, expanded and developed into strong world powers. Spain's influence, without chartered companies, did not last as long.

The notion lingers to this day that a multinational company should and will serve primarily the interests of its home country nationals and the home country government. Foreign-owned companies are inherently suspect by the people and governments of host countries. For example, witness the attitudes and concerns currently felt and expressed by the citizens of the United States at the encroachment of foreign owners in this nation's banks.

Criticism of the multinational company takes numerous forms. Host governments, finding it difficult to keep closely informed about the multinational corporations of other nations within their borders, feel concern that these foreign corporations may at times serve as convenient agents for their home government's pursuit of purposes incompatible with local policies. The assumption by governments, since the Great Depression, of major influence on internal economic affairs, implies a degree of economic nationalism. Transfer payments among corporate components of a multinational company, it is felt, provide the opportunity for artificial pricing and tax evasion. Even efficiency is often resented. Crushing or buying out local competition is sometimes alleged. Market prices may be fixed, and competitive behavior constrained by the host government. Accusations are made that local labor is exploited. Constituencies of home governments, on the other hand, complain that jobs are exported, that domestic productive capability is diminished, and that the economy is weakened. Yet, despite the crescendo of concern in both home and host countries, international investment and international trade in recent decades have grown at a more rapid rate than domestic investment and internal trade. The large corporation that has *not* acquired interests in other countries is now more the exception than the rule.

The Spread of Global Investment

At a faster pace than many realize, great manufacturing and trading companies have developed a vast interwoven network of communications and interests, of procedures for the transfer of technology and commercial intelligence, and of personnel that cuts across national boundaries and cultural patterns. Unlike the situation that obtains in a political settlement, global companies operate in a context in which their negotiations do not carry a heavy baggage of emotional commitment, and in which a resolution of a problem can be beneficial to both parties. They provide a network of interconnected conduits that facilitate the optimal utilization of financial, material, and technical resources. As a unifying influence, the multinational companies are a powerful force in the world today. Concomitantly, they provide an equilibrating tendency in the global economy, when they are able to place their production where it can achieve the lowest unit cost and sell where the returns are highest. "Business has an immense future," in the opinion of Henry Kissinger, "of opportunity and responsibility, in helping to meet the development challenge."[1]

These optimistic thoughts, however, must necessarily be accompanied by the realization that managing the multinational corporation is highly complex. The task of appraising a rapidly changing world economic order to achieve maximum efficiency and return on investment is a highly sophisticated exercise. In addition, adaptation must be made to differing social expectations in numerous cultures and to the often conflicting and overlapping political positions of competing national governments.

A succinct recitation of several of the major trends in world business will serve to demonstrate the risks as well as the opportunities for the business corporation operating on a global scale. In combination, the several basic changes now occurring, in the opinion of close observers, will result in a modified structure of world business that will differ markedly from the past. The United States has lost some of its lead in productivity and technology, first to Western Europe and Japan, and then surprisingly to the "advanced developing countries": Brazil and Mexico in South and Central America, and to Korea, Taiwan, Singapore, and Hong Kong in the Far East. As the cost of energy increases relative to the cost of labor, the comparative advantage of the developing countries will be further enhanced, especially relative to Western Europe and Japan, which are heavily dependent on external sources of energy.

Adjusting to the World Economy

The rate of economic growth in the less-developed countries has been greater than that in the developed countries, and since most of them are in the Southern Hemisphere, a shift of industrial production toward the South is occurring. Access to raw materials supports the shift. Food production, however, has lagged in the less-developed world. The availability of land to produce cereals, grasses, and forest products is diminishing relative to the growth of global population. Forward strides have been made in technology for fishing and mining the seas, but the political issues of entitlement are far from resolved. The raw materials of mines are scarcer and the real costs of their extraction are rising. The limits of the earth's energy reserves of liquid and gaseous hydrocarbons have become a matter of global concern. Though needed by all nations, their availability and cost are tied to the decisions of the OPEC nations.

All of these matters are basic to the rate of world economic growth and to the trade and investment relationships among nations and regions to each other. They imply a slower rate of total global growth, and a gradual "closing of the gap" of the less-developed world, together with a further political assertiveness on the part of the less-developed countries. The

emerging structure of the world economy will make difficult the maintenance of nondiscriminatory and liberal trade and investment policies.
Indeed, as *Business Week* magazine has observed:

> In a world . . . where the established countries are threatened by
> intensified competition from the lesser developed countries, regaining
> the momentum toward freer trade would require superhuman states-
> manship.[2]

The experience of recent years has resulted in a loss of confidence that
governments can manage their internal economic affairs without isolating
outside influences. The persistence of inflation, in combination with
unemployment and a slowing rate of economic growth, has resulted in
inward looking policies, especially in the developed world. Quotas, nontar-
iff barriers, and "orderly marketing" agreements are much in evidence. A
common currency has been proposed for Western Europe, in part to protect against the declining value of the U.S. dollar. The tentative efforts of
Europe, Japan, and the United States to carve out their own spheres of economic influence could result in the development of a regionalism, within
each of which a reasonable degree of nondiscriminatory trade and investment could occur.

In this highly complex world economy, the multinational corporation
may be the major remaining force for economic integration. But its managers must be aware that any form of integration necessarily qualifies a
nation's ability to be wholly independent. Interdependence involves adjustment costs and as a major integrating agent, the multinational corporation
cannot wholly avoid ruffling the sensitivities of foreign governments, especially in the less-developed world.

Adjusting to World Cultures and Politics

Adaptation to a rapidly changing world economy is one thing; adaptation
to the aspirations and cultural patterns of local population and to the political policies of local governments is another. Personnel practices in different
parts of the world are a crucial area that requires adaptability and adjustment to cultural differences and change. To pay wages comparable with
those of the home country would require the establishment of compounds
to keep the nonbeneficiaries out—hardly a desirable solution. Yet to pay
wages comparable with those in the host country exposes a business to
accusations of exploitation by labor leaders at home. And personnel practices differ widely among countries—from Japan, to France, to the Latin

American countries. The impact of demographic trends will differ markedly from those of the United States. Population, especially in the less-developed countries, is increasing so rapidly, it is expected that, on a global basis, the reserve army of the unemployed will reach alarming totals in a few years. It has been estimated that by 1995, or in less than twenty years, the total world labor force seeking employment may grow by a billion people from just over 1.6 billion to nearly 2.6 billion.[3] This, coupled with increasing evidence of slower global economic growth, could spell social and political instability.

In political matters, the multilateral corporation must adapt to more than one national jurisdiction. Apart from the effort of the U.S. government to impose rules on foreign affiliates through extraterritorial application of U.S. laws—antitrust for example—there have been numerous cases in which enforcement of foreign political policy has, in the past, been attempted by using multinational companies: proscribing the shipment, by a U.S. subsidiary, of Canadian wheat to China or truck parts to Cuba. Each nation-state thinks of itself as an important economic actor in its own domestic and foreign affairs, responding to the perceived political needs of its citizens. The opportunity is always present to develop adversary relationships with the quite different objectives of the multinational corporation. Yet accommodation has been and must continue to be made. Whether willing to not, the managers of multinational corporations are being forced to accept some of the conflicting pressures of world politics.

An interesting contrast in cultural attitudes is provided by recent U.S. legislation proscribing foreign payments (to obtain contract business) on penalty of severe liability. Some have interpreted this as an attempt to impose American morality on the traditional practices of other people. The *New York Times* recently quoted a British businessman in Hong Kong with the cynical remark:

> "Who are the Americans to tell us about morality? What's business all about anyway—to make money. You pay a commission to make a deal, you make a profit, everybody's happy."

And the British can write-off such a payment on their tax returns as a necessary business expense.

Managerial Innovation

The Greek god Proteus was hard to get a hold on; when seized or cornered, he disengaged himself simply by changing shape. It is in the sense of a supple innovator that the modern corporation has proven a worldly inheritor of the protean tradition. Its capacity to adapt its structure, procedures, and commitments to the requirements of evolving circumstances has confounded its critics, while delighting its supporters. Cast in the role of world developer, yet hemmed in by a wide array of cultural, political, financial, and even military obstacles, it has had to pioneer or pull out. The withdrawal of IBM from India is a conspicuous example of the latter, and it should be noted that the number of smaller divestments has tended to increase in recent years. But, for the most part, the multinational corporation has elected to stay and pioneer—in ways that some would have thought unworkable, radical, or simply absurd a half-century ago.

The earliest modification of traditional direct foreign investment was the joint venture, in which equity ownership is shared in varying proportions with citizens of the receiving countries or with the host government. In the area of natural resource industries—oil and minerals—imaginative modifications of the joint venture, including novel self-liquidating financial arrangements, have been developed to give recognition to both the home country's inherent property rights and the contributions of capital and capability of foreign enterprises.

A nonequity form of joint venture is the service contract under which the "investing" company agrees with a host representative—again either the government or private groups—to provide services for a fixed fee. When the "service" includes the creation and management of a previously nonexistent enterprise, the arrangement goes by the name of a "management contract." A variant of the management contract, the "co-production scheme," is used in Soviet-bloc countries. The private business in this setup may supply machinery, technology, management, and perhaps a market, with the host government furnishing the plant, workers, and the raw materials. Compensation for the foreign partner may be by fee or, more typically, by a predetermined share of the end product.

All of these arrangements are supplementary to the more traditional form of foreign investment: the overseas affiliate that holds indefinite tenure of title in the country of operation. Whether these practices represent transitional steps, in the development of regional or global arrangements, which will in turn diminish their necessity or desirability is a question that cannot now be answered. It is sufficient to say that, in the aggregate, they represent a significant enlargement of the capability of the modern corporation to adapt itself to a world of cultural, economic, and political disparities.

The imaginative means by which the multinational corporation has spread its commitments around the globe are an interesting part—but only a part—of the story. The complexities associated with its daily operation require comparable initiatives, adaptability, and sensitivity.

A variety of trade policies and practices have developed throughout the world regarding monopoly and competition. Adaptations to the competitive practices of a host country may, and frequently do, run afoul of the antitrust position of the United States; yet competitive disadvantages with local firms may be incurred through failure to adapt. The participation of a Gulf Oil affiliate in a Canadian government sponsored uranium cartel was a dramatic example. A host of financial problems with novel features emerges in the acquisition of new capital in foreign markets, the transfer of funds, and even in the wide variety of accounting requirements and practices in different countries. Indeed, intracompany transactions become international transactions.

New concepts of organizational structure and management control have been designed. Personnel policies for both management and labor, adjusted to personal needs as well as local custom and legislation, have been developed. Clearly there is no shortage of problems ahead for the worldwide business organization. Despite its newness as a major world influence and its vast reservoir of unsolved problems, it is pregnant with great promise. The demands and problems that will shape the multinational corporation of tomorrow relate more to political versus business values than to those of humanism versus materialism; and the impact of political influences will remain as an inextricable conditioner of their policies and practices.

A lesson can be learned from the experience of the foreign affiliates of global organizations. Whether their home base is in the United States, Europe, Japan, Latin America, or even Southeast Asia, these foreign affiliates have had to make adjustments imposed by economic, cultural, and political circumstances. It is heartening to see how flexible and perceptive business has been in its response to newly encountered circumstances. Now an additional pressure is beginning to make itself felt throughout the global business world with the recrudescence in public thinking of post-industrial concern for the individual. It will take many years for this emerging influence to be felt in a dominant manner in the less-developed world, but even there it is not without present influence.

The reconciliation of the values of science, which did so much to develop the modern business corporation, with those of the humanism now being reasserted, has caused much confusion in managing the purely domestic corporation. But that does not mean that no progress is evident either at home or abroad. A growing awareness of the values of humanism blended with those of rationalism will be a powerful influence in helping both the multinational and the purely domestic corporation to achieve productive destinies.

Notes

Beyond the Bottom Line (New York: Macmillan, 1979), pp. 130–40.

1. Henry Kissinger, address, published in *Future of Business* (The Center for Strategic and International Studies, Georgetown University, June, 1977), p. 14.

2. *Business Week.*

3. "Population," The Population Crisis Committee, Washington, D.C., September, 1977, No 7.

Selected
Bibliography

Selected Bibliography

1940

Liquidity and Instability. Ph.D. dissertation, Columbia University. New York, Morningside Heights: Columbia University Press. 298 pp.

Newcomer, Mabel. *Taxation and Fiscal Policy*, with an editor's preface by Courtney C. Brown. New York: Columbia University Press.

1945

The Combined Boards. Department of State Publication No. 2372. Washington: U.S. Government Printing Office, 1945.

1953-54 to 1957-58

Graduate School of Business, Columbia University, *Report of the Dean for 1953-54 through 1957-58.* Columbia University Bulletin, Series 58, No. 38 (September 20, 1958).

1956

Cordiner, Ralph J. *New Frontiers for Professional Managers*, with a preface by Courtney C. Brown. 1956 McKinsey Foundation Lecture. New York: McGraw Hill.

1957

The Director Looks at His Job. Edited by Courtney C. Brown and E. Everett Smith. New York: Columbia University Press. 160 pp.

Houser, Theodor V. *Big Business and Human Values*, with a preface by Courtney C. Brown. 1957 McKinsey Foundation Lecture. New York: McGraw Hill.

1958

Greenewalt, Crawford H. *The Uncommon Man: The Individual in the Organization*, with a preface by Courtney C. Brown. 1958 McKinsey Foundation Lecture; published 1959. New York: McGraw Hill.

Journey Toward Understanding, with Mrs. Courtney C. (Marjorie L.) Brown. Burlington, Vermont.

225

1959

Graduate School of Business, Columbia University, *Report of the Dean [for 1958-59]*. Columbia University Bulletin, Series 59, No. 31 (August 1, 1959).

Blough, Roger M. *Free Man and the Corporation*, with a preface by Courtney C. Brown. 1959 McKinsey Foundation Lecture. New York: McGraw Hill.

1960

Graduate School of Business, Columbia University, *Report of the Dean [for 1959-60]*. Columbia University Bulletin, Series 60, No. 42 (October 15, 1960).

Kappel, Frederick R. *Vitality in a Business Enterprise*, with a preface by Courtney C. Brown. 1960 McKinsey Foundation Lecture. New York: McGraw Hill.

1961

Graduate School of Business, Columbia University, *Report of the Dean for 1960-61*. Columbia University Bulletin, Series 61, No. 37 (September 16, 1961).

1962

Graduate School of Business, Columbia University, "The Governance of Higher Education: Drift or Direction?," *Report for the Year 1961-1962*.

Folsom, Marion B. *Executive Decision Making*, with a preface by Courtney C. Brown. 1961 McKinsey Foundation Lecture. New York: McGraw Hill.

1963

Graduate School of Business, Columbia University, "An Experiment in Academic Scheduling," *Report for the Year 1962-63*.

Plain Talk on Business and the Public Interest: Discussions from the Fall 1962 WNBC Television Series "Let's Talk Business." Moderator, Courtney C. Brown. Edited by Courtney C. Brown. #4 in the Columbia Business School Series; Series Editor, Clarence C. Walton. New York: Graduate School of Business of Columbia University. 204 pp.

The Ethics of Business: Corporate Behavior in the Market Place, with a preface by Courtney C. Brown. Edited by Courtney C. Brown. New York: Graduate School of Business, Columbia University.

Watson, Thomas J., Jr. *A Business and Its Beliefs*, with a preface by Courtney C. Brown. 1963 McKinsey Foundation Lecture. New York: McGraw Hill.

1964

Graduate School of Business, Columbia University, "Academic Fund Raising: Yesterday and Today," *Report for the Year 1963-1964*.

Rockefeller, David. *Creative Management in Banking*, with a preface by

Courtney C. Brown. 1964 McKinsey Foundation Lecture. New York: McGraw Hill.

1965

Graduate School of Business, Columbia University, "Emerging Themes in Business Education," *Report for the Year 1964-65.*

Mortimer, Charles G. *The Purposeful Pursuit of Profits and Growth in Business,* with a preface by Courtney C. Brown. 1965 McKinsey Foundation Lecture. New York: McGraw Hill.

1966

Graduate School of Business, Columbia University, "Fiftieth Anniversary Observations," *Report for the Year 1965-66.*

1967

Graduate School of Business, Columbia University, "The Corporation as Catalyst," *Report for the Year 1966-1967.*

Donner, Frederick G. *The World-wide Industrial Enterprise: Its Challenge and Promise,* with a preface by Courtney C. Brown. 1967 McKinsey Foundation Lecture. New York: McGraw Hill.

1968

Graduate School of Business, Columbia University, "A Message for Business from Columbia," *Report for the Year 1967-1968.*

Oates, James F., Jr., *Business and Social Change: Life Insurance Looks at the Future,* with a preface by Courtney C. Brown. 1968 McKinsey Foundation Lecture. New York: McGraw Hill.

The Creative Interface, with John T. Connor [and] Elisha Gray. Washington: American University, School of Business Administration.

The New Relationship Between Business and Government. Washington: American University, School of Business Administration.

1969

Graduate School of Business, Columbia University, "Management Capabilities–How Transferable?," *Report for the Year 1968-1969.*

Webb, James E., *Space Age Management: The Large Scale Approach,* with a foreword by Courtney C. Brown. 1969 McKinsey Foundation Lecture. New York: McGraw Hill.

1970

World Business: Promise and Problems. Edited by Courtney C. Brown. New York: An Arkville Press Book, The Macmillan Company. 364 pp.

"Prologue to a New World Symphony?," *World Business: Promise and Problems.* Edited by Courtney C. Brown. New York: An Arkville Press Book, The Macmillan Company. 364 pp.

1975

"The Impact of Change on Directors," *The Corporate Director: New Roles, New Responsibilities—A Report of the Corporate Directors Conference.* Boston: Cahners Books.

Corporate Directors and Managers. New York: Macmillan, [1976] c.1975.

1976

Putting the Corporate Board to Work. A volume in the Program for Studies of the Modern Corporation, Graduate School of Business, Columbia University. New York: Macmillan. 191 pp.

"Legitimacy, Objectivity, and Vitality of the Board of Directors of the Large Company," *Chief Executive's Handbook.* Edited by John Desmond Glover and George A. Simon. Homewood, Illinois: Dow Jones - Irwin.

1979

Beyond the Bottom Line. A volume in the Program for Studies of the Modern Corporation, Graduate School of Business,Columbia University. New York: Macmillan. 188 pp.

"Rethinking the Language of Business," from *Beyond the Bottom Line. New York Times,* Sunday, August 26,1979.

"A Corporate Dilemma: Materialism vs. Humanism," *The Future of Business: Global Issues in the 80s and 90s.* Edited by Max Ways. New York: Pergamon Press. 119 pp.

1983

The Dean Meant Business. New York: Graduate School of Business, Columbia University. 288 pp.

1985-86

"The Virtues of Moderate Growth." Published here for the first time.